Southern Literary Studies
Fred Hobson, Editor

Dream Garden

Dream Garden

The Poetic Vision of Fred Chappell

Pleasing thoughts —

Fred Chappell

EDITED BY PATRICK BIZZARO

LOUISIANA STATE UNIVERSITY PRESS   *Baton Rouge and London*

Designer: Michele Myatt Quinn
Typeface: Adobe Bembo
Typesetter: Impressions Book and Journal Services, Inc.
Printer and binder: Thomson-Shore, Inc.

The editor is grateful to the following authors, journals, and publishers for permission to reprint the essays noted: Dabney Stuart, "Spiritual Matter in Fred Chappell's Poetry: A Prologue," *Southern Review,* n.s., XXVII (Winter, 1991); Henry Taylor, " 'The World Was Plenty': The Poems of Fred Chappell," in Taylor, *Compulsory Figures: Essays on Recent American Poets* (Baton Rouge: Louisiana State University Press, 1992); Kelly Cherry, "The Idea of Odyssey in *Midquest,*" which first appeared as "A Writer's Harmonious World," *Parnassus* (1996); Robert Morgan, "*Midquest* and the Gift of Narrative," which first appeared as "Fred Chappell's *Midquest,*" *American Poetry Review,* XI (1982), and was reprinted in Morgan, *Good Measure: Essays, Interviews, and Notes on Poetry* (Baton Rouge: Louisiana State University Press, 1993); Peter Makuck, "Chappell's Continuities: *First and Last Words,*" *Virginia Quarterly Review* (1992); David R. Slavitt, "The Comedian as the Letter C Strikes Again," *New England Review,* XVI (Spring, 1994). A much shorter version of Alex Albright's essay appeared in *North Carolina Literary Review* (Summer, 1992).

The editor also thanks East Carolina University, Dean Keats Sparrow, and Donald Palumbo, chair of the English Department, for their support of this book. He especially appreciates the Sparrow Research Award, granted by the ECU Department of English, which provided essential time to work on the project. He is also grateful to Amy Willoughby and Heather Burt for their untiring efforts on behalf of the book.

Library of Congress Cataloging-in-Publication Data

Dream garden : the poetic vision of Fred Chappell / edited by Patrick
    Bizzaro.
        p.   cm. — (Southern literary studies)
    Includes index.
    ISBN 0-8071-2202-5 (cloth : alk. paper)
    1. Chappell, Fred, 1936–   —Criticism and interpretation.
I. Bizzaro, Patrick.   II. Series.
PS3553.H298Z64   1997
818'.5409—dc21   97-14265
                                                                            CIP

The paper in this book meets the guidelines for permanence and durability of the Committee on Production Guidelines for Book Longevity of the Council on Library Resources. ∞

For the ever-expanding community of Chappell enthusiasts,
for Jason and Kristin, my children,
and for Resa

CONTENTS

WORKS BY FRED CHAPPELL CITED

Awakening to Music. Davidson, N.C., 1979.

Brighten the Corner Where You Are. New York, 1989.

C. Baton Rouge, 1993.

Castle Tzingal. Baton Rouge, 1984.

First and Last Words. Baton Rouge, 1989.

The Fred Chappell Reader. New York, 1987.

I Am One of You Forever. Baton Rouge, 1987.

The Inkling. New York, 1966.

Midquest. Baton Rouge, 1981.

Moments of Light. Los Angeles, 1980.

Plow Naked: Selected Writings on Poetry. Baton Rouge, 1993.

Source. Baton Rouge, 1985.

Spring Garden: New and Selected Poems. Baton Rouge, 1995.

The World Between the Eyes. Baton Rouge, 1971.

Foreword

GEORGE GARRETT

It is a privilege to be a kind of porter, a gatekeeper here, to swing wide the gate with a little flourish and to welcome you to this wonderful and well-earned appreciation (in various forms) of Fred Chappell. I have known both the man and his work for a good many years, going back to a day and a time at Duke University when I was a young visiting writer and Fred Chappell was some kind of student. I had the pleasure of reading some of his work and, as I recall, awarding him a prize on behalf of the local literary magazine, the *Archive*.

In my mind, anyway, I've been awarding him prizes ever since. It was not then but on another trip down to Duke, a recent one, when I up and asked my host, and Fred's old teacher the great William Blackburn, a man who had taught a good many very good writers—Mac Hyman, William Styron, Reynolds Price, Anne Tyler, among others—who among them ("Mirror, mirror on the wall") was the best of all. We were both a little sloshed on Blackburn's good bourbon. Else I wouldn't have dared the impertinence of asking him such a thing. His answer was sober and instantaneous: "No question about it. Fred Chappell is the most gifted and the best of the bunch. Though whether he will ever 'succeed' as a writer the way they have, I don't know."

I believe Bill Blackburn would (may well be) very happy at the measure of "success" that has come along for Ole Fred, even though, as he feared, it has not been easy. Even though, to tell the truth, a mutual friend of mine and Fred's, in fact, commissioned a portrait painting of my decapitated bald head on a platter, I am not John the Baptist. Nor was meant to be. But I have been tooting horns and telling people about his work for all these years. To tell some more truth, I am relieved that there is such a big crowd of us, his fans, these days, a regular marching band of his admirers. What remains to be said is what is being said herein, here and now, and what will certainly, sure enough, be said by more and more writers and reviewers and critics—readers are voting with their feet and their wallets—in times to come. For myself, I will reiterate and oversimplify my position. We have among us a very modest number of writers who, in spite of the overwhelming trend towards specialization, write both fiction and poetry. We have only a very, very few who can do both things tolerably well. Fred Chappell is among the best American poets alive, an energetic, innovative, wonderfully imaginative master artist. Likewise his novels—always from the beginning first rate and getting better all the time, as he has been growing and changing—are among our few and finest. And do not, please, ignore or forget his marvelous short stories, of all shapes and all sizes, which (it seems to me) are among the very best examples of that form and have not been fully exposed or appreciated yet. Or the criticism, which is rigorous, intelligent, inventive, and just. A true artist leaves his mark on all he touches. Fred Chappell as teacher has exercised an enormous and benign influence on contemporary letters.

Notice that I have just described for you our preeminent man of letters. As such, he constantly teaches others, myself among them, by example and by good influence.

I reckon I know a thousand and one stories about the "real" Fred Chappell, the living and breathing, suffering and rejoicing person, the man who wrote the books. I will spare you and him, for the time being, all but one of the most recent. Which will be news to him, too. Not long ago I was in New York City, engaged in an intense and difficult discussion, the give-and-take chess moves of negotiation, with an important (and moderately imperious) editor. Someone who had her doubts—they were clear in the hard light of her eyes and the high set of her jaw—about both me and my project, my ideas. She didn't actually yawn in my face but might as well have. I was losing her interest by leaps and bounds. Somehow, entirely by accident, the name of Fred Chappell came into the conversation, only for a wink and a flash, to be sure, like the sudden flight of a kingfisher. She leaned toward me and wrinkled her brow.

"Do you really know him?"

"Who?"

"Fred Chappell."

"A little. . . . Yes, ma'am, I guess I do. Fred's a friend."

She didn't actually respond with the obligatory next line (Why didn't you *say* so?), but her whole face changed for the better into smiles and attention.

"Tell me a little about him," she said.

And I did.

And I will be sending her a copy of this happy gathering of other voices, too. Just as soon as I have one.

Dream Garden

Introduction: Fred Chappell's Community of Readers

PATRICK BIZZARO

> For me it is in the work that the final perfection
> of a life is lodged; the work is the life.
> —*Plow Naked*

Over the past thirty years, students of literature have been interested in how new audiences are developed, especially communities of readers devoted to poets whose work is innovative in treatments of subject or in use of form. As a result, when we read what poets themselves say about poets and poetry, we are nowadays quite naturally interested in what they have to say about readers of poetry. In part, an understanding of who these readers are and how they read provides insights into changing poetic tastes as well as lasting and influential innovations. In fact, by understanding readers we might even gain insight into why we continue to read poetry at the turn of the century despite the availability of music videos, virtual reality, and televised courtroom dramas that more easily entertain us.

Understanding poets—Fred Chappell in particular—and poetry itself in the postmodern age by studying readers may at first seem a *fin de siècle* preoccupation with theory. But the concern with critical reception has long been a part of poetic effort. And this concern has interested Fred Chappell. In his collection of writings on poetry, *Plow Naked,* he makes this very point in a discussion about audience. Chappell knows quite well that every poet "looks for someone to admire his work." But the search for an admiring reader is a far more complex matter than the decision to write something for that reader to admire: "The poet may have been born to produce poetry, but no one in the course of human time ever felt he was put upon the globe to read poetry. It is a catch-as-catch-can proposition, this search by a poet for his audience" (30).

In fact, this search has a long and honored history. Among poets' solutions to the problem of readership, specifically that they are not apt to have many readers—if any readers at all—is Yeats's: "Disgusted by and contemptuous of the middle class he found to be lacking in proper interest in poetic genius and nationalist literature, [Yeats] decided to invent an audience, to write for an ideal reader" (30). Chappell's interest in Yeats's invented, ideal, and, of course, invisible audience signals perhaps the best reason for this book. Unlike Yeats, Chappell has a wide and prestigious readership from whom we and future generations can learn how to read Chappell's poetry.

Chappell is not only interested in how his predecessors envision audience, but he is also conscious of the loyalty and lasting contributions of his readers. "The list of my literary creditors," Chappell writes, "is impressive both in its size and in the prestige of its names and it lengthens year by year" (13). In this group, Chappell graciously includes alongside powerful and successful writers his own students, to whom he claims to "owe more . . . than I can ever say, however much I want to say it" (13). These are Chappell's readers, certainly more tangible than the ideal reader Yeats knew as "a man who does not exist, / A man who is but a dream" (30).

What can we learn by understanding how and why these readers have come to constitute Chappell's audience? First, we can learn about his influence on the contemporary poetic scene. In the same way that we learn something about him when we read in *Plow Naked* the names of some of his influences—ranging from Poe and Hemingway to Reynolds Price, George Garrett, and Peter Taylor—we learn also about him by seeing how his contemporaries—in this volume, such eminent figures as Robert Morgan, Kelly Cherry, Dabney Stuart, Henry Taylor, and David Slavitt, among others—read his poetry. In short, we learn what Chappell's contemporaries, a prestigious group indeed, value most about his poetic contributions.

Second, that Chappell's readers are real and that their methods for reading his poetry are collected here makes it possible for us to lay a foundation for future readers, who will want some place to start in studying and understanding his poetry decades from now, generations from now. They will want to know who read Chappell's work during his lifetime and how that work was read.

It goes without saying that Chappell's contributions as a poet are far-reaching. As a literary "switch-hitter," of course, his fictional productions will merit equal time, perhaps in a book like this one, just as Fred's poetry has paralleled his fictional efforts in theme and structure. To appreciate fully Chappell's canon as it is discussed in these essays, a chronological arrangement of treatments of Chappell's poetry seems best, since themes from early volumes are echoed in later books and since he has consciously attempted to tie his volumes of poetry together structurally, often in relation to his novels as well.

In an effort to reflect accurately what Chappell's readers most value in (that is, how they read) his poetry and as preparation for readers who are relatively new to Chappell's poetry, this volume begins with an overview. R. H. W. Dillard, in his poem "Fred Chappell's Poetry: Paradox and Tension," Resa Crane and James Kirkland, in their interview with Chappell, and R. T. Smith, in "Proteus Loose in the Baptismal Font," not only establish the influence Chappell has had on them but also offer insights into how contemporary writers and critics read and respond to Chappell's verse. In the interview, conducted late in 1995, Chappell also discusses his most recent work in his book *Spring Garden.*

Continuing with this effort to provide wide-ranging and informative readings, Dabney Stuart puts forth a view of Chappell's poetry based on the idea that Chappell is concerned with the duality of flesh and spirit. Stuart studies the subject of Chappell's verse as well as the structure of his books. Henry Taylor, in "'The World Has Plenty': The Poems of Fred Chappell," shows that though Chappell's fiction has changed noticeably, the poetry has maintained "a consistency of style and approach." Taylor concentrates on *The World Between the Eyes, Midquest,* and *First and Last Words.*

The essays that follow Taylor's are arranged to reflect the chronology of Chappell's publications. Kathryn Stripling Byer's "Turning the Windlass at the Well: Fred Chappell's Early Poetry" begins with a caution: "Looking back at a major poet's first book of poems can be a risky undertaking, particularly if the poet is Fred Chappell, one of the most prolific and versatile writers in recent memory." But Byer then goes on to do exactly that by examining Chappell's first poems not as forerunners to *Midquest* and *First and Last Words* but as poetic achievements in themselves. Her essay serves as preparation for readings of the structural and thematic centerpiece of Chappell's poetic achievement thus far—*Midquest*.

The success and influence of this integration of four volumes—*River, Bloodfire, Wind Mountain,* and *Earthsleep*—are reflected by the space allotted to various readings of *Midquest*. John Lang reads for community and allusion, and at the end of his essay he provides a list of references and allusions in *Midquest*. Kelly Cherry's "A Writer's Harmonious World" follows the narrative thread—the quest motif—that links these volumes together under a single title. Robert Morgan discusses the narrative structure of the book by focusing less on the quest motif and more on other structural elements of the poem, including symbolism and metaphor.

The inevitable comparison between the structure of *Midquest* and the structure of Chappell's novels is addressed in Richard Abowitz's "Chappell's Aesthetic Agenda: The Binding of *Midquest* to *I Am One of You Forever* and *Brighten the Corner Where You Are*." Abowitz speculates that "Chappell is attempting to combine *Midquest* and a quartet of novels . . . into one mammoth work."

My own essay treats the oft-dismissed *Castle Tzingal* as a comment by Chappell on the status of the poet in the last quarter of the twentieth century. I argue that Chappell "challenges us in *Castle Tzingal* to view poetry differently in an age when all about us weep for the loss of audience."

Don Johnson and Peter Makuck offer interpretations of Chappell's *First and Last Words*. Johnson argues for the complementary nature of Chappell's "dual role as 'ole Fred,' the Carolina mountain boy, and Professor Chappell, the cosmopolitan man of letters." Makuck asserts that since the publication of *Midquest* in 1981, a careful reader can see throughout Chappell's works continuities of voice as well as "an abiding concern with Ultimates, with faith and art, love and war."

David Slavitt and Susan O'Dell Underwood offer views of Chappell's two most recent volumes, *C* and *Spring Garden*. Slavitt studies Chappell's epigrams in *C,* beginning with the view that "epigrams are not easy to do: they are, like jokes, most demanding, take talent and training and an instinct for timing, and a sense of the absurd . . . a whole range of craftsmanly and human qualities that are rarely found together." Underwood comments on both the new poems Chappell has included in *Spring Garden* and on the poems selected for republication.

Finally, Alex Albright's "Friend of Reason: Surveying the Fred Chappell Papers at Duke University" focuses not just on the mass of material available in the collection but on what those materials tell us about Chappell as literary figure and political advocate. Rather than offer a complete listing of the works available in the Chappell collection, since such a list is apt to change, Albright's goal is more to suggest the kinds of research that might be undertaken using the materials found there.

Clearly, Fred Chappell has a strong and well-established community of readers who offer a myriad of ways to interpret his poetry. Rather than simply offering a salute to Chappell, which is certainly deserved, the varied approaches by the writers in this volume should help future generations of readers as well as today's teachers of literature make insightful readings of Chappell's poems.

Fred Chappell's Poetry

R. H. W. DILLARD

It seems that more often year by year
  I ignore Ciardi's dictum
"Not to send a poem on a prose errand"
  And send them out, come
Rain, come shine, to do a proser's job,
  Not that I distrust prose,
But rather that the deadlines pass,
  The other things I do impose
Themselves on the promises I've made
  To write prose pieces, and then
I've no choice but to knuckle under,
  Give up, or call upon the muse again
To do the work at which I've failed.
  But, Fred, you must admit you
Set the precedent yourself, sending
  A poem (and more than one) to do
A letter's work in envelopes
  And on the printed page.
So, rather than an article in "MLA style,"
  I'll risk the editor's just rage
And send this poem instead to say
  A thing or two that I have noted
About your poems, your novels, about you,
  An idea or so I've floated

In both prose and conversation
       Over the twenty-five years or more
Since we first met (with George and David)
       In Charlottesville. You wore
A clip-on tie, claimed you had yet to master
       The art of the knot, but that's not
What I meant to talk about here, rather
       Another memory, another time, a hot
Late spring day at Duke when I was driving
       Sam Goldwyn, Jr. (but that's another story),
And you came walking to us across the arms
       Of the auditorium seats, or we
Had finished talking and you walked away:
       What matters is your perfect balance
In more ways than one, a paradigm, I later
       Came to see, of your talents,
Dark Romantic and Sam Johnson scholar,
       Feet off the ground but firmly planted,
Moving straight toward your goal (here or there)
       But on a course that slanted
Across the fixed seats and their rigorous demands
       "Old Fred *never* had a grain of couth,"
You had Susan say of your persona in *Midquest,*
       But he always knows where the truth
Is and how to get there, I'll add,
Of the Fred persona in *this* verse.
       But before I get to the point (if I ever do),
Another memory, one that's much worse
       And yet is of a piece. This one from the summer
Of 1970: *Hour of the Wolf* was showing
       In my film class, and you and Sue were there.
When you saw the awful baroness, even knowing
       She was one of the artist's demons, peel off
Her face and remove her eyes, you ran
       Out of the darkened room, your own demons clacking
At your skull, out into the bright hall, unmanned
       And shaking, but you could not leave. You stayed

There, your eye pressed to the crack in the door,
    Watching Bergman's nightmare to the dreadful end.
I could go on with the tale. There's more
    About your own nightmares that night and the nights
To follow, but what interests me
    (And makes me tell this story here) is the tension
You revealed between the need to flee
    And the greater need to stay and see the worst,
The very worst. Between the raw, stripped face
    And the need to see it through, to analyze and organize
And put each horror in its place.
    It is that tension and the balance you achieve,
Poised on the arms of the seats, or running
    For the door where you will stay, that, to my mind,
Are the center and the secret of the stunning
    Things you do in prose and verse: the tension between
And balance of diction and tone, content and form;
    The dark undertones of light, the light implicit
In pitch dark; to use the scientists' new term,
    The "ordered chaos" of your words. It is this paradox
That I find in Polanski's films, the pressure
    Of surface and depth, or, say, in Bergman's *Mozart,*
The Magic Flute, turbulence and measure,
    In all your novels and in your poems, language
And metre, memory and intellect, fear
    And understanding, cold sweat in the stomach
And the deep sigh that brings relief, no mere
    Literary device, but the tense rhythm and balance
Of our random lives. No wonder then
    That your poetry is so close to prayer, that love
Is at the source, a movement to "Amen."
    But before I end, I should return to that tie
Which (this, from Richard Abowitz)
    Is just the clip-on kind night watchmen wear
So that it rips away, forces (or permits)
    The criminal who thought he had you in his grip

To turn and run, or at least to let you go—
    Let you go as far as the door anyway, where
You'll doubtless stay, or go back in to sew
    Up the case, look the perpetrator in the eye.
I'll bet you've learned to tie the knot
    By now, but I hope you won't mind my keeping
That clip-on as a kind of forget-me-not,
    A reminder of the ways your language works,
How when I think I've got you safe in hand,
    You surprise me yet again, slip away, shift ground,
Sway, regain your balance, make your stand.
    Fred, I haven't seen you for a while,
Not since George's birthday in D.C.
    And certainly not enough at all,
But I hope you'll accept this poem from me
    Even if Bizzaro sends it promptly back.
It isn't prose, is not an article, won't fit
    Easily into a bibliography, but it says something
I've wanted to say, and, so, that's it.

A LIST OF WORKS CITED surely must include
    The Book of Life; *The Book of Days*;
Midquest, of course; maybe even *The Book of Changes*
    Where, if memory serves (shall I laze
Around or look it up?), *It Is Time, Lord* appears
    As by Lord Chappell, the title
Transformed to *It Is Time, Fred* (I was always
    One for an easy laugh, but right'll
Soon prevail—or late, at least—in bibliographies
    If nowhere else); *The World Between the Eyes,*
Fred read from it in Charlottesville;
    The Young Lovers which met an early demise
(Goldwyn's movie, Garrett's script).
    Only to rise again on cable—our time's
Equivalent of the final trump that will
    Bring the good, the lovely, cancelled lines, poor rimes,

Each wayward thought, each bright surmise,
    All sights and sounds, the ugly, even the bad
All back to light; and let's see, Bergman movies,
    Vargtimmen, *Trollflojten*, and other sad
Lantern shows too numerous to mention;
    The Book of Sand; *The Book of the Dead*;
The Gourmet's Guide to EAT, Virginia; *Frankenstein*;
    And all the books we've ever wished we'd read.

First and Last Words:
A Conversation with Fred Chappell

RESA CRANE AND JAMES KIRKLAND

Fred Chappell's house rests in a hilly section of Greensboro, not far from the University of North Carolina. Flowering trees bloom, and a light rain falls. The house itself is solid; brick walls support light-green trim.

Fred, dressed casually in gray pants, sweater, and brown loafers, greets us at the door and leads us to a den at the back of the house, which holds a well-used fireplace and flowered furniture. Art in various mediums by new artists decorates the walls. A piano stool holds three books—*Masterpieces of Eighteenth Century Drawing*, *François Boucher*, and *Masterdrawings from the Woodner Collection*—which demonstrate the diverse interests informing and influencing Fred's work. We talk for a few moments about everything from the state of education to the condition of the Chappells' backyard garden; then the conversation turns to Fred's poetry.

JK: I was watching a videotape of the North Carolina writers program where you were interviewed with Reynolds Price. The interviewer asked how you got involved in writing, and you said you decided to go to Duke, but something other than your high school grades got you in. Was it your writing?

FC: Yes, I wrote a lot. Great volumes of stuff. I think I wrote two or three short stories a month. I'm trying to remember.

JK: So you were writing in both mediums at the same time?

FC: Yes. Yes, I think everyone starts with poetry. Even Marx started with poetry. But most people switch over or settle on one or the other.

RC: Were there people in your family who encouraged you to write or did you start yourself?

FC: It was on my own. They discouraged me very thoroughly. They did all kinds of things to discourage me every now and then. But like most families, this was such a puzzling development to them they really didn't know how to take it. So sometimes they would encourage me. The great *encouragement* was that my folks were teachers . . . so that their house had books in it. They expected us to read and write, and they took it for granted that we would probably go to college, which was not usual at that place and time.

RC: So you could get a degree and find a "real" job?

FC: That became some small source of contention when I was in graduate school, too. Well . . . [getting a degree] just looks like an impossibly long process, you know.

JK: It wasn't like becoming a doctor, where you have some understandable goal.

FC: That's right.

RC: But in your profession you do operate on words.

FC: Like a lawyer, right. Seems to me all kinds of professions operate primarily on words.

RC: Do you do a lot of revision?

FC: Oh! As a matter of fact, I revise so much and so often that that's the part I enjoy. I really *love* first drafts.

RC: You mean you don't produce perfect drafts the first time?

FC: No. Used to. [*Chuckles.*] That is, I published 'em. I write everything in longhand. And there's some *real* revisions. Top to bottom editing. So the amount of revision is simply enormous.

JK: Do you do a lot of cutting and pasting?

FC: Yes. I do a lot of that, but that's after the day-by-day revisions. So it's just a lot of revision. I never regretted having to cut anything except when I was working on this new series of novels where it's supposed to be humorous, and it was so difficult to think of anything even remotely amusing that I just hate to cut anything that's even a *tiny bit* humorous.

RC: Are influences on your current work the same as influences on your earlier work? And if not, how have they changed?

FC: Well, I don't know. I mean, people you think—or hope consciously—are influencing you may not be the writers who are. Probably the earlier influences are pretty steady—people like Ray Bradbury and Mark Twain. Later on, they kind of flit about. Steadily, when I knew him, the late Peter Taylor influenced me. Not his work so much as the knowledge that he might actually have read my pages. And then you all have infatuations that come and go. Some writers you may have never heard of: Laurie Lee, Kenneth Graham, people like that. But I know the kind of the tone I want to hit, so I don't worry too much about it. If I were trying to head out into new material I'd pick something, then I'd consciously search for a writer that had handled this kind of thing, or something like it, or something opposite to it, and I would search out an influence that way, certainly.

RC: You've said that people who want to write should read a lot. Do you still read a lot?

FC: I do. And I write a lot. I'm not even writing right now because I've got to read so much. I read a lot of books and, of course, I read all my students' writing. And I read all my friends' books. And they publish about seventeen a week. So that keeps me busy. And then you have research. I have research for my own projects. My reading after that is for my own pleasure and benefit and is hard to get to. But in the summer, if I'm not traveling, I usually try to establish a reading project.

JK: You mention the names of specific writers—Dante, for instance—in *Midquest* and other poems. Did you get that kind of background in your own home, or when you were in college, or afterwards?

FC: A great deal of my reading in the classics was when I was a kid in my home because, simply, there they were. A lot of reading in Shakespeare, Edgar Allan Poe, Robert Louis Stevenson, and stuff like that. My fun reading in those days was science fiction, and that was about the only *modern* literature, just about, that I could find, that I could put my hands on, anyway. Other stuff I wasn't interested in. Which was probably good stuff. And then when I got to Duke! What I loved about Duke—what I love about any college—is the library. I had never seen a library like that. I spent my first two years drinking beer and reading books out of the library and not going to class. I never had a course in Dante. But I've read through a number of translations and learned enough Italian to plug along and enjoy it very much.

JK: Since you mentioned Duke, I noticed that in *Wind Mountain*, in the dialogue between you and Reynolds Price and Susan, you were talking about the symbolic versus the literal. Is that a pretty accurate reflection of the kind of conversations you had then?

FC: Yes. Very accurate reflection of a kind of a continuing dialogue, or debate, that Reynolds and Jim Applewhite and I had in those days. Usually it was Jim and I who would argue with Reynolds. And from what Reynolds said, he thought it was very accurate. So maybe it is.

JK: So his sense of it was that you go with the situation pretty much the way it is—realistic.

FC: That's what he said then; we've all changed our minds since. That's the way it was then. What's kind of left out, I think, is that he was a successful novelist with his first novel, and Jim and I were jealous and felt that *poetry* was what was *really* worth writing. [*Laughs heartily.*]

JK: I would have thought that you would favor a more symbolic approach—which brings to mind another question. I know you do a lot of readings and workshops. Do readers ever bring anything to your poems that really startles you?

FC: Usually, when I'm really startled is about ten or eleven at night, and some *sophomore* who's been assigned to write a paper—someone in Utah, usually, or in the Midwest—has had about three too many No-Dozes and is struggling with his paper and will call me up and say: "This is what I think. Is this right?" And I always say, "Oh, *absolutely!* That was exactly what I had in mind." [*Laughs.*] Most readers use their common sense and have experience of their own to bring to bear on it, but for young—real young readers—it's a different world to them.

JK: Do you get different responses from readers who are from the area, from the mountains, who really know the culture from an inside position, versus people from the Northeast, maybe, or the West, who are not as familiar with it?

FC: Well, from the Northeast, their experiences are pretty constant. Out west, you can't tell—sometimes yes, sometimes no. The West is mostly populated by people who moved from the South. The difference—going up into the mountains, into that area—is that they seem to know who the people really are and call them by name and tell me stories about them. Those are wonderful responses.

RC: Are characters in your poems a compilation of several people, or are they just one person?

FC: It's not consistent from one to another. Sometimes they're just caricatures. I say caricatures; that's how it seems to me. Actually, I suppose, they're only exaggerated a bit and not real caricatures. A lot of them are single characters, some of them are composites of more than one person. Sometimes they're part portrait and part fabrication. Now and again you can find just a fabrication thrown in.

JK: How about Virgil Campbell, for instance? Is there someone he's strongly modeled on, or is he a composite character?

FC: This doesn't take much imagination. [*Winks.*] His real name was Homer Campbell, and yes, he was a real person and a very colorful person. Everyone who ever met him remembers him. People from that area will ask about him more than anything else. And because he *was* so colorful, and eccentric, and so forth, and *very* straightforward, he seemed to me a kind of good "guide," a good pivot for the Appalachian experience, to center. That's how he's used, to center.

RC: Earlier, when you were talking about influences, you said you usually already had something in mind. When you're working on poetry, does it dictate its own structure to you, or do you consciously decide on the structure, or does it come to you already structured?

FC: Very rarely comes to me already structured. When you start with a personality . . . I'll start with a voice or a kind of sound I want to have, or I'll start with the materials, and then beyond that, I know what kind of *feeling* I want, what kind of emotional effect when I get to the end of that.

JK: In the Preface to *Midquest* you talk about persons—Ol' Fred and the "I" narrator and the speaker, versus the more generalized situation. You mention that a voice comes to you first. Are you conscious of that as you're working, particularly with some of the later collections where the thematic coherence is not quite the same as it is in the earlier collections?

FC: Yes, it's conscious. That is, I can't make myself hear the voice, but I know I have to hear it. To that extent, it's conscious. But I can't create the voice. It has to come to me. I can't figure it out. I don't know how it works, but it is a voice, an actual voice. I can hear it pretty precisely. Usually, that's when I'm at work already. But I also hear it in the morning before I get up. And when things are going well, I see a whole page of typewriting from it. That's not what I write down when I go to work, but something about it . . . Maybe just the visual patterns or something. It's all very mysterious, I reckon, still.

JK: Concerning *Midquest*, I'm interested in the combination of genres in it.

FC: I didn't worry too much about what the total form was. I knew what I wanted. I just figured it was a long narrative poem in a complicated arrangement. I thought of it as a single work in four parts. And I'm working on—I'm trying to work on—a novel that follows that form. It's going to have to be in four parts, too. That is, the last two novels are supposed to be part of quartets. That will balance off *Midquest*.

JK: The mention of quartets reminds me that when I read *Midquest* I noticed a kind of musical construction. How much of that was by design?

FC: A fair amount of it. Perhaps an artistic . . . at least one artistic cynosure for me would be Beethoven's quartets, at least constant. And then later on—even more to my own purposes, I thought—were Bartok's quintets.

RC: Did you have the idea about the four books at the time you began writing *Midquest*?

FC: Not when I first started writing it. I didn't know what the hell I was doing. I had written the first poem of the first book and sent it off to a magazine, and then I didn't think about it. Didn't hear about it, either. The magazine folded, or I just forgot. Then it showed up, and I said: "Oh. I kind of remember this." And I think it's one of those things your mind does, deliberately, without your realizing it. I recognized that there was a lot of material there that was an overture to a large structure, and by the time I'd written the second poem, I saw that. I saw the shape of the whole thing. Not the exact structure but the shape of it. So, yes.

JK: You mentioned that *Midquest* was a reactionary poem. In what sense do you see it as reactionary?

FC: Oh, I thought it was reactionary compared not only to the kind of lyric poems written, and being written, by some poets over in the New York School and the Language School but also to the longer poems which follow to one degree or another the cantos. You could list a good dozen of those, like "Paterson" and a lot of those I haven't caught up with. So I just meant reactionary in using more traditional materials and certainly traditional forms—a deliberate choice not to write the other way. The publishers asked me to put that Preface in, and I don't regret it. I just think it might be misleading or distracting.

JK: I read the individual volumes first, so I didn't get to the Preface until last.

FC: Good. I would think that that Preface was misleading because I wrote it in a terrible hurry. The first time I saw it in print I thought, "This thing looks like I really knew what the hell I was doing." But I really didn't know that much. [*Chuckles.*]

JK: The Preface was interesting because it mentioned the things that struck me as I was reading each of the four books, like the structural forms and the dramatic monologues and the interior monologues and all those other features. The Preface reinforced most of my intuitions about the collection. I would like to pursue, though, some of the issues raised in the Preface. The verse form variations in the *Midquest* poems, for example— Did you have a sense of the content or the subject matter or the personalities?

FC: Yes. I had the material and I knew the *shape* and I knew how I wanted people to feel in certain parts. And *then* there was the difficulty of matching the material to the different forms. And some of the larger decisions were easy. Most of the material in present time is in free verse so the emotional factor is very tight, but others just simply didn't want to go. There's some poems I could just never learn to handle. Never learned at all. Sapphics, for example. I tried those for a while. And there was also some material in *Castle Tzingal* that I didn't know what to do with.

RC: Can you talk about the perspective in the first poem in *River*, "The River Awakening into the Sea"? You start out with "It's morning . . . ," written from the perspective of somebody who's watching what's going on. It's morning, and even though readers identify with the "my" of the poem itself, the readers and the persona are still separate because readers must imagine the two people in bed together and the two people as one; as you say, of course, a spiritual community.

FC: Yeah. I've talked to other people, and the perspective in that poem is very odd to me, but other people had the same idea. Your point of view can be fixed in the corner of the room. Kids do that a lot. They always imagine someone watching them. Except they always imagine their parents watching them from that angle, or their teacher—maybe their Sunday school teacher—and I wanted to write it because I had to get something else. Because if I used "I," it'd just be somebody waking up and you wouldn't . . . well, you couldn't read it quite that way. So I had to use a double perspective, but I tried to hide it.

RC: The perspective makes it easier for the reader to identify what is going on in the poem.

FC: Well, it was either that or be stuck with some sort of Joycean language of semiconsciousness. "There was a little boy with a moo-cow. . . ." At one point in the series, Susan is caught like that, where she's halfway awake—no, not even halfway awake, maybe a quarter of the way awake—and she thinks and is a little bit confused. But I didn't want to do it too much because then you'd have this whole poem with this kind of baby talk, and I . . . I don't know. Choices. It's like sorting oranges. You just decide whether this one is big, medium, or small. All day long you sit at the table and say, "I don't know."

RC: Writing is not as concrete as it seems when you begin to think about asking questions about it. How does Susan feel about being the subject of many of your poems?

FC: You'll have to ask her to make sure, but she's never said anything bad about it. She thought I was making her seem goody-goody, and she didn't want that. So she was very happy to have the nude study. She thought that was funny. Then people started asking her about it, and it wasn't so funny anymore. [*Laughs heartily.*]

JK: We noticed that *River*, like the other books in *Midquest*, has eleven poems, with one about Virgil Campbell in the middle. Most of the pairings are very clear, but what did you see as the parallel between "My Grandmother Washes Her Feet" and "Science Fiction Water Letter to Guy Lillian"?

FC: Invented histories, invented histories of the world and the family. It's much the same. "Water Letter" is invented history. Creation myths. I parody those a lot. That's the fiction there. Yes, I guess that's not as symmetrical as it should be, but that's the way I thought of it.

RC: In the novel section of "Water Letter," you describe this creation, and the woman who's called Mother of the Year comes down and meets the first Dumb Joe that comes along and she says, "Now listen to me honey, / I'm only going to say this once, so try / to get it." That section reminded me of Helen Keller being taught language.

FC: Right. That's kind of what I had in mind. That's just looking at history. Some of the linguistic histories—which to me are real fairy tales—

when they list the oldest words they can track down, water is always one of them. And "wa-wa" is it, so I had to throw it in. And then, I thought as you did about teaching the deaf to speak.

JK: In the poem "Grandmother Washes Her Feet," there's a part at the end that mentions becoming a clerk or a lawyer.

FC: Oh yes. That's a pretty accurate reporting of what someone—a lady who was not my grandmother—said.

RC: With regard to occupations, in the poem "My Father Washes His Hands," the father talks about giving up farming and says something about selling furniture to poor people. The poem is written from his perspective, so would you say that this is a close representation of his personality or— as we discussed earlier—a compilation of personalities?

FC: I can't judge that. I tried to draw his personality in a certain light. The poems tend to idealize parents, of course. Filial poems do, to a certain extent. But to the best of my ability, without really precise naturalism, those are the characters as I see them.

RC: So he farmed in addition to being a teacher?

FC: Yes, he did. Most teachers still farm, I think, or they have some other job, yes. And most farmers have some other job because they usually have to support a farm. Which I *think* was the case in our family. At least the farm has never produced any tangible income—above costs—since I've been alive. In my hometown, everybody worked for the paper mill and the farm; before they got to the mill and after they got off, they farmed. And that's what supported the farm. They always felt that it was a sort of investment that you kept paying your life into rather than anything else. Because, I think, for them—and for a lot of people still—even that much land represents an independence of sorts.

JK: As a folklorist, I'm interested in the ways you use folk materials in your poems—the tall tales in the hurricane poem, for example, with the Beethoven symphony coming down the river. Did your father actually tell those stories?

FC: Not specifics. Those specific stories weren't anything to my dad. I made those up or borrowed them. But he did love to tell stories. It's just that I can't remember many that he told. I have to supply them.

JK: Like the story in "My Father's Hurricane" about the storm being so strong it blew the lid off a jar of pickles that they had tried to unscrew for fifteen years?

FC: That's something my father would say. That might even be a quote there.

JK: And the last scene where the hotel and all the lovers were carried away in the storm—that was funny, too. And then there's the voice that says: "Now don't say too much about that. Be careful what you say." There are some other funny parts in those poems that remind me of stories I've heard before—like the one where Virgil Campbell is caught by the *current* woman with the *other* woman.

FC: Oh yeah, the shroud beating. That's a folktale that I've heard for a hundred years, and I finally used it. I first heard it from a service man who told me that it happened to his sergeant. And then after that, I began to hear it from everybody, so I figured, "Ha, ha, ha."

A couple of times I did that in the making of *Midquest*. I deliberately took folk stories people would probably know and tried to reshape them into verses. Just kind of in homage to Chaucer. In fact, "Three Sheets in the Wind: Virgil Campbell Confesses" used to be in a very tight verse form—a little five-line stanza that kind of rhymes—and then when I thought Chaucer was making things in particular like that, I thought I'd put Chaucer in couplets, which is what it's in now. Somewhere or another in some magazine or another, it exists in that five-line verse—each five-line stanzas—but I've forgotten the places. Be interesting for me to compare them sometimes.

I wonder whatever made me think to tell a longish story like that in little tiny bitsy mosaic pieces. [*Winks.*] You just don't know what the hell gets into you. I make one mistake after another.

JK: The humor comes not only from the kind of incongruity you just mentioned but also from the effect produced by some of the verse forms you use. For example, in the poem "Birthday 35: Diary Entry," you say: "Multiplying my age by 2 in my head / I'm a grandfather. Or dead."

FC: That's one section that I don't like at all.

RC: You don't like the poem itself, you mean?

FC: "Diary Entry"? I like the middle part with the dog in it. But I don't like those dumb little couplets. They seem awfully clunky to me now.

JK: In other poems, though, the couplets seem exactly right for the comic effect. There are a number of passages, for instance, where I'm reminded of *Don Juan*.

FC: Every once in a while, one of those characters does kind of break into that couplet that ends Byron's *Don Juan* stanzas. What is that? Rime royal? No, ottava rima. I discovered that Byron is funny because he establishes himself in the poems very early, but in this poem, if it doesn't come from a character it's not funny; it's just miserable. But the other people can talk out of their own concerns and their own characters—then you've got a chance.

The lady with the glass eye, for example—she was a real lady. She wasn't in my family, but she was a real lady, and she did that to me when I was a kid. She came by with her eye and tried to hand it to me and said, "Stick this in." She was addicted to paregoric. She really was. That is a strange addiction, which means that she had to beg for money. But you don't . . . I never heard of anybody begging in the mountains. So that was how she did it. She would say, "Would you put my eye back in for me?" And people would say, "Why don't you go see a doctor about that eye, Annie?" And they'd give her a little money, and she'd say: "Oh, okay. Maybe that's better." At the time, I didn't understand what was going on. I figured it out years later, like you do most things.

JK: While we're on the subject of unusual characters, could you comment on what you were attempting to accomplish in *Castle Tzingal*? That book seems so distinctive in concept and technique; where did it come from, and how does it fit with your other works?

FC: Wooo! I don't know. I know the first poem in there, "The Homunculus," I woke up at three o'clock in the morning and wrote it down just like it is, except for changing one or two words. So it came to me in a kind of dream or vision or something. I have no idea. But I knew that wasn't the end of it. So I just published it—somewhere, I can't remember where—and let it lie because I knew the rest of that story would want to be told sometime. And I hit a dry spot with fiction and just happened to remember a line of that poem somewhere. But it was very difficult. It was not easy to put that story together. And it used to be much more complicated. So that you didn't know, actually, who had done the murders, and all kinds of different things were going on. And I thought, "This thing looks kind of weird already." And I knew that people would get impatient and not be able to follow it, so I simplified the story, but now I think I made a mistake. I should have left that story convoluted and complex.

JK: The book still seems complex, though, because the characters tell their own stories and the reader has to piece things together.

FC: Yeah, but I had them out of chronological order and some characters assuming other characters' voices and all kinds of other weird stuff. But I don't like to be obscure. I like to be clear. But I think I may have simplified the suspense of that story. It should have some suspense.

JK: You really get a sense of the distinctive personality of each persona in these poems. That's what interested me the most.

FC: That's what interested me, too. The hardest persona was the Queen, because the difficulty was not to make her sound whining but [to make her] one of verity's heroines. I'm not sure I solved that problem.

JK: Was the main difficulty that the characters are so different from Virgil Campbell or your father or grandfather, where you have actually heard their voices and you have some recollection of them?

FC: The difficulty was not to let it verge too closely into contemporary political allegory. My original title was *Orpheus at Watergate* or something. And the poem got a little better the farther it went, but it never entirely lost that Watergate paranoid quality, I don't think. The closer it verges toward political allegory and satire, the weaker it is, it seems to me. And the more fairy-tale the atmosphere, the more successful it is. I'd always hoped that Sendak would illustrate that poem, but he hasn't showed any interest so far.

RC: I've noticed a number of political poems in *First and Last Words* also, but there you seem to be dealing with many other themes as well. Did you have a thematic structure or just a general organizational pattern already in mind? Or did you decide on an arrangement after you knew which poems you wanted to include?

FC: I had a couple of poems—let's see if I can remember which ones. the "Book of Job" poem I had, and "Patience" I worked on for a long, long time, and "Afternoons with Allen," which I hadn't thought of for a long time until now, and then years afterward, "Scarecrow Colloquy." And it occurred to me that these are prologues. And epilogues. And that would make a nice design for a book. And that was part of it. The longer part was the Entr'act. But they should all deal with cultural artifacts of one sort or another. They should be kind of a book about books about art and that sort of thing—with less use of folk material. But I have the Mountain Mama "Book of Job" there as a lead-in from the other material into this.

RC: In that particular poem you talk about her reading and her hands and how her fingers look. There's a lot of physical or anatomical images in this book, like the hands. And that's repeated in "My Hands Placed on a Reubens Drawing" and in several of the other poems. Also the lovers' limbs in . . .

FC: "Slow Harbor"? I liked that poem, too. I don't get to write too many love poems. Except in *Midquest,* I guess.

JK: Another poem I enjoyed in *First and Last Words* was "Remodeling the Hermit's Cabin."

FC: Yeah, kind of a little allegory about constitutional reform or whatever they call it. That actually took place. This poem was a poem before I thought about it being an allegory. We took apart a wonderful old hermit's cabin up in the mountains, for this fella from Florida. He was justified because the ceiling was so low. I mean, one guy built this little old cabin. And as soon as he could reach up a little bit, he quit. I don't blame him. But he used enormous materials, and the floor beams and everything were eighteen inches square. So that was fun. And the figures in it, of course, come from *Walden*—they're borrowed from Thoreau's building his cabin, which I thought I'd stick in for fun.

RC: Some of the poems in *First and Last Words* had a strong emphasis on the elements, especially "Prayer for the Hanged Man."

FC: I'm not sure that one should be in there. That one is an overtly political poem, written during the early days of Nicaragua and El Salvador. And it was my attempt to think how revolution is carried on. That is, at first there is some political ideal, but pretty soon in the small situation we have there, it becomes a matter of family revenge. And it goes around the circle and then gets elevated to political idealism. And it just seemed to me to be the way that worked. I was also thinking a little bit about Antigone in that poem. But it's not quite as directly literary, somehow.

JK: It's connected with the pastoral tradition, too, through the Georgics poem. Of course, the poem "Patience" starts out with an idealized view of nature, then moves to the reality of war.

FC: Well, actually, I thought it would probably be read in this way, but the more warlike passages in that poem come from the original poem. They are a direct translation of the Georgics, and the other is kind of an imitation of pastoralism. But Virgil—and this is one of the things that's missing in the later pastoral poems—Virgil was careful to include the fact of war. And his picture of it, I thought, was pretty good. So I translated it and throwed it in.

RC: "Patience" also fits in with "Digs" because there is the idealized image at first, and then the second section describes the way things really are. First you're talking about the past and all this history that was in the making. Then the second section talks about the way it is now. And finally, in the end section, there's a synthesis, as in "Patience." So when I read those two poems, it seems that the structure echoes.

FC: It does. It mirrors it. I had not thought of that. But I think that one would necessarily attract the other in a volume of that size. It's also connected with a poem called "How the Job Gets Done." That was written as a kind of pendant to "Patience." I mean, specifically toward the end of the book. But I hadn't thought of "Digs." I guess it's simply because the subject—the background subject matter—is Roman material and this is Anglo-Saxon material. I thought of them as being a little bit different, but they're not.

RC: "Digs" was written in three separate sections. The first section talks about what has happened in the past—the "grave heaps" and all the things that characterize past generations—the "vallations the Romans built / and died in, before the eastern troubles / called them off to these white headlands." And then in the second part, "quite a triumph in the professor's notebook," there's "the Beaker People / the Corded Pot People / the Long Knives," and it goes on, saying in effect, here is the road, here are the train tracks, and here in between are all these artifacts that someone could possibly find, yet they're just passed over every day by people who don't even realize what's there. And then the final section pulls those details together.

JK: There is a part at the end where you satirize people who try to exploit these materials for personal gain, as when the professor discovers the citation.

FC: A little Anglo-Saxon alliterative meter in the section. Well, I was amazed when we were going through England a couple of years ago to find that the archaeology is right there, everywhere. Right next to the Holiday Inn. So that you could actually just stay in the hotel and go out and make wonderful discoveries there.

RC: You went to Italy with your family on a fellowship. How long were you there? And do you find that what you observed and did while you were in Italy frequently comes up in your poetry?

FC: We were there nine months, and I do feel its influence, but it's hard to put one's finger on it. An interest in art, of course, which I had before, but nothing like just standing there and saturating myself in it. But also a kind of realization of what European culture is really like. To be there for a long period of time is very different from taking a course. In the first place, you realize how casual people are who live in the midst of these works of art—how much they take for granted—and you also realize, thank goodness, that they don't know any more about it than you do. Just because you're born in a museum city doesn't necessarily mean you're a professor in a university.

JK: Was there some particular incident that led you to that realization?

FC: Well, my best lesson was when we were in Italy on a Sunday afternoon, and lots of soldiers were at the art museums. You find lots of them in troops there, with their sergeants lecturing to them about art. But some of the soldiers have nothing better to do because they're broke, and they take their girlfriends there. There was some perfectly normal Greek statue there that grossed these two kids out. So it's perfectly obvious that they had never looked at the statues before. It was just very interesting to me.

RC: Your interest in people and the arts is reflected in a number of poems we haven't yet talked about, such as "The Reader" and the poem immediately following it, "The Garden."

FC: Yes, literature and the word, or words. Those poems are deliberately a duo. "The Reader" is my mother-in-law, Helene, who read until the last few months just the way it was described. Her mind was still sound, but her eyesight was failing her, and she moved into a retirement home. But that's the way she was.

RC: There's a lot of physical imagery in "The Reader," too. You talk about how her body "asks a painful question of the book."

FC: She had acute scoliosis, so she was hunched like a question mark over the book.

RC: You go on to say "her fingers are so smooth and white / they reflect the pages; a light / the color of cool linen bathes her hands," and that refers back to the beginning poem, "An Old Mountain Woman Reading the Book of Job."

FC: Yeah, I tried to draw that—the picture of the hand upon the book is a very powerful force for me. I think that there are a couple of Dürer drawings that utilize the same imagery that stick in my mind. And I wanted to bring that juxtaposition of the hand of a flesh-and-blood person, lying on top of or emerging from the history that produced it. I just think that's a dominant image for me. In certain parts of the book, there are certain parts of the body—a great deal of hands and plows and swords and tools, bows, that sort of thing: anatomical imagery.

RC: In "My Hands Placed on a Rubens Drawing" you talk about art and how art struggles to get away from the person who created it and there's a carved fist—I believe it was carved in stone?

FC: That's deliberate, that shifts from Rubens there, of course. I was thinking specifically of Michaelangelo's "David," which we used to see in Florence at the Academie of Florence all that time, and his hand is about eye level, so you can get a real shot of this hand. If you look at it too much, it's bothersome; it kind of haunts you.

RC: Of all the poems in *First and Last Words* that revolve around works of art, "My Hands Placed on a Rubens Drawing" is my favorite. Even if readers don't know Rubens, the images conjure up exactly the kind of woman Rubens painted.

FC: Well, I think one of the things that happens, to me at any rate, as I grow older, is that I learned to like a lot of art I didn't care for when I was younger. Rubens was a painter I did not care for when I was in Europe, and just by dint of study—I do that when I find something I don't really care for much—I finally got to where I appreciate those ladies of Rubens. So I try hard; Rubens was a step some way—sideways—for me.

JK: There's quite a contrast between this volume and your next collection, *C.* When did you first become interested in epigrams, and what stimulated that interest?

FC: Well . . . it took over fifteen years to write. But in order to get a hundred epigrams, you've got to write about six hundred—and even then you've got some clinkers in there, as you know. There's no way out of it—it's recognized by all epigrammatists. First book of epigrams that counts was Martial's, and he said—matter of fact, I translated it somewhere—the same thing: several of them are going to be duds. [*Laughs.*]

RC: Did you decide to call the book *C* only because there are a hundred poems, or is the title meant to evoke other associations as well?

FC: It has many different possibilities. It's C—to see. It's also my initial. And there's another: I have a plan to bring out another book of fifty short stories called *L.* [*Chuckles.*]

JK: Did the fact that you included only epigrams in this volume make it easier or more difficult to organize than your earlier collections?

FC: When you have small enough units like that you can play around a lot. You have to tell a story in much larger units of thought, and you don't have as much control over it like you do with those itsy things. They're arranged sort of by motif. You'll have a bunch about literary critics, and a bunch about politicians. And the whole thing kind of takes place in the space of a day. There's a morning that goes by, and there's a serenade at night, and the seasons come in. There are youthful poems and love poems and grouchier poems.

RC: Speaking of the grouchier poems and the politician poems, we laughed at "El Perfecto."

FC: Yes, that poem got more comment from reviewers than any other poem. Nobody, nobody misidentified the subject of that poem.

JK: So do you have any politicians or critics or anyone else you satirize in the poems who speak back?

FC: No, just a few comments here and there. From the newspapers, post offices, friends, that's all. No real heavy feedback. The deconstructionists or poststructuralists never ask *me* for any aid or anything like that. They already have answers.

RC: We noticed that all of the poems can be read on several different levels. For instance, with the critics poems, if you don't know exactly who the critics are, you know enough about critics in general so you can enjoy the poem. If you do know which critic is being picked on, then it's even more fun.

FC: There are a few of those that are probably identifiable to those in the racket; I don't know. Other people might read the poems and think they know who they [the critics] are.

RC: I'm very interested in words, language use, and particularly dialect—spoken dialect—I wonder how the epigrams themselves influenced the language that you've used. The style of the epigram is prescribed, but how about the language you've used and the subject matter?

FC: Well, there is a difference. In the first place, the epigram is so brief that, generally, you don't have room to indulge in characterization at all. So that your use of colloquial speech is not to regionalize a voice or characterize the speaker. The epigrammatic language itself is rather formal language, especially if you're using rhyme forms or metric forms because you have to get the whole in a very short space, and our more formal words—even our abstractions—tend to stay that way. Probably there are more abstractions in this book than you would find in an ordinary book. That's just about all you're doing, in that case.

JK: Yet despite the formality and abstractness of the language, there is a conversational tone in many of the epigrams, such as "Rx."

FC: There I had to characterize the doctor in a very brief way using an old, rough, country doctor's speech and also to imply in the poem that there's a friendship between the two people, so that he can get away with drinking his patient's whiskey and fob it off as a joke. That's a translation from Martial. I think I'm the only person to have attempted a real translation of that poem, but you can *never* be sure.

One of the things I've found out since it's been published is that most of the letters I got were from epigrammatists, and of course, there is such a fierce little cadre of them, they made a study of these things. Well, I guess you do if you write them; you make a study of them. And they have societies, and a magazine called *The Epigrammatist.* Have you ever seen it? It's this big. [*Holds his left thumb and forefinger against his right forefinger.*]

JK: Although the epigram obviously lends itself to comic expression, I was surprised at its versatility.

FC: Well, epigrams tend to be little short jolts. Some have to be serious, and some have to be melancholy. It's like a movie that's all one-liners. So there's serious poems in there, and I suppose the form of epigrams is now what it was two thousand years ago. That's the way Martial's poems are, too. Some of them are so ambiguous you don't really know if they're funny or sad or what they are. But we've lost the tone of those.

RC: Are all the epigrams that have a name at the bottom translations?

FC: Yes, but you adapt them to your needs. I put my name in on purpose so that I could have an answer to him—a reply to him, in a sense. So his poem, which begins directly with someone talking to Martial—it says "Martial . . ."—and goes from there, I changed it to Chappell. That is one that did not need to be translated. The Earl of Surrey translated many of them, but I had to retranslate it in order to write my reply. So I put myself in competition with this great classic poem by Surrey. [*Laughs.*]

JK: Speaking of the classics, when did you first become interested in Juvenal and Martial?

FC: It came about when I was at Duke. I had a terrific Latin teacher named John Mahoney, who was a wonderful scholar and very fine teacher, and maybe the first Catholic I ever met, I'm not sure. And he was so interested in students that he decided to have a little Aristotle Club over at his house, and we went and we read *Nichomachean Ethics*. I didn't realize we were being proselytized, but so what? Under the circumstances we got to read Aristotle. Later on, I swear to God, I think he went to Hollywood. I think he got divorced and dropped out of the academy. Anyway, he struck up my interest in them. The only classical poets I knew were Homer and Virgil—that I had read in prose translation. Then when I got to Duke, there were all these other folks I had no access to at home, and I was, of course, very much taken. They were fascinating poets, especially Catullus, Martial, and—to a certain extent—Ovid. For some reason, I couldn't catch onto Horace. For some reason, I didn't begin to like Horace until just about fifteen years ago. And then I caught on and started enjoying him. He's incredibly difficult to translate. You need to figure out, sometimes, what Horace is telling you.

RC: So you're still reading those in Latin?

FC: Yes, when I have time, I like to.

JK: You've included quite a few poems from *C* in your new book, *Spring Garden*. Is that because you see epigrams as a particularly important poetic form, or do they serve some other purpose?

FC: For variety's sake, you want to improve the rhythm of the book, so there are some shorter poems. The epigrams are scattered about; I didn't want to put them all in one place.

RC: We wondered if the kind of structure found in *Midquest* is similar to that of *Spring Garden;* for example, in *Midquest* you can almost fold the separate books together and poems one and twelve go together, and two and eleven, and three and ten, and so on. Is there a similar structure for *Spring Garden?*

FC: Well, just the very loose narrative structure that it all takes place in a single day. I started the book in the garden with Susan slaving away, and I'm here foolin' with my poems, and that's about it. So that's it; it's not done geometrically. The organization is just an accident of poems composed over many years that happened to fall into these different categories.

RC: It took you several years of drinking tea in the morning to decide the organization of the book?

FC: Well, no, it took editors sending back the first version of the book for copy editing; that's soon after it was accepted about four years ago. It was my new and selected poems, just like you were asking. You know, here's some old poems, and here's some new poems. And it was very disappointing. It was like a book that was snippets of other books. I decided I had to do something with the whole thing, and so that's what I came up with. It's *Spring Garden,* of course, because that's where I work. That's the university address, and it seemed like a good idea to name it *Spring Garden.* It was particularly effective, *Spring Garden,* because I collected so many of my little flowers, and they would be like students. That's all. I just needed to make a whole volume—something to draw the poems together.

JK: We were both curious how you decided which poems to include and which to leave out.

FC: Well, some of the choices were quite difficult, but it was easy—fairly easy—to say, "Not that one! God help us, not that one!" The real dreadful ones are easy enough to spot. The ones that I kind of like—that's not so hard. But there's a whole lot of poems that I'm really not sure whether or not to use. I'd say, "Do I really want to use this thing? Maybe if I rewrite it. . . ." So a lot of them are new versions. That helps a little. And then if I write a new version I say, "I'm going to include it because I did a lot of work on it. Publish it if it's good or not!"

JK: While reading *Spring Garden,* we realized that there were very few poems from *Midquest* and *Castle Tzingal.* Is that because these volumes are so self-contained?

FC: One thing I did decide was that first of all, no poems from *Midquest.* Then I decided I would include two. Well, I needed a Susan poem, obviously, and then I decided that I wanted a character poem which would be the best to show a character's personality. Or just because I liked it—I think it's the grandmother poem. And I just kind of liked the poem, so I wanted to put that in there. It was a kind of watermark for me. The first of those narrative dialogue poems I'd written. And for something original. Most of the rest of them, all the rest of them, all the rest of *Midquest,* is not there. It's just not there. I couldn't find any way to piece it out. They wouldn't stand alone. I think they have to feed off each other, and the same is true of *Castle Tzingal.*

RC: Considering the poems you did include, they seem to be told from the perspective of someone looking back over his or her life, as if to say, "They always told me I'd get here, but I just didn't believe it."

FC: That's true. There was no way a volume of new and selected poetry was not going to be reminiscent. I don't see how you could avoid it. And that's one of the things I didn't like with the first version; they were just poems. And I needed a way to set them; I thought, there's kind of a reminiscence, a looking back to weeding my garden—throwing out the poison oak and the ragweed, and trying to keep a little thyme and ginger would be the way to do it. You're right; there is a kind of looking back saying, "Oh, Lord! It's getting late in the day."

JK: So the title, then, works on several different levels simultaneously?

FC: Yes, that's partly because of the Ronsard model; Ronsard suggested that in a poem about spring. It's about going out and gathering herbs for a salad. According to the poem, it must have been one heck of a salad. He had a lot of herbs in it, and I think he might have been in poor health, and the salad was meant to restore him. So that's the start of it, and it is spring garden. Part of the irony is, of course, that we're weeding a spring garden at a later stage of our life.

RC: Another thing I noticed in this manuscript is the same kind of intense physical imagery that predominates in *First and Last Words*. For instance, some of the general prologue talks specifically about Susan working outside; it mentions her hands. Then there's "My Hands Placed on a Rubens Drawing," the original poem which made me notice this imagery, and "The Reader."

FC: Yes, they're here.

JK: What makes the physical images so remarkable to me is the range of responses they elicit. Some are highly realistic, while others, such as "Rider," make ordinary things seem strange, otherworldly.

FC: Yes, the "rider" alluded to in that poem is sometimes called the "wild huntsman" figure from folklore, sometimes called the phantom rider. It was written for *Contemporary Poetry Review,* and it was a special issue dedicated to Heather Miller. She was married to Clyde, a forest ranger at White Lake, and she used to go to one particular place in the woods there, a dense, thicket place; it reminded her of places she had seen when she was a girl. When she was a child, she would imagine that a stranger came through there and rode away with the children. And I thought that the legend of children hiding, hiding away in leaves and waiting until the wild huntsman came by, and then when they see him and see what a force of nature he is, they join him willingly and gladly. That's what it was all about. That was the whole thing.

JK: Yes, it's like a fairy tale—except for the last line.

FC: "All fairy tales are true, all except our own." That is, all the fairy tales have happy endings. People's true lives don't have happy endings.

RC: Would you describe your ideal reader, or what kind of reader you envision? Do you envision one kind of reader for a certain poem or set of poems and another reader for another set of poems?

FC: Yes, it shifts. I don't always imagine an ideal reader, but often do, and yes, it does shift. It shifts slightly. There's probably a group of about a dozen figures, historical and personal, that I just kind of refer to eventually. Reynolds would be one; Peter Taylor was one; George Garrett I always think of. But then all kinds of people I think of. My wife, Susan, is a person I always refer to. But most of it is other writers of poetry that have been with us for quite a while.

My particular audience does get a little larger for each book of fiction, except the latest collection of short stories. It gets a little larger for each book of poetry, unless it's something really weird like *Castle Tzingal.* But who they are, exactly, I have not the faintest idea. The letters I get are kind of all over the place. They're not in the mid-range. They're usually young people who have been asked to read the book, or somebody made them read the book, and older people who are retired and are in their fifties and sixties, but I don't get the thirty-something crowd. I guess they don't know about me or don't want to read it. So my audience is kind of centralized.

RC: Someone once said that your work follows a circular pattern, returning to earlier situations and themes. Do you agree?

FC: Well, if everything goes according to plan—it's not going to go according to schedule—a novel that I've begun working on will start that process. It'll be the last book of the quartet that started with *I Am One of You Forever.* But that's about seven-tenths through the third volume now, and the last one will bring these self-consciously together.

RC: So, there's *I Am One of You Forever* and *Brighten the Corner Where You Are,* and a third volume almost finished. Is there another book in the works other than the one you're writing?

FC: I've got to finish this . . . it's not really a novel, it's kind of what they call a "fix-up." It's a bunch of short stories kind of connected but very loosely. That's called *Farewell, I'm Bound to Leave You.* After that, the fourth novel is about Jess—reminiscing rather like *Spring Garden* many years later. His parents have passed away, and he has to go back and, I guess, sell off the farm—that period of a man's life.

RC: What a terrible loss for him. What a confusing part of his life.

FC: It will be very difficult for him. He shall have become an academic by then, a classical scholar, as a matter of fact, engaged in a translation of the *Georgics*—farming poems—which will be kind of ironic and sorrowful. I don't know. We'll see how all this works out.

RC: Well, I'm sure he's taken on a life of his own, and it's only the first few pages you have to work to lead him through; after that. . . .

FC: That's the best kind of writing. When it comes alive like that and takes the bit in its teeth.

RC: Do you think you'll get a chance to write another poem again?

FC: [*Laughs.*] The next book of poetry looks like it's going to be a little book of character sketches. Another satirical book after this rather serious one, called *Family Gathering,* but I've just started this one.

RC: Is that going to be people from your family?

FC: Oh, no, it's just fiction.

RC: Will it be closer along the lines of *Castle Tzingal*?

FC: No, it'll be very light, for the most part. It's a breather between serious work. Other ones are harder to do because the technique has to be perfect.

JK: Could you comment on the changes you've seen in your poetry from *The World Between the Eyes* to *Spring Garden*?

FC: Well, one change I'd be interested in is if it got any better. I didn't think about it then, partly because I didn't know what I was doing, but I wasn't really satisfied with *The World Between the Eyes*. So *River* came about partly because I looked at that first book and thought the only way to improve was to try and change what I was doing, so I really buckled down.

RC: Being conscious of the differences in structure, I was wondering if the books you've written so far fit into an overall pattern.

FC: Now there's a possibility. I've learned that I've begun to think in terms of quartets, and I have ambitious plans for lots of things—as I was saying a moment ago—whether they work out or not. Actually, I prefer not to even talk about them. George Garrett told me he had the impression that sooner or later all my stuff would tie together. How boring. That's probably true. He was probably right about that.

RC: One final question we'd like to ask concerns a related idea—which surfaces repeatedly in your poetry—that there's one person, who is two people, who are one. You can really see that in some of the love poems, especially the Susan poems, where there's a distinction between the persona and Susan, then they seem to be one, then they're two, and finally they're one again. Can you talk about that? Some examples are "Fire Now Wakening on the River," "Susan Bathing," and in a different way, "My Grandmother Washes Her Feet." In the last one, the younger man the grandmother is speaking to is separate from his family, but at the same time he's not able to get away from them because they are tied culturally as well as familially. And then they're separate again.

FC: I believe in some sort of way that there's a community and that we are momentary manifestations, each of us. We're momentary manifestations. And—this is interesting—we're individuals and quite apart. But when we're asleep, when we're dead, before we get born, we're all a part of that same mass of humanity. And the personality rises to the surface, and then it goes back to whatever it came from.

In that sense of community and in his ability to portray experience—both lofty and mundane—lie Fred Chappell's deepest talents. As we drive away, Fred's house recedes down Walker Avenue, which ultimately gives way to Spring Garden Street, a reminder of the conversation just concluded and the poems and stories yet to be written.

Proteus Loose in the Baptismal Font

R. T. Smith

Autumnal Equinox in the Blue Ridge but November in my soul, as Melville says. What I get for water is saltless rain, a small river for my canoe. A hornet dries on the sill, and ubiquitous crickets are tightening down. A yellow finch raids the cat's food. Fenceline, hillcrest, cow-jawed lethargy, and road ruts; a train snakes under the bridge. In the next valley, a steeple shines. What I'm doing is fingering the beads, working across the landscape of chestnut, poplar, and blue spruce toward the place of writing, the calm cove where smoke from a single house steadies the day. This is Chappell territory, the region he has loved fiercely enough to possess it, as Didion has suggested one can do. It is important that Chappell is from near here—Canton, North Carolina, to be exact (his literal canton and wellspring of his cantos)—but not all that important, as he now dispatches the imagination and memory in tandem to this demesne from his cultivated Greensboro dominion. A university professor (to evade "the condescension and insularity that are the dangers of leading the almost monastic existence of a writer"), a cheerfully mischievous friend and mentor, a sincere ("without wax," true cast) husband and father, Fred Chappell is that rare creature who can wear the laurel of the poet and the mantle of the fictionist with almost equal ease, and he has been twisting himself into those two Cuchulain-like warp spasms and turning out prose and poetry distinguished by clarity, charity, surefootness, and surprise for about three decades. He has been drilling through the bedrock of the Bible belt with his loving enthusiasms and iconoclasm right in the motherlode of Jesse H. Bible's constituency, and he assaults sleepiness and laziness and downright inertia with his wry shifts of form and mask. His voices, from the vernacular to the oracular, are those of Homer's Proteus cackling, "Don't throw me into that Baptismal font, Cousin," till he lands there to cavort and thrive, to delve and spout like a whale.

That rare harmonious (but probably protean) committee we call Homer opens the *Odyssey* entreating the muse to tell him of the man of many ways and far journeys, and it was that feature of Chappell's early work that lured me to him. I was in graduate school down in Boone, also not far from here, and I was deep in the drearies over the current state of my newly embraced vocation, the voyage of poetry. John Ashbery's *Self-Portrait in a Convex Mirror* had just been awarded the literary hat-trick—Pulitzer, National Book Award, and National Books Critics' Circle Award—and I was mightily stunned. Elegant and intriguing it was, clever and informed, but it seemed like brainwork, winking solipsism passing as navigation, experimental more than experiential. I sat under the eaves of Ivy Hall, stared across the backlit firtips to the west and said, "If this is where poetry's headed, I'm in the wrong racket." What saved me was Chappell's *River*. It offered passage, traction, narrative as what the poet himself calls "the structure on which I hang the lyric moments." And, lo, I was lifted. The eleven sections gave me Ole Fred, Susan, Virgil Campbell, a brace of miraculously real grand-parents, and a quick but firm rehearsal of the history of technique, from Popish couplets to a rejoicing shower-stream of consciousness. Widsith had opened up that word hoard and sang, chanted, intoned, or prayed, whatever *mathelode* might have meant to hearthside bards and their audiences.

Sitting in a hearthside *seisiun* of traditional Irish music, when the players pause and swap instruments, each taking his turn at fiddle, flute, guitar, and bodhran, I think of Chappell's book. It was his deftness at swapping instruments around that helped me to understand more how range of pitch and pace mark that reservoir of possibilities we call a writer's voice.

Not that I didn't already know something about Chappell. Though I had found much of *The World Between the Eyes* fey and intellectual, with too much of "whim" embossed on the lintel (remember: I was young), I valued "Weird Tales," the precursor of the epistolary poems in *Midquest*, the title poem about discovery and imagination with its three elemental sympathies ("Of the elements his is water . . . ," and "Every fire is his brother") and the rural narratives, two of which—"Father" and "Mother" —are the first stage of his lifelong attempt, still clearly developing in the newest fiction, to express gratitude to the feisty and generous sources of his inborn (but Duke-refined) gifts. The two poems that had held me like that distant snapping string in "The Cherry Orchard" are "The Farm" and "February," both of which suggested that you don't have to refine a sense of ritual out of the realm of the actual (as Dickey often does) to tell your origin-reclaiming story. The relief had been significant but not complete, for Chappell, except perhaps in the opening poem, "February," had not yet caught the current of his own best fluence. That poem is visceral and visual, alternately abrupt and sinuous, witty and candid, beautiful and extravagant and musical, as it chronicles rural hog slaughter and "the child, elated-drunk / with the horror," as the victim's viscera possesses the house.

The above catalogue of adjectives easily applies to *River*'s eleven parts, and for one facet of what shines brilliantly there as theme, I'll turn, as I have often done, to Donald Secreast, who has written that in *River,* "clarity of vision is always presented in conjunction with sullied or tainted water." That act of cleansing seems central to Chappell's work—the knowledge that nothing, neither memory nor fancy, remains clean, if left untended. Though Secreast limits his analysis to the book's two most accomplished pieces, "My Grandmother Washes Her Feet" and "Cleaning the Well," the enterprise of bathing and dousing sacraments, with the documenting poems as liturgy, infuses the volume.

The whole issue of form (formula, format, performance) really lives in this text, which is a series of loving assaults on genre and convention, at once communal and transgressive. Couplets? Terza rima? Blank verse? Fred Chappell dances them all, yokes them to his purpose, which I take to be less ironic than the recent Po-Mo madness but still less rustic than Sam Ervin's wryness in mask and maze. Chappell uses the "received forms" to establish context and focus, probably conscious of how the imperial Romans used "focus" for hearth. He does not wish to "wipe the slate clean" (which once meant simply to clear the firestone), but to build his local fires in the name of his predecessors. Like the Olympic runner and the lover, he carries a torch. With it he sets the water of *River* afire, giving us breathing characters, the resonance of myth and history, refining ironies, symphonic orchestration, an orbiting drive as wildly controlled as Dale Earnhardt's Chevy, and the sweet trajectory of reminiscence, all rendered in dialect and dialectic and all aimed at the moral and aesthetic questions that haunt him and us, all undercut with a modesty and embraced bewilderment that make

Chappell the kind of writer Holden Caulfield could love: one who, when you read his books, you want to call up at night.

Of course, by this time Chappell had already published four novels, which he calls "lyrical mood pieces," and what reputation he had as a storyteller in the States had arrived frog-back—like Poe and Faulkner—as *It Is Time, Lord*, *The Inkling* and *Dagon* had found enthusiastic translators in Maurice-Edgar Coindreau and Claude Levy. In these novels, Proteus begins with fictionalized autobiography and works toward parable and character mosaic. The first and third of these quietly anticipate the translation into English of the succulent "magical realism" of the tropics but most likely find their precedents for Dagon and the Ironbird in biblical sources, where the miraculous and the mundane are twins joined at the tongue.

Perhaps the qualities of these works that make for lasting intrigue include: the lightness with which Chappell wears his anxiety of influence from Lovecraft, Hawthorne; the fascination with dream-like imagery walking in sunlight; the pyromaniacal resonance; and the willingness to appreciate the smoke of myth that hovers behind the homely.

Sometimes this homeliness is located in the literal geography of his past, as in *The Inkling,* sometimes in the locales of his far-flung imagination and wide reading, as in *Dagon,* but in each case he gives us characters determined to look straight and naked-eyed at the world in an attempt to discover some way to love it. In his determination to find the meaning that he is always certain is there, Chappell confronts the conventional systems of comfort and finds them wanting, then tempts his characters with the reliefs of solipsism, only to wrest them toward some more careful, other-admitting vision. The people of these books, whether whores, professors, adolescents, lapsed ministers, pimps, or lascivious demiurges, are all aware of the coldness of alienation, and all want to purchase some admission to the community, though they are variously aware of what coin will serve to bribe Charon to ferry them back from the practical nihilism that Chappell seems to see as one of the more seductive self-reductions of our age. It is clear that this writer possesses and embraces and invites in others the Shelleyan "moral imagination."

Although both the early fiction and poetry bristle with surprises and knuckleballs, Chappell has always seemed to prefer Frost's "old ways of being new," carefully invoking the conventions he intends to subvert. In this quest for what I'll call "humanity" (lest "humanism" activate a Jessealarm), Chappell has set about reverting, attempting to transform the inner texture of the art of writing. Unsurprisingly, he raises the banners of Browning and Chaucer over the semaphore flags of Berryman and the pennant of consistency, represented by Dante.

Nevertheless, his pursuit of Dantesque structure continued as the other three books that were to complete the *Midquest* quartet appeared. *Bloodfire* (1978) is Chappell's true Phlegathon. Introduced by a quotation from Char, it rehearses the impulses of the day that *River* chronicles, although from a different perspective. The parallels and counterbalances between the volumes are far easier to follow now, employing the author's useful preface to *Midquest,* but when the volume first saw daylight, I wrestled with its design—decoding, juxtaposing, finding my whole sensibility engaged and refusing to release the book till it blessed me. Now Chappell likes to describe the whole enterprise as a "sampler," with attendant overtones of modest Americana, but my first encounters with *Bloodfire* were cauterizing. Early ambition and that deep-rooted ambivalence toward the Klan-birthing, self-righteous, mysterious, and poverty-worn South shapes some of the undertow that complicated his fascination with love. A church burns in Saxon hemistitches, a weather-wounded father burns a dollar to escape the tyranny of its symbolism, a poet considers his vocation while splitting logs and trying to marry art to nature. Frankenstein's monster, innocent of evil intent, perishes in flame. Protestors and napalm victims burn like the tongue of Odysseus in the *Inferno*. It is all vivid, visceral, dramatic. Lustfire and firewater alike transform, as the poet admits in an elegiac epistle, "What I mostly ripped off from Rimbaud was the notion of fire / As symbolic of tortured, transcendent-striving will." It is a frenzied book, little softened by Virgil Campbell's Sut Lovingood–comic yarn about the Clay County centennial parade.

The salamander element was followed in short order by *Wind Mountain* in 1980 and *Earthsleep* the next year. By now, the intricate stitch and boldness of his cosmic design were evident to most everyone, and *Midquest* was as popular a topic in my circles as Durrell's *Alexandria Quartet*. Though Chappell was obviously a shape-shifter and iconoclast, readers began to purchase some hold on the classical / agrarian marriage in his trajectory. And a place was being cleared for him at the high table.

In homage to symmetry, the second brace of installments in the quartet begin and end with poems of home, bedroom, drifting awake, and drifting asleep on this day of his birthday suite, but the initial piece in the last, *Earthsleep,* recapitulates the earlier volumes, gathering force from their rehearsal. The new emphasis in his breeze book is raucous lying, for it performs the function of ironic praise for language and music alike. Not only does Chappell evoke the topos and tropos of rural Southern mountains and the logos of his clan, but he also mythologizes his contemporaries, colleagues and adversaries alike, placing Jim Whitehead and Bob Morgan in heaven and Jim Dickey in hell for his concupiscent compulsions. Fun, frolic, and self-irony's torrent occupy much of the volume's draft and banter, and the local guide's—Virgil Campbell's—monologue, "Three Sheets in the Wind: Virgil Campbell Confesses," is one of the most pleasing narratives in the whole matched set. Therein, the picaro, caught *in flagrante delicto,* finds hell on earth in a bushel of couplets that hold no cow sacred.

Earthsleep rounded it out, brought the imagery and wit home to roost in time to join its siblings under a single cover in 1981 and, shortly after, relieve some of my sillier anxieties by earning Chappell a share of the Bollingen Prize with that old puzzlement, Ashbery. With "heavy," "hard," "dirt," and "grave" as its touchstone words, this final installment bears little of the humor of its immediate predecessor. Grief and resignation pervade the pages, but as usual they are uplifted by the force of Chappell's imagination, his technical mastery coaxing life into even the most somber of moments. If the function of elegy is to somehow breathe new vitality into the departed, this book may come closest of the four to true resurrecting praise, in spite of much machinery that now gets called "postmodern"—all that in-joke and spiel-dazzle, allusion and ellipsis, cacophany of odd musics and metaphor that unsays itself, dream-swerve, blend of place name and myth-shadow, irony's epiphanies, blasphemy and lamentation, pastiche and parody, layered puns and holographic-seeming *dramatis personae,* word jazz and tongue-twist gems. In *Earthsleep,* the poems are no longer numbered, and they seem to meld into one another more smoothly than in the other elements where the earth is healing and decomposing the anxiety-ridden particulars. The conclusion of his symposium brings new kinds of cleansing, renders the fields Elysian, aims at Paradise and the whorled rose in spite of clay golems in the furrows and the toil-broken grandsire's entreaty for peaceful silence. Thus the last quartet rises and resolves.

Can Doc Watson play Bach? Probably, but most casual listeners of bluegrass music would be unlikely to stop and consider the question. Can Fred

Chappell, crafter of all those obviously southern narratives, despite their variety of formal modes, actually write poems and stories that step completely outside the agrarian frame? The truth is, he has been doing it all along, even though most readers associate him with the "Ole Fred" stance composed of Br'er Fred, Sut Fred, Reynolds Applefred, and Freddery O'Chappell. Legend has it that under a carefully shrouded nom de plume, the young Chappell wrote supernatural and sci-fi tales, and he has continued to flirt with those genres while adding historical fiction, lieder, satirical essays, and preludes and epilogues as ventriloquist for a variety of the Great Dead. Nonetheless, the question keeps coming home to roost: What's the point of all these rural half-nostalgic poems, even when they do not fall into the pit of unabashed romanticism, even when the southernness is as much vehicle as subject? Can irony save them from terminal *ubi sunt* in-the-cups escapism?

It gives me a personal turn of thought. Recently, an arts administrator decided to insult me by referring to my work as "squirrel on a log poems," awakening a question in me that never sleeps very comfortably: Are these southern gothic narratives, for all their wry, sly, gritty address to things I think matter, only a game, when one could be writing poems full of Italian phrases and exotic places, or poems about explicitly political issues, medieval symbols, and love of polyglot women? Many of Chappell's detractors would force the same question about his work, despite its protean quality, and I think they might find their best answer in one of those naturally appearing vehicles for metaphor that many southern poets gravitate to.

For example: two days ago I brought into the house three knobby and inelegant horse chestnuts—duff-brown, saurian-skinned, the stems rising from the rind-sequents' intersection. There on the mantle, they resembled something cows wouldn't eat, ants wouldn't trifle with, dogs wouldn't wet—tiny bell-pepper shapes that only absorb light, but tonight's hearth-heat coaxed them open, the lobes separating cleanly to reveal the sheen of red umber buckeyes within. The charmed objects—fetishes to some—were necessarily concealed, as many of the world's marvels are similarly camouflaged. Whoever thought of eating artichokes, of pressing cochineal from dead insects, of extracting perfume from a whale? Jack Gilbert writes of opening up an owl to find the colors and shapes of ancient Byzantium, and even Eliot testifies that a species of beauty loiters behind the seemingly mundane. When Chappell gives us alcoholic countrymen or sardonic grandmothers, hog slayings or boys with dynamite, we'd be wise to peer past the surface, to embrace that prickly angel till it blesses us, for usually the light of blessing awaits the honed eye, as the poet reclaims the legacy of significance and tragedy the creators of the New South have so often striven to obliterate.

When I think of this aspect of Chappell's work, the painter William Dunlap comes to mind, for his rural Mississippi, Carolina, and Virginia images have earned him some scorn from the high priests who think of him as entertaining and fulfilling the easy wishes of a sentimental public. But the iconography of the South—from Washington and Faulkner, through the artist's own family, across Civil War battle sites and into farm, river, and forest—is always lacquered with irony. Dunlap charges his work with the counterforce of iconoclastic perspectives and employs the painterly techniques of Rembrandt and Wyeth to execute his impressions. When he gives us a hound dog, it may be holding point in the direction of a nuclear reactor. His Jefferson Davis might well be in drag, as everything is grist and fodder, everything is fair game, and Chappell differs from this only in that his work undermines fashion perhaps more subtly.

In what will likely be called Chappell's "middle fictions," that honed eye is a useful apparatus for mining the ore of universal value that runs through what the quick eye might gloss as sheer costumery. The volume displays and investigates historical figures like Haydn, Franklin, and Blackbeard but also creates allegorical figures and modern, southern, moral agents working out their salvation—or failing to—in recognizable and modest surroundings. Whether the stories occur in biblical settings, Enlightenment frontiers, or the hills and dives of twentieth-century North Carolina, the reader is always aware of the possibility of moral action, the necessity to make choices and the sorrow of potential failure. As Annie Dillard writes in her excellent introduction to *Moments of Light,* "And there, in the thick of the mystery where spirit and matter meet, there is the faintly-perceived harmony, the world's great grounding in beauty: the music of the spheres" (xvi). In the most engaging of these stories, children and sojourners take important strides along the path from innocence to knowledge, discovering the absence of discernible justice in the phenomenal world and the lovely necessity of trying to act with compassion and forgiveness anyway. As in the poems, the journey toward self-knowledge and acceptance always carries spiritual implications, and the riveting imagery and convincing psychological portrayal of Stovebolt Johnson, William Herschel, the boy of "January," and the dazed narrator of "Broken Blossoms" conspire to remind us that even the most adroit and prestidigital fictions are more than games or exercises in texture.

The prose pieces in *I Am One of You Forever,* like those in *Moments of Light,* ought probably to be called "fictions," since they resist analysis as the well-made and self-contained narratives of most definitions of "short story." Yet they don't, for my money, thread together in any way I'd want to call a novel. Instead, *I Am One* satisfies me as the aesthetic echo of all the moral emphasis of *Moments of Light.* It's a series of flowers blooming off the same vine, a vine that creeps back to "Broken Blossoms" and chronicles the rusties and windies—that is, pranks and yarns—from a series of visiting uncles, from the hired man Johnson Gibbs, and from Joe Robert, the father of Chappell's young protagonist and alter-ego, Jess.

Back in *River,* a grandmother has told her acolyte about his "shadow cousins," people who come from the Other Side somehow, yet are still "of us," and in this volume they become shadow uncles and aunts of the wandering WASP variety, workers of the miraculous and testers of the stable family's tolerance, endurance, and sense of humor. There is Uncle Luden, the Don Juan; Uncle Zeno, the sighted Homer; Uncle Gurton, the Merlin; and Uncle Rankin, Nosferatu in coveralls. Although all these figures bring consternation and entertainment to the farm, Zeno is the most powerful figure, as he is forever weaving tales. Even when Jess discovers his uncle perched in a tree on the edge of the woods, he is reciting, as if the vision is irresistible: "He was talking too, out here in the grassy knolls under the soft blue sky where there was not a living soul he could have been aware of to listen to him. I crept up as noiselessly as I could. I wanted to hear what he told himself in private, thinking that maybe the old man was revealing secrets of the earth he alone was privy to."

Later, the boy begins to believe that Zeno's stories can transform—completely remove from phenomenal existence and into the noumenal stream—people just by pouring them into narratives. The entire question of the relationship between story and history shimmers into focus in a way Borges would have appreciated, a way that flashes new light on the uncle whose spied-upon beard grows like some science-fiction thicket till it occupies the whole house, as well as the uncle who sleeps in his coffin and fishes only in the doldrums but eventually plays the boldest rusty of the book.

These stories, along with those of Johnson Gibbs (whose disappearance and reappearance has always caused me slight dissatisfaction), involve anecdote and fable. They are framed by a story about an attempt to build a bridge and a garden for the mother and a story about the simultaneous dream on the part of three grown men about someone named Helen. The book takes its title from the dark figure of Johnson asking, "Well, Jess, are you one of us or not?" Whatever they are, they have conjured, these three yarners and joyous liars, the figure of a muse, one referred to in "The Storytellers" as worth striking out across the wine-dark sea after. And the boy, who is something of a thin mask for the actual Chappell, is indeed one of them. At the conclusion of the previous section, the narrator Jess recounts his having to sing to repay a musically gifted aunt for her performance, and he reports: "If I could sing—sing, I mean, so that another human being could bear to hear me—I wouldn't sit scribbling this story of a long time ago." But we know how Virgil set out: "Arms and the man *I sing*." Chappell, Cousin Tongue-in-Cheek, knows the difference is no difference at all.

In *Brighten the Corner Where You Are,* Chappell turns again to the mythologized version of his father that he has so often spun toward narrative gold. It is the story of a fabulous day in 1946 when the father as Prometheus-Scopes saves a life, faces a tragedy, and encounters a series of Mephistophelian tempters and guides, including a Devil-possum, a sophistic goat on a roof, and a shadowy custodian in his Barthian funhouse of a lair. Thus, supernatural creatures and natural forces seem to conspire with the school board, whose impending inquisition looms, threatening Joe Robert's job and forcing him to articulate his reasons for being. Evolution hangs heavy in the atmosphere of the novel, which seems willing to claim any form, from Socratic dialogue to fable, to assert its delight in surface change and serious mischief, while never endangering its undeconstructable testimony to the value of both dream and compassionate, responsible action. The book provides yet another installment in the life of Chappell's ur-self and in the unfolding weaving of what Pascal called "the heart's reasons, of which reason knows not."

Castle Tzingal, Chappell's first book of poems after *Midquest,* seems almost a deliberate refusal to submit to any description. Take medieval romance, cut it with a dose of sci-fi, meld in gothic conventions and epigrammatic wit, and one might create the "music that silvers the wind with shadow" streaming through this lovely oddity. In a series of deft dramatic monologues uttered by an astrologer, a homunculus, an admiral, a page, a king, a queen, and a disembodied voice, Chappell creates the grand guignol atmosphere of a Mervyn Peake novel in a mercurial shorthand that increasingly intrigues. As a study in evil and perversion, the volume is interesting enough, but Chappell succeeds in convincing the reader that the concerns of Kyd, Poe, Webster, Mary Shelley, and Browning still obtain. Whether or not the spirit of poetry triumphs over the dark story it discloses is questionable. *Castle Tzingal* remains my least favorite Chappell volume, more a tour de force for the connoisseur than any of his other works, but perhaps a necessary armature of the Rubik's cube of his *oeuvre,* his reminder to us that there is no consensus narrative, only the fragments we shore against our ruins. At their best, the individual sections achieve an almost calligraphic clarity, reminding one of Emerson's dictum that "every word is a fossil poem."

In the year when Yale's Wise Ones decided that Chappell should sip some Bollingen, Louisiana State University Press released *Source,* a volume of his as-yet uncollected poems that seems almost a small anthology of lyrical impulses, many with the familiar narrative voice absent or muted. The first section, however, contains poems of homage to his mountain childhood, three of them actually titled as prayers. Less raucous than much of his work, these pieces remind us of the comfort that abandoned schoolhouses (where bees sing and "their vocalese / Entrances the native tranquil dust"), milking, walking, and observing provide a respite from "the whole wide silly world." In "Humility," Chappell provides an ultimate rationale for the pastoral:

Here we might choose to live always, here where
Ugly rumors of ourselves do not reach,
Where in the whisper-light of the kerosene lamp
The deep Bible lies open like a turned-down bed.

In the book's next section, Chappell makes it clear that he has not forgotten our postlapsarian state, however. "The Evening of the Second Day" is apocalyptic, a bit like the narrative at the close of "Road Warrior," a bit like Merwin's voice in *The Lice.* This section also treats of music with a variety of approaches, from word jazz to dignified, echoing processional. "Music as Natural Resource," for instance, begins as a paean to the savannah-like nature of riverine sounds but ends in hot slang: "Go get em,

Yardbird. Git it on." In contrast, the final poems of the section delve into the gnomic. Archaic language and knotty wit abound, but the dark vision that many of these chants and riddles seem designed to undermine still shimmers.

The third section of *Source* is an even more formal excursion into music—Chappell's second published lieder cycle, entitled "The Transformed Twilight." What at first appears to be a complete immersion in lyric extravagance turns out to be an exploration of a sculptor's vision in the presence of love, war, and nature; the grim realities are mitigated but not neutralized by the art and by love.

The final section begins with the line, "I am changing shape again," soon to be followed by the willingness to eat "tatters / Of holy books or the torn blood of children" in order to "understand civilization." Darkness, the gallows, Lucretius in "the white fountain of delirium" and an angel "purely clothed in terror" collect, but the angel may create a new, communicating universe. The final poem, "Forever Mountain," returns to a transformed Pisgah that infuses him as it turns gold. *Source* then ends on the sentence, "This is a prayer." Against the dangerous swerves from our better selves, the poet offers this polymorphic litany to health and blessed candor.

The particular manifestations of Proteus that shape his most recent offering are professorial and celebratory, as *First and Last Words* provides prologues, epilogues, and meditations on classic works of art, literature, and music. This is a less unruly, less iconoclastic Chappell but one who still finds the world a scrimmage of appetite and seeks rest in the shine of artfully polished words, brush strokes, chords. Whereas in most of his work Chappell appears to believe, as I do, that art is a way to worship, the poems in this volume suggest that art can also be a proper object of worship, for Chappell constructs shrines, often in the modes of the precedent texts. Even under the professorial mantle, the poet shifts shapes, now speaking as Virgil, now as Aeschylus's watchman, now in honor of Tolstoy, Hardy, Vermeer.

The business of this book is books, which are gardens, harbors, prophecies, middens, and charms. They are stimulating and unsettling. "The Reader" testifies, "And yet, they comfort her, being all / That she could never be nor wish to be; / They bring the world . . . into her small apartment." The best three poems in the book, for my money, also bring people into the room—the unconsoled subject of "An Old Mountain Woman Reading the Book of Job," the "busted down" and garrulous bachelor of

"Dipperful," and the two speakers of "Remodeling the Hermit's Cabin," which chronicles the tacky destiny of a lovingly and shrewdly made cabin to serve as Chappell's parallel for our besieged Constitution.

In this volume, as with the others, hope and sorrow entwine and writhe together like the haunted dance of impossible hybrid creatures from *The Book of Kells*. Perhaps that symbiosis suggests Chappell's largest and most fiercely sought theme—the synthesis of all opposites gathered into the light.

So the day passes, the edge in the weather rough as whetrock, the new moon low in the evening sky, rusty scuppernong vines and the pecan's golding leaves. Late sparrows sing the fallen osage orange open, while insects try to sing time still with their dwindling. Tonight will bring Virginia wine and a fireside talk with Brontoi Bedyurov about the shamans, about the folk dress and history of his native Siberian Mountains, for these local habitations and names are the grain and elixir that always travel well. But as I close up shop for the day, I imagine nature and Chappell's writing twined together in their mysterious calibrations. *Caritas* rises with maple flame, wistfulness knots with thistle floss, anger explodes with a shadow crow's caw, and *agape* lolls symmetrically from the red spider lily's stalk. If there are sprites out there that can entertain and heal us by their fidelities and contortions, one of them sports the eternal Chappell grin, polymath and polymorphous, autochthon and autodidact. He can make words paint and make them sing, and he bears us no malice, not a shade of *schadenfreude,* but a blessing, even as he resists the lofty pun on his surname and signs himself "Ole Fred."

Spiritual Matter in Fred Chappell's Poetry: A Prologue

DABNEY STUART

> Tanto giú cadde, che tutti argomenti
> à la salute sua eran giá corti
> fuor che mostrarli le perdute genté.
> —Dante, *Purgatorio*, XXX, 136–38

> Our faith must be earned from terror.
> —Fred Chappell, *Bloodfire*, IX

Flesh and Spirit

The first two words of the title of this essay are a subdued version of Fred Chappell's more spritely rhymed phrase "attar of matter" (in "Firewood"). I intend, however, the same complementary attachment of terms. Chappell's phrase suggests, in sound as well as substance, that there is an essence embedded in matter and releasable from it—a sweet, intangible spirit inexplicably meshed in the molecular arrangement of the elemental stuff of which all things, including human and other creatures, are composed. One direction in which Chappell aims the atomistic possibilities inherent in this perspective is Lucretian. The other primary direction is not, however, subject to the contained reshuffling of atoms. Chappell is more essentially preoccupied with and hopeful of images of release and transformation, which are Christian in their orientation. The two modes of understanding are, needless to say, not always cleanly separable.

Perhaps a finer distinction is in order. The Lucretian perspective doesn't employ the complementary duality of flesh and spirit but rather transposes it into the fluid, imperceptible molecular composition of apparently solid material bodies. This, of course, was Lucretius' understanding of how the transience of individual instances of forms could be reconciled with the equally obvious recurrence, apparently eternal, of the forms themselves. Individual people die, but the human race does not; we eat this carrot today, but another grows for us to eat tomorrow; we may pulverize this stone, but stones are everywhere. Mutation and recurrence are complementary motions, rearranging the atoms out of whose coalescence particular things are made, and because of whose dispersal they disappear. But the atoms are irreducible and everlasting, as is the process of rearrangement—carried out by the forces he called Love and Strife—by which perceptible forms occur, pass away, and recur.

The interpenetration of earth, air, fire, and water is one expression of the Lucretian dispensation in *Midquest* and seems to me in no need of elaborate elucidation. The titles of the frame poems of Volumes II, III, and IV serve as sufficient indicators, as do the abundance of phrases in those same poems in which two or more of the elements cohere: "dewfired," for instance, and "Earthsmoke," "earth/with its mouths of wind," "water in stone," and "blind windcurrent of the soil." It shows more explicitly, however, in passages where Chappell uses Lucretius' terms and images. In "Bloodfire Garden," it is in the fire of love that "we are/whole again,/our atoms driven and/interlocked as heat in air" (91–92). When the "untenable trombone tones" Chappell imagines riding "out upon the blue-bleached air" pops, it lets him "slide the effervescent atoms" alone ("The Autumn Bleat of the Weathervane Trombone," 114–15). In the same poem, he refers to "the hail of impulse Nature keeps tossing over/Her shoulder" (115). The recurrent "coming apart to" constructions (as in "fire coming apart now to wind") extend this explicit evocation across some of the frame poems. In the world beyond the "four-square crucis of elements" in "Earth Emergent Drifts the Fire River" (a cold world of nothingness, which I will comment on in more detail later), "the single atoms stray/Lost and touchless" (146–47). This poem is, in fact, dotted with Lucretian infusions, perceptions more accessible because of the atomistic backdrop. As Fred wakes in the first poem of *Bloodfire,* "the seeds, ignis semina, of fire / Put forth in me their rootlets" (56).[1] *Ignis semina* is, in fact, a phrase from Lucretius, which Chappell identifies later in "Firewood."

"Susan Bathing" and "Firewood" comprise the two most probing, subtle, and thorough embodiments of the Lucretian vision in *Midquest*. They are rather miraculous poems in many ways, not least in their personal and local dimensions and in the careful psychological progression their disguised narrative lines reveal. But my space and context limit me to some brief comments on the process of atomistic transmutations that occur in "Firewood."

It is "Flame, flame" that Fred's ax strikes first; he imagines the fire in the hearth that the log he is splitting will eventually afford. The dimensions the language implies become more complex immediately, as he speaks of the "heart / red in the oak where sun / climbed vein by vein" (67). It's not until he tangles with the walnut log some seventy-five lines later that these implications begin to receive their fullest development. This time he sees "the life" of the blazing log, "yellow / red and orange and blue & hasting your dark gasses / starward, on the silverblue night splaying a new tree / shape, tree of spirit spread on the night wind" (69). This new tree lifted from the burning of the old one sifts "upward to the needle pricks of fire" of the constellations. The roots of the tree of fire

> sizzle in our fireplace, the
> ghostly arms of it embrace the moon, the lancet
> glance of the star pierces its leafage, this tree
> in our fireplace is the sun risen at midnight,
> capillaries of heat light lift out the chimney,
> the rose trellis of stars is afire, sun reaches
> homeward again to the *vacant interlunar spaces,*
> chimney is its shrunk trunk & pins our dwelling
> to the earth and to the stars equally, this spirit
> trunk in the chimney is the spine of the world. (69)

Chappell suggests at least a double cycle here: the sun's energy enters the tree, causes it to grow, and then, in the burning of the logs, is released again

---

1. Because both the author and the narrator of *Midquest* share the same name but are not identical to each other, I have used "Fred Chappell" or "Chappell" to refer to the former and "Fred" for the latter. Chappell comments on this matter in his Preface to *Midquest*.

into the vastness of space where it originated; the physical form of the tree rooted in the earth is released as a tree of spirit rooted in the hearth fire and foliated among the stars. That the stars themselves are fire spreads further the impress of transformation focused in this passage. The fire, however, remains mysterious, no matter the language invented to image it, because it gives us light in which to "read" everything but itself. It is also mortal. As the fire in the hearth dwindles so does the tree of spirit rising from it: "Lucretius'/seed of fire ignis semina is seed semina mortuis/. . . of death in that same split second" (70).

Three other sorts of transformations parallel this central one. In the brief parenthetical phrase that echoes the burden of "My Grandmother Washes Her Feet"—*"dirt we rose from, dirt we'll never forget"* (70)—human beings rise from the ground and are rooted there, no matter the changes that transpire in any individual life. Human will, similarly, may cast "forward/ into the flesh of light itself/. . . angry against the stream of time" (70–71). Perhaps the poet, too, *"can* transform all/germens with an incantatory perception of what's/what or what's supposed" (71). These palimpsest possibilities layered against the basic image of the tree of spirit follow one another in the poem pell-mell, each growing from the other, the form enacting transformation while articulating its stages. The energy of language and prophetic will, twined together, leads Fred to a credo: it can make

> every tree that stands a *Christmas tree,* Christmas
> on Earth, though even as I recall the beautiful
> manifesto my faith flickers & dwindles, we are not
> born for the rarer destinies only for the rarest,
> we are born to enter the tree of smoke, backbone of
> the world of substance, born to smear our life stuff
> against the zodiac, & as I take down in matter
> the spine of the world & will send it up again in
> spirit a feeling that these things are so indelibly
> correct overtakes me. (71)

Part of the primary drama of this extraordinary poem consists of its entertainment. It is interesting, first of all, various and full of surprising turns, holding together voice and attention (poet's and reader's), as well as holding out alternative ways of speaking about the relationship of matter to spirit.

The Lucretian focus, a naturalistic philosophy both ancient and contemporary, balances, as it were, in the middle of a spectrum.

At one end is nothingness, the terrifying possibility that a "roaming/ puddle of gravitons, a winter's night the black / hole, comes this way striding & yanks the tree / of light elongate like a sunny licorice down / the drain" (70).

Fred explicitly rejects the terror of nothingness, along with the will-less condition of Nirvana (which he has earlier called "a sterile and joyless blasphemy"), in the opening poem of *Earthsleep*, indicating by their juxtaposition that the latter is a version of the former. "What there is in emptiness," he says,

> . . . let it consume itself,
> Let it mass and flounder yonder from the skin
> Of things, let it not come nigh this hearth, this hold,
> This house, let the cloud of unbeing never touch
> Our garish boxes of fervor. (146)

In the same series of refusals he seems also to include Lucretius' eternal atomistic dispersal and configuration; he mentions "another" world, "where no water sings with / Its breath of fire, where sunlight the cloud never / Ripens to peach, where the single atoms stray / Lost and touchless" (146–47). Lucretius' vision, I think, slides to the negative end of the spectrum here.[2] The double nadir of "Susan Bathing," which produces abject fear in Fred, is first, that he will not be able to praise her adequately (in *River*'s "Birthday 35," to have his mouth stopped is "despair") and second, that Susan will vaporize and disappear. After confronting such motions toward vacuum, Fred pushes his face "more fiercely" to Susan's breast and begins a series of allusive reprises of earlier poems that have centered on experiences of healing contact with people he loves.

It is not surprising given Fred's heritage that atomistic philosophy is insufficient, since Lucretius includes the soul among material things. A central thrust of his arguments in *De Rerum Natura* is to remove from his auditors their fear of punishment after life by arguing that the soul, like everything

---

2. A complementary comic rejection occurs in *Earthsleep,* IV, where "the Ideal World," Platonic in its evocative details, "sounds like a Grand Hotel / Emptied out because of chicken pox."

else, disperses into autonomous, anonymous atoms. There *was,* therefore, no hereafter to fear. This is not only too neat and reductive for a mind as probing, doubtful, and inventive as Fred Chappell's, it also dismisses too cerebrally what he has absorbed into the veins of his imagination from birth. If Lucretius had grown up with Fred's grandparents and parents, he would have rejected atomism, too. Chappell's profound disinclination also proceeds from his sensuality and, perhaps above all, from his unstaunchable love of life. In his splendid essay on Lucretius in *Three Philosophical Poets,* George Santayana observed that at the bottom of Lucretius' insistent opposition to immortality was a fear of life.[3] Santayana called this an "untenable ideal." He asserted that "What is dreaded is the defeat of a present will directed upon life and its various undertakings. . . . To introduce ascetic discipline, to bring out the irony of experience, to expose the self-contradictions of the will, would be the true means of mitigating the love of life; and if the love of life were extinguished, the fear of death, like smoke rising from that fire, would have vanished also" (53).

Fred clearly is no ascetic. He seeks everywhere to embrace life, to fire the world with his will, in the local and temporal frame of *Midquest* to celebrate his birthday, and to continue his fundamentally hopeful, Dantesque journey toward light.

At the other extreme is the Christmas tree and its extension at the end of "Firewood" into images of marriage, procreation, and finally, salvation. The sexual and marital similes salted into the opening page of the poem (*e.g.,* "*marriage / vow* joints," "nice girls back in high school") receive more serious resolution in such phrases as "the wedge goes in like semen" and "the river-clean smell of opened / flesh comes at me as the annunciation to Mary" (73). The latter reference also echoes the more extended annunciation passage in "Susan Bathing." Immediately following these focuses is Fred's assertion "I'm washed in the blood / of the sun," a variation of "blood of the Lamb" in a context suggesting, with "Christmas on Earth," a Christian salvation, an implicit answer to the parenthetical question "but where / shall I sit when once this flesh is spirit?" (73) The "flesh! more flesh" at the heart of the riven log is analogous to the Christian incarnation and helps one understand the source of Fred's love of the earth and life on it that pervades *Midquest.* ("The flesh the earth is suits me fine" is a representa-

3. George Santayana, *Three Philosophical Poets* (Cambridge, Mass., 1910), 53.

tive instance.) The poem following "Firewood" deals with a real fire, the conflagration that destroyed Fred's grandfather's church. Its concluding passage reinforces the sacramental, transforming vision of "Firewood." In form and language imitating Old English alliterative verse, the poem presents Fred and Susan coming to the site of the fire years later to find it altogether revivified, a "victory of spirit":

> Time took it anew
> and changed that church-plot   to an enchanted chrisom
> of leaf and flower   of lithe light and shade.
>
> *Pilgrim, the past   becomes prayer*
> *becomes remembrance rock-real   of Resurrection*
> *when the Willer so willeth   works his wild wonders.* (77)

This is stated as unequivocally as "the spine of the world" passage quoted above.

Other less extended instances of the Christian mode of transformation abound. The world was formed as "the purer spirits surged ever upward, / Shucking the gross pig-matter their bodies" ("Fire Now Wakening on the River," 56). Sexual union in "Bloodfire Garden" burns the lovers "down again to the ghost of us, . . . Burnt-off, we are being prepared" (94). For the grandmother in "Second Wind," the stirring of a slight breeze becomes "the breath of life. . . . / Renewal of spirit such as I could never / Deny" (106). In a richly evocative scene on Wind Mountain, "the resplendent house of spirit bursts around the body" ("Earth Emergent Drifts the Fire River," 149). The four elements carried by the winds are "suffering of spirit, suffering of elements, / In one mass," in "Dawn Wind Unlocks the River Sky" (98). Both the poems celebrating jazz in *Wind Mountain* embody the idea from Schopenhauer that serves as epigraph in Chappell's homage to Louis Armstrong—"*Music is the world over again,*" but in impalpable sound, in another form altogether (99). At the close of that poem, man becomes "half funky animal, half pure music, / Meat and spirit drunk together" (102).

The spiritual choice I am suggesting *Midquest* reticulately and dramatically enacts is more sharply underlined by three poems at the close of *Source,* published in 1985, four years after *Midquest's* serially printed volumes (1975, 1978, 1979, 1980) were collected into one. In "Urlied," Chappell puts words (some anachronistic) into Lucretius' mouth, having him reject immortality via Rilke and the familiar anthropomorphism of Olympus. Conversely, Lucretius reiterates his "trust" in the forces of dissolution and coalescence (love / strife, Venus / Mars) and draws this comfort from his system: "There's nothing personal in it" (*Source,* 53). The evaluation is heavily ironic, however, being true as a description of the movement of matter but devastatingly false when applied to the emotional effect of losing one's identity. Chappell articulates this dreadful rift in the last section of the poem, where he evaluates Lucretius' endeavor as fundamentally courageous and integral but finally without solace. He leaves Lucretius in the "white fountain of delirium / Burning but not purified" (54), recalling both the close of T. S. Eliot's "The Fire Sermon" and the final stanza of his own "Feverscape: The Silver Planet" in *Midquest.* Once again, the Lucretian vision, for all its radically compelling perception into the material nature of things, is bleak and isolate, not transforming in a way Chappell finds desirable.

The other two poems set against "Urlied" involve ascent. "Message" employs Lucretian terminology, but Chappell's context involves three dimensions basically apostate to the Roman poet's system: the controlling metaphor of ascension; an increased understanding by the grief-stricken sufferer; and a concern with expressing that understanding in language. In choosing among his sorrows, the "he" of the poem becomes the measure of his own grief. In the opening lines' use of an angel as messenger "purely clothed in terror," there is also an implicit acceptance of this aspect of Rilke, contrasted to his dismissal by Lucretius in the preceding poem.

More telling still is "Forever Mountain," the final poem in *Source.* Chappell presents his father ascending, after death, Mt. Pisgah, about fifteen miles southeast of Canton, North Carolina—Chappell's hometown but also the mountain from which God showed Moses the promised land. Words from the hymn "Sweet Hour of Prayer" are relevant to the vision the poem renders: "Til from Mt. Pisgah's lofty height / I view my home and take my flight." J. T. Chappell doesn't fly, but he does leisurely ascend the mountain, "taking the time / He's got a world of" (57). He observes "the quality of light come over him," spends a dreamful night, "rises glad and early and goes his way, / Taking by plateaus the mountain that possesses him." He has come a far piece from the Pilate-like figure he cut when we last saw him in *Midquest.* At the poem's close, Chappell's "vision blurs . . . with distance," Pisgah becomes Forever Mountain, "a cloud / That light turns gold, that wind dislimns." The shift from the figure of his father to Chappell's blurred vision has much the same effect as would an unmitigated focus on the father's assumption into a new form. We witness an ascension of body to light and transformation, the context and perspective explicitly biblical, implicitly Christian. Between "Message" and "Forever Mountain," in fact, Chappell places a terse and rending avatar of another hymn, "O Sacred Head Now Wounded," concerned with the mocking of Jesus' suffering during his trial and crucifixion.

Prayer; Orthodoxies

I called "Forever Mountain" a vision, but in an italicized line appended to the poem, Chappell calls it a prayer. It is noteworthy that it's not a vision or a wish or a hope, but specifically *a prayer. Source*, in fact, contains three other poems so labeled, each of them depicting a merging of the one who prays with the particular conditions he prays about ("about" in the sense of concerning, and circling). In the first, "A Prayer for the Mountains," it is a peaceable kingdom he both accepts as existing and desires to exist, wanting to "share the sleep / Of the cool ground's mildest children" (5). In "A Prayer for Slowness," he seeks to be not content but filled with giving, as the cow in the poem has "her rich welcome / . . . taken from her" (6). "A Prayer for Truthfulness" concerns the poet's release of his poem from his control into its own illumination, able to say finally "its last abandonment" (7). The three prayers are, in short, not self-focused or escapist or acquisitive; in fact, insofar as they ask for anything, it is a place among the portions of other creatures into which Chappell may meld his being and talent.

Prayer is, of course, as complex an area as the other spiritual matters in Fred Chappell's work. I'm no expert on it by any stretch of the imagination, but a few thoughts may at least serve to disperse its associations beyond mere petition.

The extraordinary act of paying conscious attention may be considered a form of prayer. Prayer may be a tonality, an indication in declarative statements or questions that the speaker is tuned somewhere to spiritual dimensions he may not be addressing directly. "Where've you been?" asked in a certain way, for instance, can be a prayer, as Kathy Mattea's recent song by that name shows. A lived life can be a prayer, though that is difficult to specify, except perhaps in the cases of some saints. Prayer is not necessarily even supplication but may be homage, or gratitude, or acceptance, or lament, or bewilderment spoken or enacted or felt toward the immanent presence of a power greater than oneself. It may be a habit or an attitude. In *Hamlet,* Claudius' prayer, though his thoughts "remain below," is still a prayer. That which impels our attention away from the self or turns the will toward imagination may, speaking as broadly as possible, be considered prayer. Chappell refers to *Midquest* in his Preface as "in its largest design a love poem" (xi); from a number of these perspectives, the book could also be thought of as a prayer.

Individual poems, too, embody this possibility. "Susan Bathing" is a prayer of worship, praise, and adoration, "My Grandmother's Dream of Plowing," a prayer for release and forgiveness, "My Father Allergic to Fire," for acknowledgement and continuance. And so on.

The prayers per se dispersed throughout *Midquest,* though not explicitly indicated as the ones in *Source,* are not so much disguised as diverse. Chappell composes and aims them variously.

"Birthday 35: Diary Entry" concludes with a prayer in the more traditional mode of petition: "Please, Lord. I want to go to some forever / Where water is, and live there" (7). Until the final three lines, the poem is a plea for an anthropomorphic afterlife (part of the pattern "How to Build the Earthly Paradise" and "At the Grave of Virgil Campbell" later extend) where current pleasures pertain, an "Elysium . . . plentifully planted / With trout streams and waterfalls and suburban / Swimming pools, and sufficient chaser for bourbon" (8). Its tone is wise-ass jaunty, its diction hip, its beat and varying line lengths accumulating a pseudo music-hall effect that seeks to minimize the prayerful imploring, much as a sophisticated dude cultivates a cool exterior to cover his sensitivity. But in the last three lines, the more serious underlying concern breaks through: he wants the water of heaven to wash away sin.

The going up in flames of Fred's grandfather's church (*Bloodfire,* VI) and the site's transformation seventeen years later "to the stark beginning where the first stars burned" (77) becomes the ground for the definition of prayer that ends the poem. What has been a catastrophe is subsequently seen as part of a reenactment of the resurrection of Jesus.

> *Pilgrim, the past   becomes prayer*
> *becomes remembrance rock-real   of Resurrection*
> *when the Willer so willeth   works his wild wonders.* (77)

"The Willer," presumably not a human being, is involved in the process of prayer defined here. The experience itself is prayer, in which the divine will is inextricably woven, suggesting that God's involvement in history is not limited to the incarnation of Jesus.

I'm not sure if the more dire self-immolation of the Buddhist monks in "Bloodfire" should be included in this context, but it seems possible. What miraculous renewal may be hidden in the most awful destruction is part of the dread mystery of God's will.

Chappell uses fire as an agent of transformation again in connection with prayer in "Bloodfire Garden." In a remarkable merging of garden and bed, brushfire and loinfire ("the disease / necessary to know God"), Fred remembers praying as he watched the blackberry vines, scythed and "raked up in barbarous heaps," put to the torch (92). It was, he says, a moment in which

> I went stark sane, feeling under my feet
> the hands of blackberry fire
> rummaging
> unfurrowed earth. (93)

What, if anything, he prays for is unspecified, but his act is imbedded in images that suggest not only fire as incipient plow ("rummaging": the area is being cleared for planting) but also the burning of human bodies ("frying lattice / of dry bones") and the incarnation of spirits ("ghosts began again to take flesh") (93). In the other half of the poem's context of burning—the bedroom—after the lovers' climax "a cool invisible smoke goes up / from our bodies, it is grateful / prayer, sigil / of warm silence between us" (94).

> In this garden our bed we have burned
> down again to the ghost of us . . . (94)

In both contexts, the burning down has resulted in renewal or the readying for it. "Burnt-off," the lovers "are being prepared"; the burning off of the wild blackberry vines is a preparation as well for new growth. The image of dry bones suggests the vulnerability of the apparently solid human body and has driven young Fred to sanity and prayer; the aftermath of the fire of sexual union is prayer as well, associated with gratitude. In this context, the fresh rain blowing up "out of the green isles / of Eden," with its implication of renewed creative harmony with the Creator, seems entirely appropriate (94).

Fred's first prayer, the one in "Birthday 35" to which I've referred above, follows a vision of Time in which he sees "nothing human,"

No man, no woman,

No animals or plants; only moon
Upon moon, sterile stone

Climbing the steep hill of void. (7)

This waste land (part of a longer passage that I think consciously echoes T. S. Eliot's poem) leads to Fred's admission, "I was afraid." This process of a fearful vision of bleakness leading to prayer occurs again in at least two noteworthy places. In *Earthsleep* I, Fred talks to himself or, more accurately, to his "Mind," which he calls "Old Crusoe." In the context of wondering if they are both lost on "this bright and lonely spark" (149), he asks three questions about their eventual fate. The questions are directed at "Earth" but involve the other three elements central to *Midquest*. All of the alternatives are terrifying: "black waters streaming / Deathward," "In wind to suffer shorn of flesh," and "fire . . . the raging ecstasy / . . . of burning foreknowledge" (149). After such imagined vistas, the next utterance is a prayer.

Do not us Earth
Remember.
Leave us, mud jumble of mirk
And humus, tucked in the rock heart
Of the mountain, in these stones are seeds of fire,
Dream-seeds which taking root shall renew the world,
Tree of Spirit lifting from the mountain of earth. (149)

I take this prayer to be a refusal to identify the human creature as simply a concatenation of elemental substances. We are no more fully accounted for as such a composite than we are as Lucretian molecular aggregates or energy diminishing toward the cold will-lessness of Nirvana. Human creatures are elemental, yes, but also infused with spirit. Fred's prayer here is childlike in its desire that Earth simply forget him and Susan and tend to some other business. They'll take a spiritual form (the tree of spirit from "Firewood") analogous to the earthly tree—an appeasing gesture?—and grow on transmuted, as spirit mysteriously grows. This eases into two afterprayers, asking "Earth" for gentleness and "Destiny" for sweet treatment. The tone and focus here is relief after the exhausting effort of imagination that precedes it.

The same process occurs finally in starker, more condensed form in the closing poem of the volume (and the book):

> Here where I find
> I am I founder.
>   Lord Lord
> Let this lost dark not. (186)

Not what? is the inevitable question. Swallow us up, as the sea overwhelms a foundering ship? That seems the most immediate likelihood. The prayer itself is so close to the terror that impels it that it cannot be completely uttered. The pattern of zeroes that occupy the volume (the "darkest vowel" of the well opening, for instance, the drains in the grandmother's and Susan's tub, the black hole in space in "Firewood") has been perhaps the best preparation for what is most feared here from the dark.

These various spiritual radiations are rarely orthodox in any sense. But institutional Christian orthodoxies, too, occupy a substantial place in the spiritual experience of *Midquest*. The most accessibly presented are made part of the lives of Fred's forebears. Concerned for his salvation, his grandfather changes denominations (*River,* VII) and is baptized in the West Fork of the Pigeon River. Later, speaking from the grave (*Earthsleep,* IX), "Here where it's / Still not Absolute" (181–82), he awaits "Judgment Day / When we can see once more in the Judgment Book / All that we've seen already, each nook / And cranny of us forever on display" (182). The tone of the latter poem is nettled and testy, a strong modulation of the comic surface of the former one; in both poems, the man is of two minds about the perspectives the church has saddled him with, but there's no doubt he accepts its terms and forms, and takes them seriously.

These two poems deal with sacraments: baptism and burial. Fred's grandmother confronts another—marriage (*River,* VII), seeing this commitment as analogous to Caesar's Rubicon: *"If I cross this river I won't turn back."* When her husband dies (*Wind Mountain,* III) and she is faced with the public anonymity of everything, as well as the distracting hodge-podge of the funeral gathering, she wants to join him. Immediately, however, she aborts the idea on orthodox grounds: "It's a sin to want yourself to die" (103). She utters this fundamental belief before the poem is well begun, then suffers the family and their best intentions until, unable to take any more, she walks outdoors, away from the house, to a place "where the rose / Vine climbed the cowlot fence and looked away / Toward Chambers Cove" (105). It is also a place in her spiritual life "where everything is hard as flint: breathing, / Walking, crying even. It's a heathen / Sorrow over us" (105). In such a condition, she is unable to help herself, but in the immobilizing heat of the day, she feels a breeze stir, coming cornstalk leaf by cornstalk leaf across the field toward her. She understands this to be "the breath of life . . . / Renewal of spirit such as I could never / Deny and still name myself a believer" (106). This utterly convincing account ends with the freshening wind touching her face "so strong it poured on me the weight of grace" (106).

At the other extreme from this visitation of saving grace, Chappell places Fred's father's guilt over the manner in which he's buried Honey, an old mule dead after generations of labor on the farm (*Earthsleep,* III). Because the clayey ground makes the digging of a grave nearly impossible, J. T. breaks the animal's legs so he won't need so deep a hole. What he does and is witnessed doing is ineradicable, however, from his memory, in his "head for good and all and ever" (155). It's no wonder, given his account of it:

> I busted her legs.
> I busted her legs with the mattock, her eyes all open
> And watching me crack her bones and bulging out
> Farther slightly with every blow. These fields
> Were in her eyes, and a picture of me against
> The sky blood-raw savage with my mattock. (154)

"Heavy is how / I felt," he says, "empty-heavy and blue as poison" (154). The context of the poem is J. T.'s washing at the pump two weeks later. He scrubs his hands for "maybe seven minutes," dries them, and when he gives Fred the towel back, "there was his handprint, / Earth-colored, indelible, on the linen" (155). The figures of Pontius Pilate and Lady MacBeth lurk in the shadowy background here, and for the moment anyhow, no grace pours down on anything.

The mule is already dead when J. T. breaks her legs, and his sense of guilt is mostly a projection of his sensitivity and compassion. The experience revealed in the grandmother's dream of plowing (*Earthsleep,* VIII), however, is a fundamental sin, the bearing of a child either prior to her marriage to Frank or through adultery during it. The skillfully dovetailed phases of her dream show her progressively unsuccessful attempts to disguise her act, its issue, and their consequences. Frank's plowing, itself an unprecedented vision for her, provides an apt contextual metaphor: something hidden is uncovered. Frank both unearths the object and asks the question that pitches the dream toward its identification: *"Is that your baby that was never mine?"* (179). Anne—the grandmother, too, is named for the first time in the book, becoming a person not wholly identified through a role—"expects" at the start of her dream a church bell to be turned up by the plow, an object associated with Frank's past misfortune (the burning of his church) rather than with her own sin. This is the first of the dream's series of displacements. The object turns out to be in its first incarnation a lump of gold, which she cradles "to [her] breast." Following Frank's question, Anne denies (to herself) it's a baby, but then suddenly "I knew it *was* a baby in my arm, / The strangest baby" (179). The displacements continue: the infant is compared to Jesus as he is depicted in the *Upper Room*—a daily devotional publication—and then becomes a "golden child" who will "bring us luck." The creature she holds, however, continues to metamorphose toward the truth the dream is unlayering, finally becoming " 'an ugly little man,' " "an evil little goblin / With an evil smile" (179). This truth is, of course, how Anne feels about the child, a slow revelation of her shame and awful self-condemnation projected outward into the form the dream work has presented as separate from her. She wishes it dead, and—"the awfullest part" (180)—it dies. It's only after this that she is able to say, "It was my fault," but her admission of responsibility is focused only on her desire for the figure's death. Her guilt, insofar as she articulates it to Fred, to whom she's recounting the dream, seems focused on this, too; she also considers the child as separate from herself in its innocence at this point: "Whatever harm had the little goblin done?" (180). There seems no conscious owning up to her responsibility for its birth. Whether we are to take the death in the dream as indicating what happened to the actual baby is inconclusive, but the guilt is real enough: she has never waked from this dream. Incidentally, the revelation of this buried secret from her past casts a sharp light on her preoccupation in previous poems with the "Shadow Cousins," the profound hesitation she experienced before committing herself to marrying Frank, and our seeing her in two situations where she is washing something (her feet, her milk cans).[4]

These poems compose behavior and attitudes derived from sectarian Christian assumptions undergirding central aspects of what one might call primary theology. Suicide, adultery, and the wish to murder are sins; guilt is inevitably consequent upon sin; grace is God-given and mysterious, coming in unpredictable forms and at unpredictable times; the sacraments are inviolable, no matter how one might seek to hedge one's bets through them, their seriousness ingrained in the soul.

One of the assumptions inherent in *Midquest* appears to be that human beings, as Fred's grandmother fears, do grow away from their sources (this occurs both to individuals and to generations), but they appear to do so as a tree grows away from its roots, remaining one organism. Human beings are mobile, of course. I mean this analogy more to suggest temporal than spatial wholeness: as a tree grows in space, so a person grows in time. Human beings can make disorienting and potentially destructive choices, but there is as well a genetic and behavioral determinism woven into their development. *Midquest* embodies Fred Chappell's fulfillment of the grandmother's vision by becoming a professor and author, leaving the farm behind, deserting, as he says, "manual labor for intellectual labor." But the restless, doubt-ridden entertainments of his imaginative mind are largely informed by and directed at the physical, religious, and moral dimensions of the farm environment in which he was raised. I think this is the source, finally, of the spiritual and psychic healing and regeneration that *Midquest* seeks in its widest intention. In my context here, the central orthodox beliefs

---

4. Fred's guilt at turning his back on the voices of the poor (*Wind Mountain,* IX) may be considered part of this pattern.

that define the family members seep into Fred's ways of probing his own diverse options.

This is clearest in the preoccupation with the relationship between matter and spirit—how to view incarnation—that pervades *Midquest* and informs much of Chappell's poetry subsequent to it. His terror in the face of nothingness and the anonymous dispersal of atoms is bearable because the Christian mode of understanding affords him a richer, more hopeful alternative. He is, of course, predisposed toward it, but too given to the mind's uncertainties to accept it without first testing the abysmal ontological possibilities that contradict it. His use of Dante's *Divine Comedy* as model and guide further underscores the influence orthodox configurations have on his work. (Below I comment on Dante more specifically.)[5]

Other more local instances arise frequently throughout the book. I have mentioned both the transformation Fred witnesses in *Bloodfire* VI and the serious note ("Washing away sin") toward which his prayer at the close of "Birthday 35" tends (8), and I will discuss his use of Jonah, Lazarus, and Joseph. Not surprisingly, in the pattern of praise for Susan in "Susan Bathing," phrases from the Christian vocabulary of belief appear: *"plenia gratia"* (from the Catholic "Hail Mary" and Luke 1:28) in the Madonna passage; *"let there be,"* from the creation story in Genesis. As a whole, the poem and the narrator's role in it are informed by the conception of God as Word (John 1:1ff.). In "Firewood," he alludes to man "in his fallen state." In *Earthsleep* VI, he tells the dead Virgil Campbell, "All the world is lit for your delight, / old Buddy, hook it to your hulk both hands, / It's a worship of God, though kinda primitive / I admit."

These last two examples are drops in the larger welter of Fred's ruminations about the afterlife. They range from the pleasant, relaxed, anthropomorphic excursions in such poems as "The Peaceable Kingdom of Emerald Windows," "At the Grave of Virgil Campbell," and *Wind Mountain* V, to the bleak visions of nothingness in "Firewood" and *Earthsleep* I. What can be envisioned in familiar terms we can project ourselves into, evaluate and decide about, but a Christian vision of the soul's form after death is more troublesome. A genuine transformation—the Pauline idea of the "body imperishable" of I Corinthians, 35–57, for instance—is, like grace,

5. The musical aspect of this part of Chappell's quest may be as crucial as the philosophical. The absence of jazz in Nirvana is another telling argument against its appeal.

a mystery and therefore by definition cannot be imaged (though the conditions of its mystery may be). Consequently, the alternative, desirable vision is only vaguely implied in *Midquest,* a spindrift of thought and faith.
This quandary is sharply presented in "Birthday 35":

> But, Lord, You stand on one side
>
> Of the infinite black ditch
> And I on the other. *And that's a bitch.* (7–8)

Fred is as fascinated, however, with how life may have begun as with
what may follow it. From the touching desire to uncover with his grandfather "the final source of West Fork Pigeon River," through the brief
hints in the opening poem of each volume about "how the world was
formed," to the more complexly developed myths of creation in *Wind
Mountain* V ("a slightly different Big Bang theory") and *River* IX ("The
Novel"), he reveals an inventive, fervent desire to be present at beginnings
(which in the myths at least, he is). The title section ("Two") of *Source*
elaborates this impulse, being composed of scattered, disparate myths, many
dealing with first causes, each apparently seeking to embody an "explanation," but finally explaining nothing.

In this preoccupation with the unknowns that border human life at either
verge, he keeps in uneasy balance his inventive, informed intellectual curiosity and his spiritual tendency to accept the unknowable, or at least his
place outside it. Here, as at so many other junctures of *Midquest,* a passage
from "Birthday 35," the true prelude to the volume, is pertinent:

> I'd sleep in the eiderdown of the True Believer
> And never nightmare about Either / Or
>
> If I had a different person in my head.
> But this gnawing worm shows that I'm not dead.
>
> Therefore: either I live with doubt
> Or get out. (5)

Structures

One may enter Chappell's *Midquest* at any point and find, as with all coherent visions emanating from a center, the basic terms and images that
shadow the whole. The poems radiate from and revolve around a hub—

though within most of them there is a nicely composed narrative linearity sometimes (*e.g.,* "Susan Bathing," "Second Wind") reinforced by a psychological progression—so that one poem or a sequence of poems may enact the volume.

"Cleaning the Well" offers an instance of this, embodying in a single piece the general construction of *Midquest* as a Dantesque descent into hell and a rising toward light and redemption. Fred assists his grandfather in cleaning the well, the literal experience graphically presented from the double perspective of a young (eight- to ten-year-old) boy doing the work and an adult creating a shape for his memory. Chappell gives various indications of the figurative perspective from which he sees the experience and by which he wishes it evaluated. Dante's descent is, of course, the fundamental metaphoric enclosure, the "soundless dreaming/O" (14) of the well's mouth functioning effectively as a fearsome gate to the netherworld, prefiguring *Inferno's* circles and the further possibility that nothingness may be at the bottom of things. The grandfather lowers Fred on pulley rope and harness, thus supporting him and becoming a "guide" (like Virgil) in a way appropriate to the context. The well itself is a version of the well at the center of the declining valleys of Malebolge through which Dante enters Cocytus, the frozen wasteland of the final circle of *Inferno.* Two of the boy's phrases particularize the broad connection. As he hits the water, he cries, "Whoo! It's *God/Damn* cold!" (14) and later, in response to his grandfather's asking how it's going, thinks, "It goes like Hell" (15). Two italicized phrases express more formally the implications of these colloquial ones: at the terrifying point where the boy has been reduced to the condition of a non-creature (nerveless, sexless, breathless, mindless, and bodiless) occur the words "*I shall arise never*" (15); similarly, at the other extreme of readjustment to the ground above, we read, "*I had not found death good*" (17).

Within the Dantesque frame, Chappell has Fred compare himself to Jonah, Joseph, and Lazarus, adding a biblical lens through which the homey, local experience is considered. A particularly telling merging of psychological insight and literary allusion takes place in this stanza (14). Fred's return to upper earth has disoriented him as much as had the earlier descent into the gelid water. He recalls the foreboding dark as "holy" and tries, in his new disorientation, "to fetch [it]/Back" (16). He then wonders if the three biblical figures had also been "ript untimely/From black wellspring of death" (16). There is the understanding of the human psyche's conservative nature, to want to remain in the condition to which it's become accustomed, so that the usual view of the miracles of the restoring of Jonah, Joseph, and Lazarus to the world is given an unexpected twist. In terms of the other allusive dimension here, Fred's resistance to his return recalls the resistance to waking with which each of the four volumes of *Midquest* begins, itself derived partly from Dante's tendency to sleep or swoon when faced with the pressure of attention and discovery (*e.g.,* *Inferno,* I, ll, III, 136, and V, 142; *Purgatorio,* XVIII, 145). Finally, "wellspring of death" encapsulates the paradoxical understanding the *Divine Comedy* assumes, eventually tracing back to the *felix culpa* of Christianity.

Poems VI, VII, and VIII of *Wind Mountain* accomplish as a series what "Cleaning the Well" does as a single poem. A comic inversion of the poem it precedes, "My Father's Hurricane" is a tall tale with which J. T. regales eleven-year-old Fred over "the ruins / Of an April supper" (116). The hurricane is immortalized as "Bad Egg," which suggests it is the destructive opposite of "Egg," the source of all life that Fred refers to hyperbolically in "Birthday 35." It is a five-layer conglomeration of all the stuff its power has uprooted and carried who knows where. J. T. travels upward through each layer, fending off young Fred's common-sense questions, until he reaches layer five, composed of "'Lovebirds, honeypies, sweethearts— whatever / You want to call them'" (119). The mother stops the story at the point where it tends toward raunchiness, the lovers "'Rolling and sporting in the wind like face cards / From a stag poker deck'" (120). The simile indicates the more serious substance the poem makes light of—lust and the gamble one takes with one's soul when one gives in to it. Paulo and Francesca are among those J. T. sees in layer five, and the potential cost of lust becomes even more sharply focused by Fred's question, "'But how did you get down without / Getting killed?'" (120). The answer to the question never comes, for the poem ends with J. T.'s voice cut off. Getting out is another story.

These last three details—the reference to Paulo and Francesca, the figurative implication that lust is a high-stakes gamble, and the allusion to death—would be sufficient to key the spiritual implications of this inverted hell. It is humorously presented, of course, and a dazzlingly inventive entertainment, but it is also from the outset suspiciously unsettling, beginning as it does with the comparison of J. T.'s cigarette smoke to a "dust cloud over a bombed-out city" (116).

The corrective to this odd *ascent* into a layer of "honeypies," begins with the title of the next poem. "In Parte Ove Non E Che Luca" is most of the final line of Canto IV of Dante's *Inferno,* and the poem it labels is a pretty fair country translation of Canto V. The chaotic uprooting of the previous poem becomes the "storm infernal" (Dante's "*bufera*" could be translated "hurricane") of the second circle of Hell. Here the winds also conflict, unceasingly driving the damned Spirits "onward with brute force":

> Up they go to the very edge of the Course
>> Of Ruin, complaining, lamenting, aghast.
>> For them the Word Divine is sheer remorse.
>
> Into this pain the lovers of flesh are thrust,
>> All those who gave their human reason over
>> To the delicious fever of carnal lust. (122)

In short, J. T.'s "lovebirds" are here, hovering "in the torn air," and this time no humor relieves their predicament. Chappell, however, updates the population by adding Casanova, a couple of poets, and from his own book, Virgil Campbell.

Campbell, in response to Fred's request that his Master and guide, the *other* Virgil, stop and bring him over to them, becomes the subject and speaker (à la Francesca) of the third poem in this group, "Three Sheets in the Wind: Virgil Campbell Confesses." He tells his own tale, balancing formally J. T.'s hurricane story. It concerns his getting caught by his wife and the preacher *in flagrante delicto* with a willing country "gal you always hear about / And generally never meet" (124). It's another funny experience, well stitched together, but for all Campbell's ingratiating humor, cajolery, and wit, it is finally quite serious because of the context in which Chappell sets it. Ironies proceed from that context, too. The poem, a confession, begins with Campbell calling himself "a solid by God citizen," but his country is the second circle of the Inferno.[6] He understands his youthful

6. I have taken Virgil Campbell's placement in the second circle of Dante's Hell so literally because of the sequence of these poems, particularly the segue between the second and third. The presence of J. T. Chappell as listener in the dramatic monologue of the

penchant for moonshine and women as "a kind of crazy" in his blood that "nothing but / The worst that can happen will ever get . . . out" (124). He then says, "The worst that can happen never happened to me," which is a lie, given his condition of damnation; it is also a sign of the rationalization and evasion of the truth that is traditionally characteristic of the damned. Virgil Campbell could have sold cider to Eve. His story leads him to make the familiar promise of those caught in a terrifying trap—he believes, sewed up in one of his wife's sheets, that he's died and gone to hell, and so he thinks

> how I'd do it all different if
> I could only live my earthly life again:
> I'd be a sweet and silent religious man. (126)

He gets out of the story's *contretemps,* of course, and the final line of the poem, in which he decides to have a drink, indicates how ineptly he's kept that rash promise. "'Well, where's the harm?'" (127) he asks rhetorically, ready to bend his elbow, repeating the same question he's asked earlier in the poem in justifying with wonderful sophistic logic his adultery. The harm is perdition, no matter the charm of the lothario; Campbell is a convincing embodiment of the giving over of human reason "to the delicious fever of carnal lust." In the larger series of poems centering on Virgil Campbell in *Midquest,* it's clear that Fred is affectionately and generously disposed toward him; Fred feels great kinship with Virgil in the last of these, "At the Grave of Virgil Campbell." But a lovable reprobate is still a reprobate, and in a book that takes seriously the fallen nature of humankind and traditional modes of dealing with that condition, the implications of this trio of poems are inescapable.

This group, then, repeats in extended form and with more widely varying tonalities the descent motif of "Cleaning the Well," using Dante's model more pervasively, making explicit the dimension of Hell's eternal enclosure. These four poems focus also *Midquest*'s recurrent entertainment

---

confession complicates this choice, however. Is J. T. damned, too? Perhaps he is a *nonce* extension of Fred, a "listener" of context, no more trapped in hell than Dante was. Or perhaps we are gradually to ease back into the familiar general-store setting of "Firewater."

from different perspectives of the possibility of an afterlife and what spiritual alternatives face its central figure, the pilgrim Fred Chappell on his thirty-fifth birthday, pressing toward "the love that moves itself in light to loving."

This essay is for Amanda, Scott, Anna, and Lynwood.

The World Was Plenty: The Poems of Fred Chappell

HENRY TAYLOR

When *The World Between the Eyes,* Fred Chappell's first book of poems, appeared in 1971, he had published three novels and completed a fourth. The first three (*It Is Time, Lord,* 1963; *The Inkling,* 1965; *Dagon,* 1968) revealed not only a thorough command of the ingredients and conventions of southern gothic fiction but also a view of the world shaped by wide-ranging and tireless reading. They are brilliant, brief, allusive, densely textured, and difficult. They found skilled translators and came to be widely respected in France—a fact that Chappell acknowledged gratefully when Bob Edwards brought it up on National Public Radio's *Morning Edition* a few years ago. Chappell added, "But it should be remembered that this is a people with admiration also for Jerry Lewis and snails." In an afterword to *The Fred Chappell Reader* (1987), Chappell points out the shortcomings of his early fiction (though without disavowing it) and says that his ambition has shifted away from excessively intellectual experiments with form: "I have got to where I should like for my work to be humane, and I do not much care if it even becomes sentimental. Perhaps it would be nice if a few artists in our time decided to rejoin the human race, and I think that I would be glad to do so, however much I disagree with its politics" (486).

The humanity, clarity, and apparent directness of Chappell's more recent novels, *I Am One of You Forever* (1987) and *Brighten the Corner Where You Are* (1989) would seem to bear out this statement, though one begins with a narrator swimming through a teardrop, and the second begins with the protagonist's theft of the moon. If Chappell's fiction has undergone a noticeable transformation, his poetry has maintained a consistency of style and approach, even as its scope has extended to the book-length *Midquest* (1981). The title poem of *The World Between the Eyes* presents a speaker who, in various guises and at various ages, continues to be the means of perception throughout much of Chappell's poetry. In this poem, he is a boy caught between the world his body inhabits and the world he finds in books. More precisely, he lives in a larger world that includes both:

> The house is chill, he wanders room and room,
> October is seething at the windows.
>
> Hands lax in his pockets. He sees
> Through it all. Man of the boring world,
> He dangles his cigarette and his dangerous charm.
>   "Ah, Comtesse, it's all too apparent,
>   you know little of the ways of the Hindoo";
> Insouciant in jade cufflinks,
> While the skyline flickers with the Big Guns. (12–13)

Here he shifts between the "real" world and his imagination, a little like Stephen Dedalus wishing he were the Count of Monte Cristo. As the poem proceeds, however, October works its magic not only on the house but also on the landscapes drawn in the books. Time is "charged past endurance with the future"(14), but the poem ends with the boy "blest in his skins, an old stone / House, and a sky eaten up with stars" (15).

"February" and "Weird Tales" emerge more purely from the two realms of rural childhood and literary fantasy, respectively. The first recounts a hog butchering from the boy's point of view; he is "dismayed / With delight"(3), "elated-drunk / With the horror"(4), as the hog is killed, scalded, gutted, cloven. For a while, the poem looks like something vegetarians might use to gain converts, but it takes in the brisk air, the joy of community ritual, and ends with a nostalgic tableau:

> And his bladder and his stomach sack! puffed
> Up and tied off and flung to the kids,
> Game balls, they bat them about,
> Running full tilt head down across the scattered yard.
> And then on a startled breeze

The bladder's hoist, vaults high and gleams in the sunlight
And reflects on its shiny globe
The sky a white square
And the figures beneath, earnest figures
Gazing straight up. (5)

Imagination and recollection combine here into something more durable
than the experience itself; and in "Weird Tales," it is finally friendship that
is the theme rather than the fascination with the obscure writers of horror
and fantasy who supplied that magazine with material. The poem begins
with an evocation of Lovecraft and proceeds to a kind of honor roll of

. . . those who witnessed, away
From the rant of commerce, the shriek of lying newsprint,
The innocent intimate truths that gnaw the marrow. (40)

But the poem ends with love and gratitude expressed to Richard Dillard,
author of *News of the Nile* (1971), the title poem of which makes beautiful
and elaborate connections among sites along the Nile, flowing north as a
train runs north to Wisconsin:

Where August Derleth prints the books
Of Lovecraft. . . .

And east of this train, south of Virginia,
In western North Carolina, Fred Chappell
Has written a novel, *Dagon,* and all these things
Come together, turn together, and will pass on
To come again. The Nile flows sluggish
And is thick with mud. It bears the news.[1]

Chappell's poem, in turn, becomes a letter, signed "Fred," and makes more
connections; to add to them, I acknowledge here that Richard Dillard provided me with the information that Farnsworth Wright (1888–1940) was
the editor of *Weird Tales*.

1. R. H. W. Dillard, *News of the Nile: A Book of Poems by R. H. W. Dillard* (Chapel Hill,
1971), 27.

This news too the Nile bears, Richard Dillard,
Flowing past "Dongola, Kerma and Wawa";
Past Karloff double features, Lugosi revivals,
The spiderwebbed offices of Farnsworth Wright:
That rather than injustices and generals,
We choose to live with vampires, demons, ghouls. (40–41)

Even the slighter poems in *The World Between the Eyes* are fine examples of the delight to be taken in finding the right words, in the power of words and literature to transform the everyday. Near the end of the book there are five poems about baseball; their true subject is wit and the similes available to a person who has done some reading. The first of the five, "Third Base Coach," begins and ends with literary comparisons:

He commands as mysteriously as
the ghost of Hamlet's father.
. . . .
Like an Aeschylean tragedy he's static; baffling;
Boring; but.

                        Urgent with import. (48)

Farther into the sequence, as a quotation from Ty Cobb describes a fast ball, and invented similes and jokes combine with those that appear to have originated on the field ("Trying to hit Wednesday with a bb gun"—"Junk Ball," 51), the poems begin to revel in their slightness, reminding us that "it's just a game" is about the most ignorant statement that can be made to someone who takes a game seriously. In other words: people who think it's just a game had better play among themselves.

II

In 1963, a few months before Chappell published his first novel, Duke University Press published *Under Twenty-five,* an anthology of "Duke narrative and verse" edited by the distinguished creative-writing teacher William Blackburn.[2] Chappell is represented by two prose pieces and ten

2. William Blackburn, ed., *Under Twenty-five: Duke Narrative and Verse, 1945–1962* (Durham, 1963).

poems, only two of which were later collected in *The World Between the Eyes*. Others are interesting primarily as evidence that Chappell was committed at an early age to using traditional forms, sometimes combining them with free verse or very loosely cadenced lines. "Familiar Poem" is in many ways the most ambitious of these poems; it is the meditation of a man lying awake beside his sleeping wife. The first of the four sections sets the scene, in a dark bedroom where "rain is sound"; the lines, moderately regular iambic pentameter, drift among rhyme schemes based on the quatrain, on five lines, and on seven. In mid-sentence, the section ends, and the form becomes looser iambic pentameter, unrhymed. The speaker's thoughts wander more noticeably, from his love for his wife, through poetic ambition as alchemy, to the knowledge of the writer's struggle to find, against "the onyx mirror of history past and future," the "bitter poison of salvation."

The third section is a sonnet. The octave addresses the sleeping wife and tries to characterize her dreams; the sestet addresses God and prays "that I may / Not be insane":

> Let my love's dreams as spies
> Into that trackless wild. When I trace back
> My life, thought seems the suffering, slack
> Thread preserving my self from the gray, gay
> Narcotic mazes and hysteric skies. (200)

In the fourth section, dawn arrives, and "reality" overcomes "imagination." As objects become discernible, "light is sound," and free verse embodies random observations of the waking world:

> The sunlight shapes all objects, destroying images to being.
> I rise and turn and unravel
> The ghost of myself from among the sheets. (201)

"Familiar Poem" is sometimes self-consciously ambitious and contains more nearly "confessional" passages than Chappell has since allowed himself. He may have admitted some youthful follies and drawn upon autobiographical material, but he has done so without the self-importance that sometimes reveals itself in this poem. Most of the time, inhabiting the worlds of imagination and of dailiness is a source of joy in Chappell's work.

The poem's chief interest now, aside from its demonstration of a twenty-five-year-old poet's enormous promise, is that it is a clear forerunner of *Midquest* (1981), the superb long poem that first appeared as four separate volumes: *River* (1975), *Bloodfire* (1978), *Wind Mountain* (1979), and *Earthsleep* (1980).

Like "Familiar Poem," each part of *Midquest* begins with a speaker awakening beside his sleeping wife; the phrase "light is sound" also appears at the beginning of *Earthsleep,* in "Earth Emergent Drifts the Fire River." Furthermore, each of the waking poems rings some variation on the idea that in waking, the speaker must lose or abandon some essential part of himself. But the speaker of *Midquest* is ten years older than the author of "Familiar Poem," and the author, most of the time, is older than that. At the Dantean midpoint of his life, the speaker takes stock and meditates—on his love for his wife, Susan; on the selves he has been and is becoming; and on the significance of place and family, of friendship, music, and literature.

As Chappell points out in a preface to the one-volume edition, each of the four parts of the poem consists of "eleven longish poems . . . covering four times the same twenty-four hours of the speaker's life" (ix). The date is May 28, 1971, his thirty-fifth birthday. Chappell goes on to declare that the speaker, named "Fred," is no more or less Fred Chappell than any of his other fictional characters and to explain a few of the principles according to which the poems are arranged. The organization allows the gradual unfolding of a life, a loose narrative, yet it also retains most of the advantages of a collection of shorter poems. There is little here that is not enriched by its context, but there is no single poem that could not stand outside the context. For this reason, the order imposed on the poems, though satisfying and persuasive, is not inevitable. Chappell's remarks set the reader up to notice certain large rhythms:

> And each of the volumes (except *Wind Mountain*) is organized as a balancing act. The first poem is mirrored by the last; the second by the next to last, and so on inward. But the sixth poem in each volume is companionless in that volume, and concerned with a garrulous old gentleman named Virgil Campbell, who is supposed to give to the whole its specifically regional, its Appalachian, context. The fifth poem in each is given to stream of consciousness and these interior monologues become discernibly more formal as

the speaker begins to order his life. Each volume is dominated by a different element of the family, *River* by the grandparents, *Bloodfire* by the father, and there is a family reunion in *Earthsleep,* the part most shadowed by death. (In order to suggest the fluid and disordered nature of air, *Wind Mountain* was exempt from some of these requirements.) (ix–x)

It turns out that in *Bloodfire* (the second part), Virgil Campbell holds forth in the seventh poem, "Firewater." In the more loosely arranged *Wind Mountain,* he gets the eighth poem, as it happens; he does not settle back to the middle of a part until *Earthsleep.* My point is not to suggest that there is a mistake in the order of the poems or even in Chappell's description of it but rather to note that giving Virgil poems VI, VII, VIII, and VI, is just as effective as giving him VI every time. Only Chappell's prefatory remark brings attention to this matter. Other "mirrorings" and the consistently stream-of-consciousness fifth poems are perhaps regular enough in their recurrence to evoke recognition, but several of Chappell's self-imposed rules were more useful to him than to his readers, in something like the way in which syllabic meter can be useful: it is in itself inaudible but gives the poet something to work with and against.

Many of the poems are in loose blank verse or free verse. Various traditional forms are also used, from the Anglo-Saxon strong-stress meter of "My Grandfather's Church Goes Up" to the elaborate chant royal of "My Mother's Hard Row to Hoe." The several voices in the poems and the fully realized characters behind them help to keep the formal variety from becoming obtrusive; so, too, does Chappell's command of meters that range from the stately to the rollicking and his ability to work in many tones and genres.

The central "balancing act" in *Midquest* is the speaker's steady exploration of the tensions between his rural Appalachian childhood and his urban professional adulthood. His grandmother is perhaps the richest source of the earlier values and attitudes. She speaks most of four poems given to her, and Fred listens, occasionally asking questions or commenting; at times, she seems conscious of her role as informant but often she drifts from there into a spoken re-creation of a moment in the distant past. Her strength and independence, and the ways in which she accommodates these to marriage and widowhood, provide some of the most moving passages in *Midquest.*

The anecdotes and recollections of Fred's parents are either wildly funny or a sweet blend of nostalgia and a wish to be true to the difficult times. When his mother recalls their first meeting, she vacillates between the warmth of a funny story and insistence that their early life was "hard, hard, hard, hard, / Hard" (109). In "My Father's Hurricane," his father indulges himself in a tall tale of being blown around in a wind that had everything on earth airborne, whereas in "My Father Allergic to Fire," he tries to assume a heavy weight of guilt for a childish and ignorant initiation into the Ku Klux Klan.

Against the background of these poems and the rowdier episodes involving Virgil Campbell, Fred addresses love poems to Susan, beholds the changing landscapes of his past and present, recalls his attempts to play the trombone, and with graceful freedom from self-indulgence, explores the sources and nature of his literary ambitions. "Science Fiction Water Letter to Guy Lillian" begins as a thoughtful discussion of the genre's limitations and ends with a précis of Fred's own unwritten sci-fi novel; "Rimbaud Fire Letter to Jim Applewhite" is a painfully humorous evocation of youthful pretensions arising from misapprehensions of Rimbaud's life and work. If these poems were required reading in creative writing workshops, student writers would have less trouble understanding what it really means to take one's work seriously.

Throughout the book, there are echoes, sometimes respectful and sometimes parodic, of other writers: Wordsworth, Cummings, Eliot, Frost, and others come in for brief and witty allusions, and Dante, who stands behind the whole poem, is both translated and transformed in *Wind Mountain*. "In Parte Ove Non E Che Luca" begins as a somewhat colloquial but perfectly honorable rendering of Canto V of the *Inferno* and holds its own against other translations for fifty-one lines. When Dante begins to introduce individual victims of lust, however, building toward Francesca da Rimini, Chappell loosens his diction gradually as he introduces Casanova, Lord Byron, and James Dickey before turning back inward to his own poem:

"Master, wait!" I said. "I recognize
　　From childhood the round form, the red face
　　Of Virgil Campbell, one of my father's cronies.

"May I not hear what brought him such disgrace?"
　　"Of course," he said, "I'll bid him to this place." (123)

Among the best of the literary poems is "Hallowind," the tenth poem in *Wind Mountain*. It is a "playlet," reminiscent of Yeats in length and metric but set in Durham in 1961; the characters are Reynolds Price, Susan, Fred, the rain, and the wind. In an argument about the nature of fiction, Fred pushes for the paradigms and myths discoverable in stories and Reynolds argues for each story's particularity until Susan enters with tea and cakes. She shifts the conversation toward conclusion, but the rain and the wind interrupt them. The wind's closing speech is a surprising and moving argument for what might be called the humanities:

It's soon enough that we dissolve
Their names to dust, unmoving move
Against their animal powers to love
And weep and fear. It's all too soon
They grow as silent as the moon
And lie in earth as naked bone.
We'll let them sit and sip their tea
Till midnight; then I'll shake the tree
Outside their window, and drive the sea
Upon the land, the mountain toward the Pole,
The desert upon the glacier. And all
They ever knew or hoped will fall
To ash . . . Till then, though, let them speak
And lighten the long dim heartache,
And trifle, for sweet trifling's sake (139)

This inclusive and loving recognition of the world we inhabit is the foundation on which *Midquest* stands. What this world is to us is touched on in a brief passage in *Brighten the Corner Where You Are*. The protagonist, Joe Robert Kirkman, is loosely based on Chappell's father; his son is the narrator. One full and fateful morning at the school where Joe Robert teaches science, he is visited by the parents of Lewis Dorson, a former student who returned from the Second World War unable to pick up his life and at last committed suicide. Joe Robert has just learned this from Lewis' mother:

It was over between them forever now, but my father felt the need to say something, knowing there was nothing to say, yet knowing, too, that she would listen. It came out lame and hoarse: "I thought the world of him. More than that."

"More than the world." She looked into his face. "I count on more."

But that wasn't what he meant, whatever he meant. The world was what my father knew, nothing more or less, better or worse. The world was plenty. "We all do," he said. (65–66)

III

In the ninth poem of *Bloodfire,* "Burning the Frankenstein Monster: Elegiac Letter to Richard Dillard," Fred acknowledges a perception of Dillard's and adds, "But *The Inkling* is long out of print, bemuses not even my mother. / Let it smolder to ash on whatever forgotten shelf" (85). As luck would have it, my copy of *The Inkling* is holding up very well. Between the front cover and the flyleaf, there is a paper napkin on which in April, 1966, at the Pickwick in Greensboro, Fred Chappell scribbled these lines:

When it's
Ginsberg on the Ganges,
Him with His hairy phalange,
I'll be back
Again, sweetheart,
In the following stanges.

None of the other writers there assembled could rise to that challenge, which is quoted here for the fun of it, as an indication of Chappell's restless interest in saying the world and as an epigraph to the question of how a poet still in mid-career might follow a book as strong and deep as *Midquest.*

Writers tend to be more interested in their recent work than in work that has receded somewhat into the past. On the one hand, a young writer can be daunted to realize that a recent work is a vast improvement on earlier efforts; one wonders whether one can rise to that level again and what the writing life will be like if one cannot. On the other hand, a writer in middle age can sometimes face with relative equanimity the thought of having written already that work which he or she may not surpass. Gratitude for having achieved that work can even be liberating: now it will be easier to take greater risks or pursue more idiosyncratic impulses. By this time, the writer knows that one must first of all be interested in what one is doing. These notions arise from contemplation of the startling oddity and the surprising success of *Castle Tzingal* (1984), a poem consisting of twenty-three dramatic pieces, most of them monologues. The nine characters are occupants of a mythical principality under the rule of a mad king, remote in time and place. The imprecision of time, especially, is that of dream or of vaguely researched costume drama; the speakers use such words as *arras, florin, villeyn, catamite, scranny,* and *grutch,* but they also use words of more recent origin, as if to remind us that they are detached from real history.

As they certainly are. The first monologue is spoken by "the Homunculus," an eighteen-inch creature named Flyting but called Tweak. His account of his origins is a fine, humorous example of alchemical fantasy:

> I was born
> On a table bright with flame and glassware,
> And had no childhood except an ignorance
> Of politics and gossip. And what a boring year
> My childhood was. No company
> But the pottering alchemist, his cat
> Who wanted to gobble me up, and three
> Disgusting nodules of melting flesh
> That were earlier attempts at being me. (1)

Tweak is a gleefully wicked spy for the king, who suspects everybody of plotting against him. His queen pines for one Marco, a troubadour from a neighboring province, who has disappeared. Petrus, an envoy from Marco's father, gradually comes close to discovering that young man's grisly fate and in three poems sends reports back home. The Astrologer, the Admiral, and a Page all take their turns exposing their fears and treacheries, and they are all disturbed at times by the disembodied voice of Marco, who still manages to sing from his place not far this side of the grave.

The poem is another balancing act, and the reader teeters on the line between standing well back in arm's-length apprehension of the self-consciously literary language and allegory and being drawn into the melodramatic story. Among the forces that draw the reader in is the skill with which Chappell sometimes echoes the sound of anonymous balladry:

As the lone long wind unwinds
     Her bobbin of white thread
She sings a song rejoicing
     That she never wed. (5)

But if this were a bedtime story, it would be saved for the nights when the children had been very wicked, indeed. That is another of the forces that draw us into these seeming improbabilities. The disloyalty, self-interest, madness, and grief of Castle Tzingal are common enough in realms with which most of us are better acquainted. Marco's disembodied voice is that of poetry or even truth, and he wonders at the enormity of his punishment:

No crime against humanity or God has yet deserved
Such unimagined punishment, no black sin
Received such frozen penalty.

Until a mad king dabbled in chemistry.
. . . .
So I live on, if live I do,
To wrinkle and pull tense the minds of those
Who have created me what I am now
Until a thorough justice arise. (31)

In our time, such words cause a chill of recognition. Our alchemy is farther-fetched even than that of Tzingal, and it has rendered us more vulnerable to madness. Many a poet in such a world has reason to feel like a disembodied voice, but Chappell tells his story with too much skill and too much pleasure in the resources of poetic form to be accused of losing hope.

IV

Source (1985) was Chappell's first full-length collection of short poems since his first book, though the publication history of individual poems shows that many of them were composed by the way while he was working on *Midquest* and *Castle Tzingal.* Furthermore, in 1979 he published *Awakening to Music,* a chapbook of fifteen poems, and in 1981, *Driftlake: A Lieder Cycle,* an elegant limited edition. *Source* contains five poems from *Awakening to Music; Driftlake* is left uncollected in favor of "The Transformed Twilight," a second "lieder cycle" similar in form and length to the first. Between the two small books and the larger one, there are some important differences of tone and apparent intention. These are particularly evident in the revisions of the five poems from *Awakening to Music* and one, "Seated Figure," reprinted from *The World Between the Eyes*.

Awakening to Music is characterized by imaginative play carried toward extremes of verbal ingenuity, startling similes, and weird situations. A few, like "Delayed by Mongol Forces at National Airport," posit wonderful premises but trail off into unsatisfying endings. Nonetheless, the title poem, a recollection of the pleasures and trials of caring for cattle, and "Music as a Woman Imperfectly Perceived" handsomely sustain their ambitious figures.

In one view, *Source* is concerned with such literary gains as may be extracted from various other kinds of losses. The first section of the book, "Child in the Fog," evokes scenes from a mountain childhood in poems simultaneously regretting their disappearance and rejoicing in the power of words to recall their shadows. Here, "Awakening to Music" has been enriched and simplified. Between the following two versions of the same passage, a strained simile has been taken out and the syntax eased:

Or:

> with hands frost-grained
> from the bucket bail I'd clutch the brood-warm
> teats and mother of God how
> a cow would kick.
> > The leg
> like a diving board snapping off on second bounce.
> As sudden as a door blown shut.
> (In August they'd lash out
> when thistle-thorns hid in the udders.) (*Awakening*, 9)

Sometimes:

> with hands frost-grained
> from the bucket bail I'd clutch the brood-warm
> teats and God help us how she'd kick a shapely
> leg as sudden as a door blown shut.
> Or just as quick in August when
> thistle-thorns embedded in the udders (*Source*, 10)

It is at the end of the poem that the most thematically significant changes have been made. The first version's ending is explicit in stating the loss attendant on living past those days of herding and milking:

And all those years I went clothed in this sleep,
odor and heat of cows
blanketed about my head,
blear low fever I breathed passionately.
How would I get it back? Go to blood
again, sleep the light green sleep?
How can anyone live truly, waking without cows?

Then
no more music. (*Awakening,* 10)

And all those years I went clothed in this sleep,
odor and warmth
of cows blanketed about my head.

How would I get it back?
Go to blood again, sleep the light green sleep?
How can I wake, not waking to music? (*Source,* 11)

The new last line allows for a paraphrase like "How can I help waking to music?" The emphasis shifts from what has gone forever to what has been retained.

In the second and third sections of the book, "Source" and "The Transformed Twilight," Chappell moves beyond instances of personal loss to portrayals of the kind of destruction our age has taught us to consider. "The Evening of the Second Day" reports the vague movements of a band of people who have reverted to tribalism among the ruins of a city blasted almost beyond recognition. The lieder cycle is a love poem, but the speaker "can imagine no brutal history that will not be born" (43) and describes a few that already have been. Yet even the darkness of these poems is mitigated by the pleasure of "Recovery of Sexual Desire After a Bad Cold" or the wit of "The Story." The story thrives among such people as a farmer's wife and children and a jolly merchant but falls drunkenly among poets; when it is thoroughly derelict, the novelists find it.

The poems in the final section, "Forever Mountain," find various kinds of consolation in the knowledge that death is an eternal separation. The poem from which the section takes its title ends with the words *"This is a prayer"*; it is an affecting farewell to the poet's father, who is visualized moving in a leisurely way through a day and night on the mountainside until he is out of sight. "Urleid" revives Lucretius and his ideas of basic atoms free of supernatural will. The poem revels in anachronism, as Lucretius dismisses Olympus as a "drawing-room farce" and takes Rilke to task for his angels.

Lucretius is treated with more affection in *First and Last Words* (1989). In "How the Job Gets Done," subtitled "an epilogue to Lucretius," a real battlefield becomes a literary battlefield, and the soil of a garden becomes a page. After the corpses and bones and weapons are dust, there is still

> in his garden the poet who labors to line-end,
> turns back like a sweating plowman to fold
> another loamy furrow over the crumbled palaces. (52)

The title of the collection arises from what Chappell is about in the first and third sections, which are devoted, respectively, to prologues and epilogues for various works of literature—*The Georgics* and *The Dynasts,* Livy and Lucretius, Goethe and Tolstoy, *The Wind in the Willows.* Chappell makes us at ease with what he is talking about, however familiar or unfamiliar the works he addresses. These poems are, for the most part, refreshingly accessible without being simple or simple-minded. Like most of the poems I have been looking at, they hover between the world of literature and the world we live in, as if it were sometimes hard to tell the difference.

The middle section of *First and Last Words,* "Entr'acte," contains a few miscellaneous poems—not closely related to the book's central concern but too good to have been left out—and a few poems that come at the life/literature dichotomy from the other direction. "Word," "Literature," "The Reader," and "The Garden" are witty texts in which the world itself becomes a text. It would be tempting to say that the poems and the world become one, but Chappell seems to like that shimmering margin between them. The two propositions of "The Garden" are, first, that "The garden is a book about the gardener," and, second, that "The gardener is a book about her garden":

She walks among these leaves as easy as morning
Come to scatter its robins and tender noises.
As the plants inhale the morning and its green light,
The book is open once again that was never shut.
What now we do not know we shall never know. (30)

The apparent directness of that passage, the casual paradox of the next-to-last line, indicate some of the qualities that keep these poems, with all their colloquy with other books, from being too literary to be believed. Chappell's intelligence has always been among the gifts he puts to most powerful use, because he knows how to keep it from being too showy. He learned this, as *Midquest* makes clear, from hanging around very bright but nonliterary people who speak their complicated minds in memorable country words. "Dipperful" gives us an encounter with an old man on a porch, under which his hounds are "warm spotted lumps of doze and quiver" (35). He speaks of walking for pleasure and walking to work. Then, echoing the wind at the end of "Hallowind," remarks "'But if we didn't have the triflingness / To think back on, nobody would come this far'" (35).

"Remodeling the Hermit's Cabin" presents words of a builder named Reade who has accepted a contract to desecrate an old cabin for the new owner, who likes certain modern amenities. This is the poem's conclusion:

"It looks kind of sad and busted, what we've done,"
I said.
        "That Florida feller will tack up plastic,"
He said, "and put him in an ice machine,
And have him a radar carport and a poodle
He's trained to count his money. These modern days
We're all a bunch of cowbirds, you know that?" (51)

This wonderful poem is presented as an epilogue to the Constitution of the United States. As with many of the other poems in *First and Last Words,* the connection is not forced or required for understanding. But the connections—even when we do need to make them before the poem is clear—are rich with amazing possibilities. A certain occupational hazard troubles some poets. As Tony Connor once put it, they "find poems in everything" and fear the failure "to feed silence to death." But Fred Chappell has long since learned that durable poems, whatever perception or occasion gets them started, occupy a mysterious realm somewhere between where we are and what we speak. The difference between the trees among which he grew up and the trees in the sacred wood diminishes with each of his strong advances upon the wilderness.

Turning the Windlass at the Well: Fred Chappell's Early Poetry

KATHRYN STRIPLING BYER

Looking back at a major poet's first book of poems can be a risky undertaking, particularly if the poet is Fred Chappell, one of the most prolific and versatile writers in recent memory. Knowing what developed from Chappell's early poems and seeing, we think, so clearly the outline of that development, we may be tempted to approach a re-reading of *The World Between the Eyes* as little more than a search for precursors to later, more accomplished poems and thereby fail to appreciate the artistic struggles that created those first poems, some of which are the most intense in contemporary poetry, almost overwhelming in their obsessive imagery and unrelenting rhythms. These early poems deserve to be re-examined on their own terms, not solely as forerunners to the great work in *Midquest*, *Source*, and *First and Last Words*. They deserve to be approached as the powerful introductory outbursts of poetic energy they are, outbursts that once carried the shock of initiation for the poet himself and still do so, more than twenty years later, for the reader.

In his essay "Feeling Into Words," the Irish poet Seamus Heaney has written convincingly of a poet's breakthough into finding a voice. He describes his own initiation into "this poetry thing" through the composition of the poem "Digging," which begins his first book, *Death of a Naturalist*. Heaney says that "Digging" was the first poem in which he felt he had made more than an arrangement of words and had at last "let down a shaft into real life."[1] He goes on to differentiate technique and craft in a young

---

1. Seamus Heaney, *Preoccupations* (New York, 1980), 41.

poet's development. "Learning the craft," he says, "is learning to turn the windlass at the well of poetry. Usually you begin by dropping the bucket halfway down the shaft and winding up a taking of air. You are miming the real thing until one day the chain draws unexpectedly tight and you have dipped into waters that will continue to entice you back" (47).

This is the point, Heaney declares, at which we may begin to speak of technique, that "dynamic alertness that mediates between the origin of feeling in memory and experience and the formal ploys that express these in a work of art" (47). It is this dynamic point, or at the very least the drawing nigh to it, that one looks for in *The World Between the Eyes,* that exciting moment when the chain draws tight, and the voice we know as Chappell's, Old Fred himself, begins to speak as only it can. That some of the poems in Chappell's first book are miming the real thing should come as no surprise. One expects as much in a first book, expects that, as in some of the book's shorter poems, for example, the poet will be playing with craft but not as yet drawing up a full bucket. The poems that do seem to reveal this dynamic alertness and to do so consistently are the long poems in which the living waters of Chappell's imagination come spilling over the rim of the bucket. Revealing a restless and inventive poetic vision, one "dismayed with delight" at what it sees, these poems come sharply alive in their tangle of memory and experience, their momentum often overwhelming the shorter lyrics, rolling on a flood-tide of words and images that promise to carry the poet as far as he wants to go, provided he can sustain his equilibrium, that is to say, his technique.

The first poem in the book, "February," introduces this tangle of memory from which the boy-witness (that "eye" so frequently doing the observing in Chappell's work) recoils yet can't stop watching, "elated-drunk / With the horror"(4) of that most familiar of rural Southern rituals, a hog-killing. Although feminine imagery is present at the outset in the gauzy frost and blue aprons of the women, the poem's emphasis is on the brutal, the hard, the *difficult,* that word bringing the others, slam-bang, up against it in line twelve. There is much masculine straining in this poem, as if indeed the poet knows he has hit pay dirt and is hauling, hauling for dear life the weighty contents of his poet's bucket up into the light of consciousness. In his rush, he sometimes ignores sentence structure, syntactical clarity. There is so much to be hauled up, so much to tell! The strong rhythms, reminiscent of the Anglo-Saxon at the heart of our language, go "wow wow across the gravel, / The cast iron pot; settles on the flame, / Black egg in its scarlet nest" (3). The fire and iron give a sense of forging, sparks flying, an image somewhat more active than Heaney's turning of the windlass and surely just as active as Heaney's phallic digging.

The rhythms of "February" call to mind the hammering of Wagner's Niebelungs toiling underground to forge the magical gold in *Das Rheingold,* those introductory poundings of a music that would swell and shift through the whole of a lifetime's sustained composition. Chappell's own percussive music shies away from nothing as he hammers out the bloody details of his ritual. His pig, its entrails gleaming in rich piles, fills every cranny of the poem. Has ever a young poet's bucket been fuller than this? No wonder the language heaves and sweats and grunts. This is labor! And what a racket it makes, filling the boy's ears till they are fit to burst. Even the women, who earlier stood silent and passive at the edge of the action, begin to yammer as soon as they receive the buckets of pig, busy in the kitchen "with the great clouds of oil and steam," taking their places at last in the ritual. Only near the end of the poem does the noise begin to subside, as the pig's bladder and stomach sac are "puffed / Up and . . . flung to the kids," and the bladder, rising on a "startled" breeze becomes, astonishingly enough, a mirror reflecting the white square of sky and the people beneath, silent now, struck dumb at last, "earnest figures / Gazing straight up" (5). What reflects is not something outside the scene, something cold as glass, but internal membrane transformed and set aloft. Forging the Rhine gold into magical rings and caps seems ordinary indeed compared to Chappell's transformation of a pig's bladder into an image reflecting reality itself!

The world in "February" is powerfully masculine. The women are present to be sure, waiting—though not for long—to take their places in Chappell's poetic world. (Think of the voices of grandmothers, mother, aunts in the later work!) But for now, to quote the old church hymn, "This is my Father's world," one in which there often seems no escape from that ancient, terrifying presence. In "The World Between the Eyes," the child, "lonely in the house of his fathers," carries "whole galaxies in his grandiloquent head," galaxies gleaned from books, for this Fred is a devourer of books and stories. They seem his only escape from the future's rooms that hold him without mercy.

Reading. The book lies on the floor.
He laces his fingers, elbows on knees.
Hour on hour he makes a queer genuflection.
Eyes that starve. Slow growth, slow
                growth of things,
                words bloom
                and burn. (13)

As in "February," images of fullness abound, of seas glutted with continents, maps crammed into bottles, rivers threatening flood. In the face of such menacing fullness, the ancient "hoodoo words" pour from him (*Gobbet, Excalibur,* Kronë), the poet's magic to fend off—what? The rage of the fathers? Among other things, this poem seems to be about the slow growth of poetry, its words that bloom and burn. In a line that echoes Theodore Roethke, he sings, "Every fire's his brother." He is forging a new kinship; everywhere he sees signs and declares the poet's duty: "to read aright / To know" (14). And as he reads, he enters the worlds of his reading, or rather *they* enter him: "Unfinished islands, broken moons, / The ships that ply between the suns: / Idols buoy in his head" (15).

The image of water runs through the poem "Wind River" at the start, swollen and dangerous as the troops try to cross. Then the river becomes the boy's seething perceptions, then language itself, a tidal wave of image and sound in which he could be washed away. (" 'Water's heavy, sir. Wrong. Time of year.' ")

Likewise, in the poem "Sunday," the preacher's voice rides on numbing waves, "rides forward mounting; / mounts up," and the boy is "battered not laved / In the undertow of stunning vowels" (45). This boy must learn, as he has in the book's title poem, how to outfit himself "for the virgin river and the savage traffic," for the memories and threatening perceptions lie heavy as a river in flood-time. The poet must wrestle with it, gentle it down before moving on into the voices of Ole Fred in *Midquest* and the ever-listening Jess, free of father-terror, in *I Am One of You Forever*. These are the voices we have come to think of as unmistakably Chappell's in their resonance, control, and passionate tenderness, but it is well to remember that this voice had its rough and tumble genesis in the flood tides of *The World Between the Eyes*.

One can hear this voice beginning to win its way through in "The Father," a poem in which the archetypal father-son relationship is expressed

most straightforwardly of all the long poems in *The World Between the Eyes*.
The father sits rock solid, his legs smelling of earth, some prehistoric earth-
god, taking his measure of creation. When he moves, the house and those
in it respond. The table quivers. The chair frets. The boy trembles. When
he commands the boy, "'Tomorrow / You come with me, maybe I'll show
you something'" (24), the words carry both threat and a grudging promise
of secrets to be revealed. The secret the two tramp through the fields to
find is nothing less than the source itself—the spring welling from the
clumped alders. "'This is what we drink,'" says the father, simply (24).
Then he reveals the danger that must be acknowledged, dealt with—the
alkali poisoning the water. In one of those seemingly casual comments that
can haunt a child for the rest of his life, the father declares in his matter-
of-fact way, "Not much a man can do when the source goes bad" (25).

Like any imaginative child, his senses more vulnerable than most to the
onslaught of the world, this child is ripe for haunting. Back home he
watches the drops plump from the watertap, counting off the rhythm, "one
one one now," and wondering how much of it will poison. He becomes
so obsessed with the tapping water that when the father says, "'Doing
nothing you. . . . Why don't you find another spring?'" (25), the charge
lies before him like his father's razor waiting on the bathroom enamel. In
one of the most disturbing scenes in the book, the blade so mesmerizes the
boy that he opens the "rending blade" and confronts his own fear in the
mirror.

> Finger-whorls rasp on the blade-edge, his skin
> Shudders, eyes open in every nook of his body.
> His face is streaked on the blade, eye
> Dripping melting; face salt-white
> In the mirror. The drain is an empty eye.
> Fair bone handle, he can get a purchase.
> Drops keep tapping, tapping,
> Tapping, tapping. His skin is wet, stiff. (26)

"So gently stroking with the eye / Edge of the razor his wrist" (26), the
child survives this trial by terror and acquires a "darkling wisdom" that
shows him what death is—"merely a peering backward from outside" (27).
Having withstood death's nightmarish vision in the mirror, he can fold the

knife away and go find the spring the father has earlier challenged him to find, a spring that although brackish, can be dug through to clear water. "'What makes you so sure?'" the father asks. "'I just know, that's all,'" the boy replies, needing no other reason (27). For hasn't he said earlier in "The World Between the Eyes" that his duty is to "read aright," to know? (14). His mind's "surcharged with the future." He cannot fail.

The same suffering through to a sense of destiny and control is expressed in the companion poem "The Mother." Not surprisingly, the threat in this poem is that of absorption into the suffocatingly intimate feminine. The mother can "strip him, put him cowering," in all of his infantile dependency. Her face "over the new one's crib" can "wash out his whole sky," leaving him easy prey for the archaic threats of Old Snarly: Which child will he eat?

Whereas the boy earlier stood his ground and confronted his father-terror in the mirror in order to survive it, he understands that to survive the Great Mother, he must flee to a safe distance. There, sitting on a nearby hill, he can get a sense of perspective on his childhood. Seeing his house, the green shingles, the white frame, he ponders this "corner huger than his life" until he finds enough courage to go deeper into the woods of his fantasies, spinning them out as the young must—those longings to run away and live in the wilderness, trap animals, eat bugs, strangle a panther! The fantasies unwind to their inevitable, unmentionable desire to murder his mother and conquer the world. And more: "Rob banks and live rich on the loot / In Huge City, and drive, / like a godamighty hurricane. . . . Gargle gin for breakfast while Cocaine / Moll polishes the tommy" (30). On and on he raves until the fantasy spins out of control in a shriek—ORITECHU GUYS LESSEE YEH GUTS, and windy imaginings die, having worn themselves out. He is left to concede: "That's no good." The real night is falling, and he must go back home.

How many poems have been written about a young boy's confrontation with the Father, his fantasies of escape from and dominance of the Mother? Surely, too many to count. But how many have been written with the urgency and abandon of Chappell's poems? More to the point, how many have been able to achieve the crucial resolution that, out of sheer emotional and artistic necessity, these poems achieve? Reading them is like walking through fire and, amazingly enough, coming out whole on the other side. Each poem concludes with a real, earned breakthrough into a life-sustaining vision. In the conclusion to "The Mother," the ground beneath the runaway boy's feet "grows still and cold in his bones"; shadows cup the trees. His fantasies spent, he turns toward home but not in despair. He goes back to what he has earlier called "the talons of the gingerbread house," with determination and discipline, his pace "deliberately fashioned," as if describing not only the human task that lies before him but the poetic as well.

Both "The Father" and "The Mother" seem to be clearing the way for later poems in which a similar sort of initiation through fear takes place, most notably "Cleaning the Well" from *River*. In this poem, one of Chappell's best known, the grandfather sends the young Fred down the well in hard December, saying, "'Now clean it out good'" (14), his face blazing above bright as steel, bright as the threatening razor blade in "The Father." The reason the boy gives for going down is as simple as it might have been in "The Father": *"He told me to go. I went"* (16). As in the two mother/father companion poems, the way is harrowing ("'It goes like Hell,'" he thinks, from which *"I shall arise never"*) (15), but in this later plumbing of the depths, the menacing fury of memory has been brought under complete artistic control. The rhymed lines move with confidence, a sure sense of technique, as if the boy who at the end of "The Father" can say almost jauntily, "'I just know, that's all'" (27), is reeling them in and having some good-natured fun at his own expense while doing so.

In its union of narrative line and tight form, its blend of terror and humor, "Cleaning the Well" seems as likely an example as any of how in later work Chappell has been able to merge the two poetic styles in *The World Between the Eyes*—the long, emotionally complex poem about childhood and the short, oftentimes amusing poems on diverse subjects. In contrast to the longer poems that so often suggest a poet obsessed by his childhood, the short poems reveal a poet who can also write about baseball, movies, music, politics, and the everyday matters of domestic life, such as coughs and two-year-old sons. The poem "Heath's New Drum," along with two other poems about his son, falls between "The World Between the Eyes" and "The Farm." They provide both emotional relief and metaphorical connections, as when he tells his son to "rumble like my childhood's churchbell" (18). Some of the excruciating tension created by the longer poems is consequently alleviated. This does not mean, however, that the best of these shorter poems lack intensity. In "Seated Figure," Chappell succeeds in concentrating to a white-hot point the image of a woman "crouched to her needle," while outside a storm rages, rages so hard that the roof itself rises, "like an owl, tumbling the thick light" (57). Each of the four quatrains keeps the poem snug and tight around a figure who, in her vulnerability and in the violence of the night around her, might easily be placed in one of the longer poems. There, however, her vulnerability would have been expressed at greater length and in more emotionally colored language. Here her endurance and stoicism hold sway, the poem as tight-lipped and strong in its reticence as she is. In "Tiros II," a poem taking as its subject one of the numerous satellites launched in the 1950s and 1960s, the same knife-sharp imagery enlivens the lines: "Space is real, / Near and cold, black as India ink, / Frightening as falling down a well" (32).

In the main, however, these shorter poems seem less accessible, most of them unable to counterbalance the rugged, almost engulfing long poems. Perhaps it is unfair to expect them to be able to do so. They are by and large lighter poems, and they run the risk of seeming inconsequential when juxtaposed with a poetry in which life-and-death emotions are expressed in such a no-holds-barred style. But they are not inconsequential. What they reveal is the young Chappell's passion for experimentation and wordplay, a yearning for the control of form amid all the ebb and flow of memory. They also introduce us to Chappell's distinctive humor and boyishness, qualities that will ultimately gentle down and humanize the violent outpourings of his imagination. What continues to fascinate any reader of *The World Between the Eyes* is the range of voice, tone, and style the book displays. Although the poles between the two kinds of poems in the book seem too far apart for it to be a coherent collection, in the great work of *Midquest* that follows, the styles that seemed so divergent in *The World Between the Eyes* merge and become one full, rich voice.

Chappell himself recently remarked during a discussion of a young woman's first work of fiction that a beginning writer must be allowed to write the way she has to write, otherwise how is she going to get where only she can go. For the beginning writer besieged by formulae, advice and workshops, this is generous, wise advice. It is also advice those who read *The World Between the Eyes* would do well to keep in mind. These poems of the young Fred Chappell do what they have to do, be it rage, wallow, joke, leer, snicker, or terrify. Yes, some of them fail, but when they do, they fail on their own terms. When they succeed, they burn through the page! They have the courage to take on the dark side of inheritance, the chaic stone-cold house of ancestry, as well as the seething lava of memory, to express its terrifying richness and finally to get free of its hold, free enough to reach a safe distance where the poet can continue to develop the art that will carry him through the journey of *Midquest* into the later novels and on to the bellringing clarity of *Source* and *First and Last Words.*

When we look back at Chappell's poetic development, it all seems so straightforward, doesn't it? The signs were right, the talent so prodigious that we are tempted to ask, "How could it have turned out otherwise?" Surely, Fred Chappell was destined to become Old Fred, the master.

But wait a minute.

Go back to *The World Between the Eyes,* to when Fred Chappell was only in his twenties and everything, poetically speaking and maybe more besides, was on the line. In these first poems, the struggle to forge a voice is as intense as it can possibly get, a struggle to the death, it sometimes seems, and no doubt seemed to the poet himself when he was writing these poems. Perhaps we should respect that struggle and acknowledge the possibility, ever present in any young writer's first work, that Fred Chappell might not have found his way through and beyond these first poems. Only then will we be able to read *The World Between the Eyes* with the urgency and growing sense of excitement that the book deserves. Only then will we be able to ask *how.* How did Fred Chappell make it from the cowering boy in "The Mother" to the writer George Garrett has called one of the finest of his time, "one of the rare and precious few who are truly 'major'"? If there are any answers to that mystery (and the growth of any poet is always a mystery), the best place to look for them are in the poems themselves, starting with the conclusion of "The Mother," the homecoming after the dangerous, yet cathartic fantasy in the woods, when the poet understands that whereas at the start of the poem he had to escape to survive, now he must go back home to go on. What matters is that he has learned *how* to go back.

> His pace is deliberately fashioned, his strength
> Unbreakable and holy in the moment.
> He stops to take the measure of the family door.
> And then he enters. (31)

What an entering it has been, one that is ongoing, the windlass still turning, drawing up from the depths of the well some of the most vital, indispensable poetry being written today.

Points of Kinship: Community and Allusion in Fred Chappell's Midquest

JOHN LANG

To view Fred Chappell as principally a "regional" writer is to overlook the varied communities on which he draws and with which he identifies himself, especially in his greatest poetic achievement to date, *Midquest*. Those communities include not only the author's relationships with his wife, Susan, with other members of his family, and with the local storekeeper Virgil Campbell, but also his larger social-political identity as an American citizen in the twentieth century. Moreover, through *Midquest's* literary and philosophical allusions, Chappell creates a series of wide-ranging communities, from the poet-friends to whom he addresses several epistolary poems to the broader literary tradition implicit in his extensive use of Dante and other writers. By organizing each of *Midquest's* four volumes around one of the elements the pre-Socratics believed to be fundamental to life, Chappell also identifies himself with a philosophical community that enables him to probe the origin and nature of human existence, particularly the relationship between mind and matter, body and spirit. Throughout *Midquest,* Chappell repeatedly weaves the personal and the "widely representative" (x). His allusions and themes link the local and the national, the regional and the universal.

Such interconnections are evident from the very beginning of *Midquest,* whose first volume, *River,* takes its epigraph from *Moby-Dick.* Chappell opens his book with the markedly regional but with the placelessly personal

The author wishes to thank Robert Denham for his valuable contribution to the Appendix of this essay.

and the directly allusive. "The River Awakening in the Sea" sets the self in relation to the beloved in a bedroom that could be anywhere. No doubt this generalized location is meant to reinforce the poet's status as a representative figure. Like Whitman's persona in *Song of Myself,* "Ole Fred" is intended to be a modern Everyman in his search for love, community, and spiritual renewal. Yet this initial poem, like the first and last poem in each of *Midquest*'s four volumes, is addressed to the poet's wife, Susan. Susan also appears in at least one other of the eleven poems in each volume. Fred's marriage to Susan is thus the principal relationship in *Midquest,* a relationship that provides the poet with one crucial experience of community.

But Susan is not simply Fred's wife. In the larger Dantean structure of the poem, she is also his Beatrice. Similarly, marriage itself becomes one of *Midquest*'s central metaphors, as it testifies to the union—often a difficult one—of distinct personalities or qualities. *Midquest* depicts not only Fred's marriage to Susan but also his grandparents' and parents' marriages. In addition, Chappell describes life itself as originating at the moment "when void and atom married" (41). And the nearly impenetrable "*marriage/vow* joints" of "Firewood" (67) lead the poet to reflect that

> when man and nature
> got married they agreed never to divorce although
> they knew they could never be happy & would have only
> the one child Art who would bring mostly grief
> to them both. (72)

These repeated references to marriage remind the reader that the search for love and the desire for order and harmony are central to *Midquest,* a book in which the concept of marriage has the kind of significance it attains in Kierkegaard's *Either/Or* and Wendell Berry's *The Country of Marriage.*

Family ties other than marriage are also extremely important in *Midquest,* as is evident in the many poems devoted to the poet's grandparents and parents. Some of Chappell's liveliest, most entertaining writing results from his portraits of these people and from the distinctive voices he creates for them. Certainly, these portraits reinforce a number of *Midquest*'s distinctively regional elements, especially in their description of the difficulties of surviving on a hardscrabble mountain farm. Yet even before Fred's grandparents first appear in the third and fourth poems of *River,* Chappell has already invoked the name of Dante in the book's second poem, "Birthday 35: Diary Entry." That poem also alludes to Plato, St. Francis, and Kierkegaard, thus establishing the philosophical and religious nature of the poet's quest. Moreover, "Birthday 35: Diary Entry" also introduces the first of Chappell's many allusions to other American writers—in this case, the waste land vision of T. S. Eliot and his Prufrock (7). Like Eliot's various personae, Ole Fred seeks to escape the spiritual desolation of contemporary life, its emotional aridity and lack of connections. The quest for love and community as a means of defining the self are crucial to the thematic structure of *Midquest.* For Chappell, genuine selfhood exists only in and through relationships to something outside the self. As he remarks in *Midquest*'s opening poem, "Everyone begins slowly to reach toward another" (1). In many respects an autobiographical poem, *Midquest* rejects the intensely private confessional mode of much American poetry of the 1960s and 1970s.

It is Fred's grandmother, first introduced in the third poem in *River,* who emphasizes the role family plays in defining the individual and who urges her young grandson not to forget his roots: "'It's dirt you rose from, dirt you'll bury in'" (12). Yet as she reveals to the boy the comic catalogue of the family's black sheep, Chappell draws not only upon the tall-tale tradition of his native Appalachia but also upon such literary ancestors as Mark Twain. The glass eye of Aunt Paregoric Annie is an heirloom from Chapter 53 of *Roughing It.* Similarly, when young Fred's grandfather orders the boy to clean the family's well in *River*'s fourth poem, Chappell depicts the experience as a version of the archetypal descent into the Underworld, with its imagery of death and resurrection. "Jonah, Joseph, Lazarus, / Were you delivered so?" the adult poet asks (16). Although he has plumbed the well's depths, he is unable to communicate whatever it was he discovered there. Echoing Bottom in Shakespeare's *A Midsummer Night's Dream,* he can only conclude inconclusively: "I could not say what I had found. / I cannot say my dream" (16). Such allusions are typical of Chappell's artistic strategy in *Midquest.* Only rarely are they obtrusive. Instead, they work together to suggest the underlying unity of human experience despite differences of place and time.

Virgil Campbell, the local storekeeper, is the character in *Midquest* "who is supposed to give to the whole its specifically regional, its Appalachian, context" (x). Yet even in "Dead Soldiers," the first poem devoted to Virgil

(*River,* VI), Chappell inserts a literary allusion. While Virgil shoots at the empty liquor bottles, a flood has liberated emptied whiskey jars from his basement. Chappell notes the "load on load of bottles rumbling out" (27). The phrase echoes Frost's "load on load of apples coming in" in "After Apple Picking." Moreover, the reader's introduction to Virgil is preceded by *River*'s most explicitly philosophical poem, "Susan Bathing," a single-sentence, stream-of-consciousness, free-verse meditation addressed to Susan. In both style and content, "Susan Bathing" has none of the simplicity and directness of "Dead Soldiers." Yet in his juxtaposition of these two poems, Chappell again harmonizes apparent opposites and indicates the inclusiveness of his poetic vision.

"Susan Bathing" also reinforces the connection between the particular and the universal in its movement from Fred's personal relationship with Susan to more general questions about physical beauty and humanity's responses to it. The poem begins and ends with the word "you," thereby affirming Fred's tie to Susan. But Fred's consciousness also moves freely through time, invoking "a Renaissance poet's wish, to be the pleasing/ showerhead touching you with a hundred streaming fingers" (18). From this sensual response to Susan's presence the poet moves on to establish her identity as an emissary of the divine. Not only does he conjoin his praise of Susan with Gabriel's annunciation to Mary, "Ave, plena gratia" (20), but he also depicts Susan both as divine intermediary and as *deus absconditus.* When Susan's body vanishes in the steam from the shower, the poet declares, in lines reminiscent of Donne's anguished prose,

> Why do you go away? where do you go? will you
> again return from behind the spiritual mists & acquaint again
> my senses? or are you for good ascended into ideal spaces & rely upon
> my hurt memory to limn your shape my heart starves to join, do not
> so scar my will I plead you, for my will is stricken and contort,
> its own most effort has fouled & burst it & only intercession from
> without can restore it . . . (21)

Although Susan's allegorical function remains subordinate to the poet's personal relationship to her, Susan reminds Fred of the powerful claims of both body and soul, the physical and the spiritual. In response to her, the poet gives voice to "speechpraise," for "unattending beauty is danger & mortal sin" (19). Praise becomes Chappell's "instrument of unclosing and rising toward light" (19), a light that brings spiritual illumination, "for once the mind prepares to praise & garbs / in worshipful robe it enlarges to plenitude" (19). "Susan Bathing," like *Midquest* as a whole, moves toward an affirmation of love: marital love, love of family and friends, love of nature, love of language and literature, love of God. As Chappell writes near the end of this poem,

> it is praise, love is praise, Susan, of what is, and if it be prisoned
> in low earth it shall bound in high air saying like howitzers its
> name and if it be scurried to & fro over cold waste of skies yet
> shall it touch with all its names blade root stone roof . . .
> . . . nowhere would you escape it. (23–24)

Chappell's credo here echoes that of St. Paul in Romans 8:38–39.

The interpenetration of the distinctively regional and the extraregional that I have been tracing in *Midquest*'s first half-dozen poems recurs throughout the volume. From the firmly established network of relationships with Susan, with his grandparents and parents, and with other members of the mountain community like Virgil Campbell, Chappell reaches out to affirm his literary kinship with writers both inside and outside the region, writers both living and dead, European as well as American. *Midquest* is anything but insular or provincial. Just as the book's sense of place involves *both* the mountains and a broader natural landscape suggested by Chappell's use of the four elements, so the literary communities in *Midquest* build upon both the local and the global.

Each of the four separately published volumes that compose the book, for example, bears its own epigraph. Two of those epigraphs, the first and the last, come from American writers: Melville and Hawthorne in *River* and *Earthsleep,* respectively. The other two are drawn from European writers: René Char and Dante in *Bloodfire* and *Wind Mountain.* The epigraph from Melville is taken from *Moby-Dick* and includes the apt statement, *"Meditation and water are wedded forever"* (xiii). The lines from Char, *"This is the hour when windows escape / houses to catch fire at the end of the / world where our world is going to dawn"* (53) are equally appropriate both to the natural element emphasized in Chappell's second volume and to *Midquest*'s theme of regeneration. Moreover, Chappell's use of a modern French poet of symbolist techniques is especially apt in a volume in which Rimbaud is a central figure. Char may also appear in *Midquest* because of his fascination with Heraclitus, one of the major pre-Socratic philosophers. The stanza from the *Inferno,* Canto V, quoted both in Italian and in English translation, that appears as the epigraph to *Wind Mountain,* extends the series of allusions to Dante that began in *Midquest*'s second poem. The stanza reappears, the wording of its second line slightly altered, in *Wind Mountain*'s seventh poem. Dante might be said to be the guardian spirit or the muse of the whole of *Midquest,* but he is an especially effective source of *Wind Mountain*'s epigraph because of the traditional association of wind with the divine, whether the breath of God by which Adam was created out of the dust or the mighty wind of the Holy Spirit's descent at Pentecost. Similarly, the epigraph in *Earthsleep,* taken from the final paragraph of Hawthorne's "The Haunted Mind," not only returns the reader to the American literary tradition that Chappell so ably represents but also introduces the imagery of sleep and dream, death and the passage to eternity that pervades this final volume. Hawthorne's prose portrays the spirit wandering *"without wonder or dismay. So calm . . . so undisturbed, as if among familiar things"* at the moment of death (143). The serenity of this passage sets a tone that Chappell repeatedly invokes in *Earthsleep* as he attempts to reconcile himself and his readers to the fact of mortality. Yet death remains problematic in the final volume of *Midquest.* For both Chappell and Hawthorne, the human mind is "haunted." In the words of the sentence from Hawthorne's sketch that immediately precedes the passage Chappell cites, "You emerge from mystery, pass through a vicissitude that you can but imperfectly control, and are borne onward to another mystery."

As has already been indicated, Dante is the single author whose work is most significant to the architecture and the thematic development of Chappell's poem. Even Virgil Campbell, the most "specifically regional" figure in the book, functions also within the larger literary structure Chappell gives to *Midquest* through his extensive use of Dante. After all, Campbell's first name is that of Dante's guide in *The Inferno* and *The Purgatorio*—although Chappell's Virgil represents a homespun oral tradition, not the highly refined literary tradition of the author of the *Aeneid.* Dante's Virgil embodies the best that human reason, unaided by divine grace, can achieve in the realm of moral virtue. Campbell, in contrast, embodies the earthier values of food, drink, sexual desire, and comic story-telling. Yet both Virgils are artist-figures. And the Roman Virgil who celebrates humanity's ties to the earth in the *Georgics* clearly anticipates Chappell's insistence throughout *Midquest* on the value of the physical world that Virgil Campbell represents.

Nevertheless, in keeping with the structure of *The Divine Comedy*, Campbell is not Fred's ultimate guide. Susan is the Beatrice of *Midquest*, to whom the poet turns in the book's last two poems. Thus, after Fred visits Campbell's grave in the sixth poem of *Earthsleep*, the seventh poem opens appropriately with lines from Canto XXX of *The Purgatorio*, the canto in Dante's epic in which Beatrice appears and Virgil vanishes, and one of several cantos Dante devotes to his visit to the Earthly Paradise. Yet Chappell's own seventh poem, "How to Build the Earthly Paradise: Letter to George Garrett," continues to focus on the physical world whose spokesperson Campbell has been. Moreover, Chappell asks near the end of that poem,

> what if it's true already? and
> we have but to touch out to see it
> among our amidst. (177)

lines that recall the poet's earlier references to his waking with Susan "in the dew-fired earliest morning of the world" (51) and to their feeling the wind and rain advancing "out of the green isles / of Eden" (94). For those whose vision is cleansed by love, Chappell implies, paradise is here and now. But the love that Susan embodies is both human and divine love, "the love that moves the sun and other stars" (187), as Chappell translates the closing line of Dante's *Paradiso* in his own final poem.

Chappell's use of Dante involves more, however, than the poet's quest for spiritual renewal, more than his depiction of Virgil Campbell and Susan as spiritual guides. At times, for instance, usually for comic effect, Chappell employs the terza rima of Dante's original, as in "My Grandfather Gets Doused" (*River*, VII) and "In Parte Ove Non E Che Luca" (*Wind Mountain*, VII). The former recounts the conversion of Old Fred's grandfather from Methodist to "hard-believer / Baptist" (30) and contains such humorously inventive rhymes as moues / ooze / bruise (30) and Methodist / pissed / exhibitionist (31). The latter poem, whose title is taken from the final line of Canto IV in *The Inferno*, draws heavily on Dante's description of the damned in Hell's Second Circle, home of the carnal. The punishment of the lustful is described in Canto V of Dante's masterpiece, and better than half of Chappell's poem simply paraphrases its Italian original. The reader has been prepared for this descent into the Dantean underworld by the reference to Paolo and Francesca near the end of the preceding poem (120), where the allusion appears in the context of a tall tale narrated by Fred's father. But what surprises and delights the reader of *Wind Mountain*'s seventh poem is Chappell's daring updating of Dante's cast of sinners. It includes not only Casanova and Lord Byron but even, in Dantean fashion, one of the poet's contemporaries—James Dickey. In fact, Chappell devotes more lines to the castigation of Dickey's vices than he does to those of either of the other sinners. Moreover, at the end of this poem, Fred glimpses "the round form, the red face / Of Virgil Campbell" (123), who is then asked to explain his presence in the Second Circle.

The ensuing poem, "Three Sheets to the Wind: Virgil Campbell Confesses," is one of the funniest in all of *Midquest,* a book filled with a humor all too rare in contemporary American poetry. Chappell creates here a set of circumstances entirely appropriate to Virgil's character while drawing upon the humor of physical discomfort that was the stock-in-trade of George Washington Harris' Sut Lovingood. In fact, Virgil's plea, *"Feet don't fail me now"* (126) as he attempts to escape from the scene of his illicit lovemaking, comes directly from Sut's mouth. Thus, Chappell once again embeds Virgil in *both* the literary and folk traditions of the mountain South *and* in the wider Western literary tradition represented by Dante.

While Dante is the author whose work is fundamental to *Midquest,* Chappell fills his book with dozens of allusions to other writers (see the appendix to this essay). The Old Southwest humor that shaped not only George Washington Harris but also Mark Twain appears at various points. "My Father's Hurricane" (*Wind Mountain,* VI), for instance, draws upon Twain's account of the Washoe Zephyr in Chapter 21 of *Roughing It.* And Fred's term "Old Hoss," used to address "Uncle Body" (114), derives from Sut's nickname for Harris. But Chappell also incorporates in *Midquest* a series of four epistolary poems that call attention to contemporary southern writers who are personal friends of the poet. In addition, *Wind Mountain* includes a playlet, "Hallowind," in which Fred converses with Reynolds Price. Taken together, these five poems define yet another of *Midquest*'s many literary communities while providing insight into some of Chappell's major poetic concerns. In their epistolary structure, furthermore, these poems re-emphasize Chappell's refusal to be trapped within the isolated self, the personal ego.

The first of these poems, "Science Fiction Water Letter to Guy Lillian" (*River,* IX), details the literary failings of much science fiction writing: its abstractness, its underdeveloped sense of the past, of history; its disregard of saints and heroic suffering; its departure from myth. Written in thirteen-syllable lines, the poem also contains Old Fred's excerpt from his own science fiction novel-in-progress, an excerpt that offers the first of *Midquest*'s many myths of origin, in this case a myth of language's origin. Such creation myths attest to Chappell's desire to probe the mystery of creativity in all its forms, a desire that may in part explain his use of the pre-Socratic philosophers in *Midquest.* Fred's novel presents a wildly improbable account of the primeval relationship between word and thing, an account that nevertheless affirms the transformative power of words as the human imagination interacts with the physical world. That novel also reinforces the poet's earlier pronouncement, "Fresh wonders clamor for language" (40), a statement Chappell makes to criticize the loss of the objective world, the realm of nature, in much modern literature. According to Chappell, this retreat into the subjective self, this detachment from nature,

> is a fashionable oddity left over from
> the '90s (Wilde, Mallarmé, & Co.). Marvell
> or Donne or Vaughan wouldn't let such opportunities
> rot on the stalk; . . .
> they had senses
> alive apart from their egos, and took delight in
> every new page of Natural Theology. (40)

Sharing Eliot's diagnosis of the modern "dissociation of sensibility," these lines also echo the concerns raised in Emerson's "Blight," with its insistence that human beings recover a right relation to nature.

The other poetic epistles in *Midquest* raise additional literary concerns that help define the diverse communities in which Chappell situates himself. In "Rimbaud Fire Letter to Jim Applewhite" (*Bloodfire,* II), Chappell recounts his youthful infatuation with Rimbaud and Baudelaire, an attraction that led the young Chappell to practice such derangement of the senses that eventually he was expelled from Duke, where he had first met fellow poet

Applewhite. Quoting in French from Rimbaud's poems "Barbare," "Comédie de la soif," and "Le Dormeur du val," Old Fred acknowledges his debt to his predecessor's craftmanship while recognizing the self-destructive elements in Rimbaud's life. After returning to Canton from Duke, Fred "watched the mountains until the mountains touched / My mind and partly tore away my fire-red / Vision of a universe besmirched" (60–61).

But the mountains were not alone in helping the poet reorient his life. He also started the concordance to Samuel Johnson that became his M.A. thesis and began reading "folks like Pope" (61), whose rationalism one can well imagine as a partial antidote to Rimbaud. Chappell concludes this letter with the playful valediction, "Yours for terror and symbolism," but the discussion of literary symbolism in "Hallowind" together with Chappell's own poetic practices in some of his work reveals the continuing influence of Rimbaud, whose relationship with Verlaine had also served as a point of departure for Chappell's second novel, *The Inkling*.

"Burning the Frankenstein Monster: Elegiac Letter to Richard Dillard" (85) returns in part to the realm of science fiction introduced in the first of *Midquest*'s epistolary poems. Chappell's point of departure in this poem is not Mary Shelley's prophetic novel but the film version of *Frankenstein* starring Boris Karloff. It is from the film, not the book, that the poet draws his description of the monster's fate. The story of Frankenstein and his creation, as Chappell recognizes, is both a version of the Prometheus legend and a cautionary tale about "the will made totally single," the "tortured, transcendent-striving will" (85). To image that will, Chappell quotes Virgil's description of the newly blinded cyclops Polyphemus in *The Aeneid* (III, 658): *"Monstrum horrendum, informe, ingens, cui lumen ademptum"* (85). The line is one Chappell had used as his epigraph to *The Inkling,* and here, as there, it suggests the blindness of the self's desire to dictate the conditions of its existence.

In this poem, then, Chappell unites the figures of Polyphemus, Prometheus, and Frankenstein as he meditates on the hapless monster's destruction. His allusion to Virgil is followed by others to Rimbaud and Percy Bysshe Shelley, to the horror films of twentieth-century popular culture, and to the apocalypses of modern politics.

Why must poor Karloff be born out of fire, and die, fire-fearing,
  In the fire? Is he truly our dream of Promethean man?

Does he warn us of terrible births from atomic furnaces, atomic
    Centuries, shambling in pain from the rose-scented past?
Having been burned and then drowned, reversing the fate of Shelley,
    The lame monster brings back upon us the inverted weight
Of the romantic period. Whose children we are, but disinherit,
    Stranded in decades when all is flame and nothing but flame. (85)

The misguided deification of the will, the desire for omnipotence combined
with the assumption of omniscience, is a tendency that Chappell's allusions
discover throughout human history. Frankenstein and his creation, like
Lear, "are bound to a wheel of crazed fire" (87), and the poem's closing
image of "the hilltop mill . . . always burning" (87) recalls not only Canton's
polluting textile mill but also Blake's "dark Satanic mills" of reason unil-
luminated by the imagination.

By evoking sympathy for Frankenstein's creation, Chappell achieves several poignant moments in this poem. Recalling the monster's first glimpse
of light, for example, the poet inquires:

What wouldn't *we* give to undergo in our latter years the virgin
    Onslaught of light? To be born again into light,
To be raised from the grave.
. . . .
Faith calls to faith, but our faith must be earned from terror, consummate
    Love must be thirsted for, light must be wholly desired. (85, 87)

Ultimately, this poem testifies to the responsibilities imposed by the power
to create. Frankenstein is held accountable by and for the "son" whom he
fathers, just as modern science bears the responsibility for its inventions—
and each of us for the lives we invent for ourselves.

Midquest's final epistolary poem, "How to Build the Earthly Paradise,"
is addressed to George Garrett (*Earthsleep,* VII). Its thirteen nine-line stanzas
are all end-stopped, a device that reinforces the poem's building-block
structure as Chappell lists the materials needed for this project: stone, sand,
earth, the dead, water, air, plants, animals, people, "the troubadour atoms /
dancing / full" (176). The precision of these stanzas' appearance on the page
gives the reader confidence in Chappell as builder (a poet is a *maker*) and
successfully prepares for the imagery of rebirth in the poem's closing lines:

New
   now you
see me a new man, unshucked from
my soiled hide, I'm coming belchlike out of
the cave. (177)

This cave recalls both Plato's famous allegory in *The Republic* and the dwelling of the Cyclops to whom Chappell alludes in "Burning the Frankenstein Monster." That the poet has grown by this point in his quest is clearly evident. Yet Chappell forestalls any mystical heightening of this moment by using the self-deflating simile "belchlike."

Almost as important as the varied literary communities with which the poet identifies is the community of metaphysical speculation represented by the pre-Socratics and the many other philosophers and religious thinkers to whom Chappell refers or alludes. As has already been noted, each of *Midquest*'s separate volumes revolves around one of the four elements that pre-Socratic philosophers such as Thales, Anaximenes, and Empedocles believed to be the origin of all existing things. Chappell's decision to use these four substances—earth, air, fire, and water—in this fashion reflects his commitment to exploring the elemental, to investigating what is fundamental to human existence. In *Midquest,* as in his early poem "A Transcendental Idealist Dreams in Springtime" (dedicated to Jim Applewhite) (*The World Between the Eyes,* 6), Chappell implicitly rejects the abstraction of Plato's world of Ideal Forms, returning for his key concepts to the earlier naturalistic phase of Greek philosophy. And Chappell also challenges the spirit of abstraction in modern philosophy, from Descartes on. The Emerson of *Nature,* for instance, distinguishing between the Me and the not-Me, relegates his body to the category of the not-Me. Chappell's creation of "Uncle Body," whom he jovially addresses in both "The Autumn Bleat of the Weathervane Trombone" (*Wind Mountain,* V) and "The Peaceable Kingdom of Emerald Windows" (*Earthsleep,* IV), seems to derive from the poet's impatience with the loss of the Creation, whether in Platonic idealism, Cartesian idealism, Emersonian Transcendentalism, or Protestant fundamentalism, with their tendency to denigrate the physical world.

In addition to the pre-Socratics, Chappell cites directly a dozen other philosophers and theologians ranging from Lucretius and Aquinas to Jean-Paul Sartre. Although many of these references occur in humorous contexts, particularly in Ole Fred's tongue-in-cheek invitation to Uncle Body "to swim from Singapore / To Hermeneutics and through the Dardanelles / To Transcendentalism, back through the Straits / Of Hegel right on to Greasy Branch" (113), Chappell is clearly staking out a poetic terrain in which metaphysical speculation is at home. If "the existentialist Dead Sea's a mush / Of murk" (113) and if few readers would welcome circumnavigation on Ole Fred's terms ("Around the World in Eighty Tractates aboard / The good ship Wittgenstein" [114]), *Midquest* nonetheless naturalizes philosophical thought. Chappell's poem moves comfortably from the homespun philosophy of Virgil Campbell to the *ignis semina* of Lucretius (70), from Hogback Ridge to the Mountains Outside Time, from "flesh-tree" to "tree of spirit" (145). The poet's humor undercuts *both* Uncle Body's reluctance to hike "the slopes / Of stony Heidegger" (114) *and* the unyielding abstraction of the German philosopher's writing. In "The Peaceable Kingdom of Emerald Windows" it's a *horse* named Maude who decides to make the Kierkegaardian "Leap of Faith" (161). Yet such humor and irony do not prevent Chappell himself from repeatedly probing the complex relationship between mind and matter, soul and body, time and eternity. In fact, among the greatest poems in *Midquest* are the long stream-of-consciousness pieces "Susan Bathing" (*River,* V), "Firewood" (*Bloodfire,* V), "The Autumn Bleat of the Weathervane Trombone" (*Wind Mountain,* V), and "The Peaceable Kingdom of Emerald Windows" (*Earthsleep,* IV). These four poems are interrelated philosophical meditations that articulate the metaphysical dualism central to Chappell's poetic vision.

The first two, "Susan Bathing" and "Firewood," are single-sentence poems that run to seven pages *each*. To call them "interior monologues" is something of a misnomer, since "Susan Bathing" directly addresses Susan, beginning and ending with the word "you," while "Firewood" too incorporates elements of direct address. But both poems adopt the technique of free association that often characterizes such "stream-of-consciousness" writing. As noted earlier, "Susan Bathing" celebrates not only the body but also the poet's "speech-praise" in response to the beauty of the physical world. Yet this Beatrice-Susan's "flesh the synonym of love" also causes the poet to profess, "I do believe your spirit has power" (22), words that link Susan to Ariel and thus adumbrate a realm beyond the physical.

"Firewood" is far more explicitly philosophical in its meditation on the relationship between matter and mind. As the poet works to split the oak log that will feed his fireplace, he reflects on the transformation of the material into the immaterial, the wood into heat and light. The log with its hidden knot yields only to great effort. In its future burning, it will become a "tree of spirit spread on the night wind" (69). Yet the very burning of this fire forces the poet to confront "the problem of mortality" (69), to consider that "we are not / born for the rarer destinies only for the rarest, / we are born to enter the tree of smoke" (71), there to vanish. As in Frost's poem "Westrunning Brook," with its "white wave [that] runs counter to itself," so here the knot in the wood "is the man or the man's / will angry against the stream of time" (70–71). Like Frost, Chappell is adept at using the hypothetical and the conditional. Frost's familiar "as if" here becomes a more open-ended "who knows" (70). For Chappell, "man in / *his fallen state* is condemned to split the tree / with his intellect all alert and doubtful" (72). Ole Fred's animal, as he remarks, "cannot . . . wallow within himself content" (71); for the poet finds himself asking, "but where / shall I sit when once this flesh is spirit?" (73).

"The Autumn Bleat of the Weathervane Trombone" extends this series of philosophical meditations but with less urgency and more humor. Unlike "Susan Bathing" and "Firewood," this poem is broken up into separate sentences, a structure meant to mirror, Chappell states in the Preface to the book, the increasing order in the speaker's life (x). Here, as throughout *Midquest,* the range of Chappell's diction and allusions establishes a bridge between the regional and the universal. The adolescent Fred, perched atop the family barn in the mountains of North Carolina, is "woodshedding a Bach partita," for instance, and contemplating "Ideal Forms of creek-glint, / Sennet and tucket of beech-leaf" (110). Blissful Guernseys may be his principal audience, but he is capable of an apostrophe to Bach himself: "Johann, thou shouldst be living at this hour"—a line that in turn echoes Wordworth's own appeal to Milton in the sonnet "London, 1802" (110). In this poem, Chappell first introduces "Uncle Body" and plays with the names of philosophers as diverse as Aquinas, Spinoza, Hegel, and Chang Hzu.

Despite its autumn setting, imagery of birth and rebirth pervades the poem. "The sun is hatching the world, what new creature / Will emerge?" the poet inquires (111). Elsewhere he lists the contemporary poets he expects to encounter in the afterlife (112). Nevertheless, "The flesh the earth is suits me fine," he declares, "Nirvana / A sterile and joyless blasphemy"

(113). But the wind that presides over this volume of *Midquest* and the music that such wind makes possible remind the poet of the fundamental reality of the invisible and the insubstantial. Combining the four elements around which the whole book is organized, Chappell testifies to the complex mystery of life: "Wind-river, river of flesh, spirit-river, / Fever stream, all these the Ocean of Earth" (113). In its final stanzas, "The Autumn Bleat of the Weathervane Trombone" offers yet another of the many creation stories Chappell employs in *Midquest*. "I've got a slightly different Big Bang theory: / In the beginning was the Trombone" (115), exclaims the exuberant, adolescent Fred, altering St. John's Gospel, with its celebration of the Word. The reader needs to remember, however, that *as a poet,* the Chappell of *Midquest* is both wordsmith and musician. Word and song marry in poetry, so that the claims Chappell makes for music apply as well to his own art. And certainly Chappell is at home in the world of music, as his references to musicians as diverse as Bach, Sibelius, Louis Armstrong, Jack Teagarden, and Bob Dylan demonstrate.

"The Autumn Bleat of the Weathervane Trombone" closes with a question addressed both to the nubile girls about whom young Fred fantasizes and to the reader: "You wouldn't let the music of this world die. / Would you?" (115). The prospect of death, first raised in "Firewood" but largely muted in "Autumn Bleat," comes to weigh more heavily on *Earthsleep,* though not oppressively so in its meditative poem "The Peaceable Kingdom of Emerald Windows." The title of this poem suggests a utopian vision like that in Edward Hicks's famous painting. Instead of the rose windows associated with gothic cathedrals, these windows are emerald, a color that suggests both their gem-like value and their connection with nature's green, the hue of seasonal rebirth. This bond between the emerald windows and nature is reinforced by Chappell's equation of the windows with raindrops (156). As in "The Autumn Bleat of the Weathervane Trombone," the season is fall. The poem's action revolves around harvesting hay, an activity whose success is threatened by the prospect of rain. Yet the poem is also a celebration of rain. "The single raindrop gives us light enough / To read whole acres of Debussy, Thoreau" (157), declares the poet, a statement that again links music and literature. Chappell's music in this poem is incantatory, invoking a paradisal state. Despite the threat of rain, despite the threat of mortality ("Goodbye I perceive to be a human creature" [156]), the tone here is one of serenity. The poem's quiet confidence is evident in the image of the empty house into which the family enters, a meal already prepared, a Bible resting on the table open to "a chapter of Psalms" (157). The poem continues, "The rainsoaked sun settles in the form / In the hay in the world in the green green hand" (157). The window imagery may also be meant to recall Emerson's insistence that the poet turns the world to glass, creating a new means of vision through which the material world, with all its opaque physicality, becomes transparent. For Chappell, however, that visionary world remains essentially unfulfilling as long as it is embraced at the expense of the physical, a point the poet re-emphasizes by concluding *Midquest* with lines quoted from *Twelfth Night,* a passage of Shakespearean comedy of the body that balances the book's Dantean "divine" comedy. To Uncle Body, who appears once again in "The Peaceable Kingdom . . . ," Old Fred remarks,

> There's some have told me, Uncle,
> This world is not for real, and maybe it's so.
> . . . An Ideal World
> They say reposes in Heavenly Peas somewhere
> 'Midst the *Azur,* a sleepy flea market of Forms,
> . . . .
> The Ideal World must be mighty fine,
> Man wouldn't ever have to mow the lawn,
> But say, Uncle Body, wouldn't our fingers starve? (158)

The Elysium that Fred envisions in this poem is populated by naturalists like Gilbert White, André Michaux, and William Bartram, by Colette, and by Ben Franklin—all of them people attuned to the physical world. Fall and spring, death and life, "matter aye and spirit too" (160)—all are included in the poet's embrace as he sings the reader "home." Returning to the "Renaissance poet's wish" of "Susan Bathing," Fred becomes "the cloud that sluices these hills" (162), themselves imaged as a woman. Love of Susan becomes love of beauty, becomes love of nature and of "dear death-life" (162). Acceptance of life on its own terms marks this last of Chappell's four meditative poems, a poem that also reflects its author's sense of the harmony between humanity and nature by personifying the horses Maude and Jackson, whose love for one another reinforces *Midquest*'s marriage motif. The varied communities with which Chappell identifies himself are ultimately unbounded in either space or time. From the intimacy of his marriage to Susan and the bonds of familial love, the poet reaches out toward a community of the moral and philosophical and literary imagination and toward communion with all creation. Although the mountains of western North Carolina and the people who live there are central to Chappell's poetic vision in *Midquest,* it is the poet's interweaving of the particulars of his region with materials drawn from outside Appalachia that creates the book's distinctive resonance. *Midquest* belongs primarily not to Appalachian or southern literature but to the larger Western literary tradition. The book's astonishing variety of poetic forms, its range of literary and musical and philosophical allusions, its intermixture of lyrical and narrative and meditative verse, and its social-political concerns all demonstrate the breadth of Chappell's sensibility.

Nor is that breadth of mind and imagination a characteristic of *Midquest* alone. Chappell is one of the modern masters of the historical short story, as *Moments of Light* (1980) reveals. That volume includes stories in which Judas, Blackbeard, Benjamin Franklin, the composer Haydn, and the astronomer Herschel all appear. *Castle Tzingal* (1984) draws its inspirations from the myth of Orpheus, from Elizabethan revenge tragedies, and from the gothic fiction of Poe. Chappell's more recent volumes of poems, such as *First and Last Words* (1989), a collection of responses to his reading and to other artistic compositions, simply confirm the range of his interests and his excellence as a poet. But *Midquest* remains his masterpiece, a book that deserves wider recognition as one of the greatest achievements in contemporary American poetry.

Appendix

References and Allusions in *Midquest*

Explicit References to Other Writers, Their Characters, and Their Works

Explicit References to Philosophers and Theologians

References to Musicians

References to Other People (Living and Dead), to Films, and to Other Works of Art

Allusions to Other Authors, Philosophers, Theologians, etc., and Their Works

References to the Bible

The Idea of Odyssey in Midquest

KELLY CHERRY

These four book-length poems—*River, Bloodfire, Wind Mountain,* and *Earthsleep*—by Fred Chappell taken together are titled *Midquest.* Each covers the same day—the author's midlife birthday, May 28, 1971—tracked from morning to following morning. Each has its own dominant metaphorical motif—water, fire, air, earth—but picks up, refers to, and develops ideas, characters, and events from the other three books. The four voices, then, if each book may be said to have a voice, are distinct in timbre but parallel in time and harmonious in structure: *Midquest* is not a sequence; it is a quartet. This astonishing undertaking and Chappell's success with it are cause for applause.

The Idea of Odyssey

Midquest! The narrative thread that binds these four books into one is that of the journey, the voyage, the long wandering among events that edify and reveal. Chappell's "long wandering," like Leopold Bloom's, is condensed to a day; like Dante's, it occurs in the middle of his life; like nobody else's that I know of, it takes place in North Carolina. Each of the four books recounts the same journey—a journey through self and society—on a different metaphorical plane (water, fire, air, earth). The end of these travels, as in any traditional odyssey, is, of course, a homecoming. Ulysses returns to Ithaca.

I have to say something here about the odyssey as a home-going. I've long had a special fondness for the idea or theme of odyssey, a fondness that stems from the coincidental fact of having spent part of my childhood in Ithaca, New York, a town I was glad to get out of but whose name has always haunted me.

Naturally, I've often wondered what course the odyssey might have taken had it been made by a woman. A simple inversion of the Homeric odyssey wouldn't do, because a woman who commences a voyage of curiosity into the world is doing something riskier than a man who sets sail under the same flag.

Chappell's odyssey is closer to Dante or Virgil, perhaps, than to the Homeric archetype or Joycean elaboration, but like all of them, it is masculine, in the fullest and richest sense of the word. His persona, "Ole Fred," interprets his voyage to himself in terms of a masculine bias. If there is one quality that is missing from this long poem, it is—therefore, I want to say—the quality of risk, a sense of insecurity, of living at the edge of the known world, the awareness that it is possible to be lost forever or that all the world may be lost. I'll come back to this.

I'll come back to it, but I don't want it taken as a negative comment—only, I hope, as a necessary clarifying one. I want to offer praise for an impressive poem and suggest a key for reading it.

Three main statements, then: First, the narrative is odyssean; second, the locus of metaphor is the Greek notion of the four basic elements; but third—or first—the structure, as I said at the outset, is musical, and the key to the four books is to read them as a quartet.

Reading Quartets

My parents, now retired, were professional string quartet players, violinists. They especially loved the late Beethoven quartets, and they made a point of including both a Beethoven quartet and a contemporary quartet in every concert. My favorite childhood memory, as early as Ithaca, is of waiting up for them to come home after a concert, my father in tails, my mother in her long net evening gowns and stoles. But the dailiest memory I have is of rehearsals; they were always rehearsing.

I remember also some of the things they used to say about music, things that seemed to me even then and seem to me still to hold equally true for writing. One was that the test of a string quartet is its slow movement; just so, no piece of writing is better than its middle. Beginnings and endings can be effective in a number of ways and are in any case relatively malleable, but the middle must make a logical or credible connection between the two without collapsing into itself.

Something else my father liked to say was that a great composer gives himself a theme small enough to work with. In other words, it is how the theme is developed—and this obviously is related to the preceding point—that provides liveliness, interest, and finally, scope. Development is the opposite of bombast.

I happen to know that Fred Chappell has a highly knowledgeable love of music, and it doesn't surprise me that music should be a major influence on his aims as a poet. The structure of *Midquest* and each of the poems in it convinces me that he wouldn't disagree with my father, if they could sit down and discuss the matter.

And now let's sit down and open the quartet.

Opening the Quartet

River opens:

Deep morning. Before the trees take silhouettes.

Bloodfire opens:

Morning.
First light shapes the trees.

Wind Mountain opens:

Early half-light, dawnwind driving
The trees.

Earthsleep, quoting an early line from *River,* opens:

Shoves us landward, straining and warping like
        kites.

Yellow ring of earth bobs up to eye-level
At the blowing window.
                    The cool deep morning
Begins to fashion the trees.

The speaker of all four poems, "Old Fred" himself, moving from "the margin of dream" (*Earthsleep,* 146) onto the unwritten page of day, moves into history. With each waking day, "History is being reborn" (*Earthsleep,* 148), and the speaker, tumbling willfully or predestined from sleep into time, into death and love and life, must "begin to scratch for clothing" (*River,* 2). Beside him is his wife—"the inspiration of your bright hair" (*Wind Mountain,* 98)—from whom he must separate, become other, "be exiled . . . / To be fresh born at thirty-five" (*Bloodfire,* 57). This starting point between the worlds "of half-sleep, / . . . of waking" is "where the four-square crucis of elements / Cuts clean across" (*Earthsleep,* 146). It is a cross, this cross of elements, that is shadowed by its unthinkable opposite,

> where no water sings with
> Its breath of fire, where sunlight the cloud never
> Ripens to peach, where the single atoms stray
> Lost and touchless, where even the longdrawn shriek
> Of history sounds a thin sigh merely, it is
> That world we send our fireships to destroy.
> Not death, no, there is no
> Death, only a deeper dreaming. But there is
> Nothing,
> The black egg seedless hatching its harsh wings.
>
> (*Earthsleep,* 146–47)

But that is Nothing; here in the historical world to which we wake there are "dream-seeds which taking root shall renew the world" (*Earthsleep,* 149). Morning burgeons from sleep like a tree from earth, like the "Tree of Spirit lifting from the mountain of earth" (*Earthsleep,* 149).

The Day

The day of the poem—history itself—begins with an act of love. It is love—as everyone knows, the poem seems to say—that plunges the poet into being. In the course of the day's odyssey, we move from this beginning through the eleven sections in each book-length poem, which extend the poet's being into the larger world, a world composed of friends and relatives, the Old and the New South, and ultimately all humanity.

Though there's no direct correspondence between these sections and the eighteen Homeric episodes, they work to emphasize the narrative progression of the poem. These internal movements also grant Chappell's virtuosity with meter and rhyme a wide diapason. The poems fairly exult in their technical invention: blank verse, rhymed couplets, set stanzas of varying length and rhyme, free verse, terza rima, verse epistle, Anglo-Saxon alliteration.

The range is extraordinary, but what is even more so is the poet's willingness to subordinate all this play and display in the service of voice—that of Ole Fred and of his family and friends. For even though these are not confessional poems, they are social (as southern fiction is social); their autobiography is particular yet typical, allowing us to see the speaker in the context of his own home and history: his parents and grandparents, the legendary events of childhood and youth, the poet's marriage echoed by the marriages of his parents and grandparents, and the back-home friends and college-and-after friends who share in the poet's art. The context expands. Modern science, the Vietnam war, pop and country culture all find places in the world of the poem, often in casual or oblique reference, sometimes in diction, sometimes in movingly demarcated passages, set pieces, as the poet's eye and mind encompass them. Even this larger world is extended by the basic odyssean narrative of the poem and its literary antecedents.

The writing everywhere is remarkably vivid, by virtue of its concreteness of image and specificity of voice as well as by the variety and depth of characterizations and the relationships among the people of the poem. (How often do contemporary poems show us people not only being together but also talking together and doing together? Nearly always, the speaker's companion, if he has one, is barely known to the reader. But in these poems, other people are allowed to speak for themselves.) This vividness is sustained through all the forms and even through swings in style— for Chappell mocks his own high literary allusions. He realized the human predicament of living in tension between faith and doubt, including self-faith and self-doubt, in the technical tensions between, for example, hill-country dialect and evangelistic rhetoric, true rhyme and slant, syntax pulled and released, said eloquence and self-mockery. Again, this technical inventiveness is of almost musical interest, capturing the ear's attention at the same time the mind is following the narrative.

In this way, the day lengthens to include more than itself; all human time resonates through it.

We need to look at each book separately, however, to see how the four play together.

River

Meditating on the first metaphorical mode or plane of being—*River* takes its epigraph from *Moby-Dick*: *"Yes, as every one knows, meditation and water are wedded for ever"*—the poet prays: "Please, Lord. I want to go to some forever / Where water is, and live there."

> I want a sky that rain drops from,
> Soothing the intemperate loam;
>
> An eternity where a man can buy a drink
> For a buddy, or a good-looking chick.
>
> If there's no hereafter with hot and cold running
> I'm simply not coming.
>
> Not that I doubt Your willingness to provide,
> But, Lord, You stand on one side
>
> Of the infinite black ditch
> And I on the other. *And that's a bitch.* (7–8)

Here on this side of the great ditch, we are in a world where there are no absolutes, only that unending pendulum swing between faith and doubt. The poet perceives his job in part as one of pinpointing relative distinctions, within those parameters, between right and wrong and good and evil— locating the real, contextual truths in the real, contextual world. This is a projection of the poet's domain—into the realm of morality—that we have not much seen of late. It is perhaps a natural consequence of Ole Fred's sense of familial and social history; it is certainly southern and Protestant. The voice here is tough, colloquial, humorous ("rain drops," "intemperate"), uneasy, but stands its ground. What is at issue here is not revelation but relation: the straightforward dickering of man with God, rather than the preciosity of a special claim to knowledge. Similarly, instead of small, personal lyrics arising from isolate moments of poetic consciousness, Chappell gives us a precisely detailed account of the world around him and is himself brought into sharp confrontation with its needs, its offerings, and the daily necessity to choose among its aspects and possibilities.

A precisely detailed account: in *River* we are introduced to the poet's grandparents, to his wife Susan, to his writer-friend Guy Lillian. We meet for the first time the fortuitously first-named Virgil Campbell, "unabashedly drunk again" and shooting—literally shooting—at the river that is flooding his house and store and at the bridge. We participate in a well-cleaning, in a baptism. A foot bath. Imagine, a poem about a foot bath! One comes away with a new respect for feet.

Near the end of the book, "at midnight," in a reflective mood—a kind of musical repeat—the poet writes that "water, like human / history weeps / itself into being."

> Mostly I dare not think it:
> slow rain twitching wounds and eyelids
> of murdered soldiers,
> daily snail-white corpses
> bloating the Mekong and Hudson,
> muskrat drowned chewing his leg
> in the iron purse-snap,
> rivers rotting to lye where
> the mill-drains vomit inky venom,
> . . . .
> babies thrust into sewer pipes. (48)

But "we are moving still," and in the final coda, as it were, "The River Seeks Again the Sea":

> The earth is shoving us to sea, the sea shoulders us
> To another earth.
> So we stand naked and carefree and holding
>
> In the dew-fired earliest morning of the world. (51)

It is as if human history may be said to heal itself in its own process of constant becoming.

Bloodfire

The players in a string quartet must all be as technically proficient as soloists, yet they have to possess a certain sweetness of temper and austerity of soul. Each must be willing to serve the ensemble before himself. If there are times when Chappell wants to show off a bit, they carefully occur in the second and third books: *River* announces and *Earthsleep* completes themes, whereas *Bloodfire* and *Wind Mountain,* less constrained by specific jobs though located in quieter positions, are paradoxically freer to do the unexpected, even to indulge themselves. Both books comment on the nature of art itself, and possibly this is not unexpected. There are musicians—my mother was one of them and so, for that matter, was the Crown Prince of Japan—who prefer playing second violin or viola because it lets them sit down inside the music, where it is made, where it comes together.

Bloodfire includes a wonderfully funny letter to fellow poet Jim Applewhite, "Rimbaud Fire Letter," about the influence of French symbolism on a young and impressionable "Haywood County hillbilly"—Ole Fred, of course. But what is unexpected is that art for art's sake, that celebration of internal combustion, leads out of itself to the idea of the world itself as art. What makes this transition possible is that people are never far from Chappell's poem: they are there as ballast, as if it were people who hold the planet in place and not gravity. Listen to these lines from Section VI about the burning of the poet's grandfather's church, with their beautiful dappling of alliteration and the singable closure:

> Again it was given   to the Grace-grain that grew it,
> had gone again   gleaming to Genesis
> to the stark beginning   where the first stars burned.
> Touchless and tristless   Time took it anew
> and changed that church-plot   to an enchanted chrisom
> of leaf and flower   of lithe light and shade.
>
> *Pilgrim, the past   becomes prayer*
> *becomes remembrance rock-real   of Resurrection*
> *when the Willer so willeth   works his wild wonders.* (76–77)

Bloodfire is a book of wild wonders. The wonder of art is the wonder of the world, and the wonder of the world is its people. The wildest wonder of all is love, and love means—must mean—martyrdom. The culminating Section XI of *Bloodfire,* "Bloodfire Garden," joins the religious and political or pacifist themes—joins them as the image of the praying Christ in the garden of Gethsemane is fused with marvelous economy to that of the Martyr wearing his crown of thorns on Golgotha. "I prayed then by the thorn fire." The garden is also the garden of the bed, as trial by "thorn fire" or any martyrdom—religious, political, personal, or artistic—is a trial of love.

> Love, after the snap
> and the deep shudder
> a cool invisible smoke goes up
> from our bodies . . .
> . . . .
> The seeds of fresh rain advance,
> wind bearing from the south,
> out of the green isles
> of Eden. (93–94)

Wind Mountain

Which brings us to the third member of this quartet, *Wind Mountain.* In the Edenic beginning, *"bedroom curls and uncurls with breath"* (97). Alas, there is a visitor in the bedroom. The bedroom, the bedroom, is visited by death. The poet can't help knowing it. If he escapes for a time, the people around him don't. When the poet's grandmother buries her husband, "It's a heathen / Sorrow . . . / And that's the bitter end of all our loving." Death makes atheists of us all. Then a wind rises "at the far end / Of the far corn-field," and the old woman, feeling that "cooling wind" on her withered cheek, says,

> It was the breath of life to me, it was
> Renewal of spirit such as I could never
> Deny and still name myself a believer. (106)

In the third metaphorical mode, wind is the bearer of grace, the breath of the spirit. It is the force that outwits our own determined intention to be unhappy, to be "true" to fact, and fills us with laughter when we least mean to laugh.

> Impure world taking purest shape in the
> Bubbles of breath Bach-blown . . .
> . . . .
> We'll laugh our mortality to death, we'll laugh
> Our frailty off. (111–12)

It is word, it is song. Genius and inspiration. It is the magic carpet. The poets and philosophers, the musicians, the scientists, and the mystics "ride . . . / Out upon the bluebleached air" (114).

Wind is what carries us beyond ourselves to knowledge of the world, what brings us to the sheer pleasure of learning, of growing, of the use of our senses and brains. It is the Fall seen as a release from hermeticism.

"Let's disport it, you and I." A general joy in its own art pervades *Wind Mountain,* yet this is not the naïve pleasure of children's art nor the autism of surrealism. The poet in his third metaphorical mode is well aware of the consequences of meaning his metaphor entails. Breath must mean death. *Wind Mountain* is exhilarating, a poetic disporting of the idea of freedom, but—there is a but; for all their clarity, nothing in these poems is sacrificed to simplicity—freedom has its fearful side, and one thing on that side is its ultimate unfixability. Freedom just won't stay where anyone, even a poet, wills it to—in, say, the third line of the fifth stanza. It transcends poetry, goes beyond the idea of itself. And this lends *Wind Mountain* a sense of poignancy, a gentleness in its wildness that is so convincing it seems as if the flowers themselves know they are doomed to fold at night. And maybe we do. At the last, in what might be described as a playlet or miniature opera, "The Wind" speaks (about speaking humankind):

> It's all too soon
> They grow as silent as the moon
> And lie in earth as naked bone.
> We'll let them sit and sip their tea
> Till midnight; then I'll shake the tree
> Outside their window, and drive the sea
> Upon the land, the mountain toward the Pole,
> The desert upon the glacier. And all

They ever knew or hoped will fall
To ash . . . Till then, though, let them speak
And lighten the long dim heartache,
And trifle, for sweet trifling's sake. (139)

And now,

Where have we not drifted in fire,
In water, in air?
But Earth is the mouths of wind. (140)

Earthsleep

In Section IV of *Earthsleep* ("green beans / Are fast asleep in the lukewarm oven"), the poet makes a point—a bottom-line point, so to speak, that is crucial to the quartet as a whole:

I'll say this about the *Book of Earth,*
The guy who wrote it didn't cheat a jot,
Even the footnotes are brimming over with matter,
Matter aye and spirit too, each
And every page is chock to stupefying. (160)

That may be taken as an ideal for the writer of this poem: this is not the closed poetry, so common today, in which the "poetic" is achieved or ostensibly achieved by the rather elementary process of blocking out the "prosaic"; this is a poetry that dares to be inclusive, to deal with the whole of our lives. *Earthsleep* is a cornucopia, a kind of praise and thanksgiving for all that is. In *River,* the poet had said to his wife, "It is praise, love is praise, Susan, of what is, and if it be prisoned / in low earth it shall bound in high air saying like howitzers its / name and if it be scurried to & fro over cold wastes of skies yet / shall it touch with all its names blade root stone roof and if / it be locked solid at both poles there it shall say its name with / infinite unthinking purity" (23–24).

Praise of "what is" for this poet is of "matter aye and spirit too" (no mind / body dichotomy here); and the Book of Earth bounds "in high air," physical and metaphysical: "Mother and father we are distilled, the golden / Sweats of eternity surround us" (156). Sweats of eternity. There is that fine love of the real again and of the reality of abstraction. But the phrase itself is as exact, as down to earth, as a foot bath. A musicologist (but we steer clear of musicologists) might want to say something about how music is both the most primitive and sophisticated of art forms, the foetal heartbeat in mathematical fancification. But in explaining the conjunction of abstract and concrete, particular and universal, one can just as easily point again to the peopleness of Chappell's work, to his unwavering awareness of the world as populated, to his persona as a mortal among others. We will all be "distilled."

Earth, then, is both Hello and Good-bye, beginning and end. *Earthsleep* is the poet's speech on the passing of Virgil Campbell, who by now is an old friend to the reader as well; it's a song about "the troubadour atoms" and the "homebrew of creation"; it's a long "Dream of Plowing." (And in the dream the bell becomes gold, becomes babe, becomes old, becomes hobgoblin, dead goblin, stone, a dream of despair that's ever there.)

The penultimate section of *Earthsleep* returns us to Stillpoint Hill. Midnight. "The moon / signs the firmament / in the steady hand / of the faithful dead" (183). But Ole Fred's allegiance as a "confessed" confederate of the human condition (I put "confessed" in quotes to mark the enormous difference between what he is doing and confessional poetry) is now and always no to barren "time," to time unbearing: the poet is pledged to history, to change; indeed, to the corruptible. To that which, moving, "moving still," elicits our compassion, because we know it—and we—will be—are ordained to be—stopped.

Finally, the poet cries,

Who's used?
Who's not scrawled upon
By the wilderness hand of
Earth and fire and water and air? (186)

But—again but—oddly but truly, this is also a loyalty to hope, since there is no beginning without an end, no awakening without "sleepgrip," and no past without the remembrance of resurrection, no journey that does not end in arrival somewhere. Earth is Good-bye and Hello.

The love that moves itself in light to loving
Flames up like dew

Here in the earliest morning of the world. (187)

A Note of Affirmation

Midquest affirms the resurrection power of art. Against the unthinkable Nothing stands the Poem itself, whose existence testifies to Mind. The new day dawns, and the poem is there to witness sunrise, even to prove that the poet witnessed it. This is what art can do, surely: it can take nothingness into itself and make of it something, or it can leave Nothing out altogether. A string quartet, touching sublimity, does this by making the very process of thinking its own subject. And next to such bravery—audacity, even—Nothing can only howl, mere noise at the portals of sound.

Chappell's quartet is not, of course, a string quartet, and the analogy will serve only so far. But for that far, it is valid.

Midquest holds Nothing at bay by creating a self-contained world. The poet's four metaphorical planes or modes—the four books—come together to establish a world, as if each were one of the four necessary elements for that world's being.

My father also liked to say that the four voices of a string quartet supplied all that were needed—anything else was superfluous. Maybe some Greek had a similar notion about the four elements. Even today, our scientists talk about various forces at work in the universe. Chappell clearly has such a notion. Four is the number of harmony, completion, totality.

In *Midquest*'s four books, Chappell creates a complete or total world, a world containing, in order, history, passion, freedom, and death and hope. His people are alive; they move around in his pages and talk with one another. Ole Fred—who is neither young nor old hayseed but adopts this mask as revelatory of his roots—is alive, as both a feeling center and a spectator, as above all a listener. This live world—will North Carolina know itself?—hangs together because its structure—the quartet, disposes each part in such a way as to uphold the other parts. Each part is defined by its relation to the others.

That the final note, then, is one of affirmation should not be surprising.

The work is its own answer to despair. To create, particularly to create with such internal logic, is to demonstrate that Nothing is nothing.

Reintegrating the World

My father would agree with that, too. Where I (and my mother, playing second fiddle) might disagree with both men—and so far as I can tell, with all men—is in their assumption that the wanderer, including the artist-wanderer, will find his way home again. For a woman, Ithaca may remain on the map as a point of *possible* return, but nothing is guaranteed. Rarely will there be a Penelope sitting there to make things all right in the end. No one is keeping the home fires burning. The woman wanderer faces a far more frightening if no more arduous journey because she is, as it were, unanchored. Odysseus is domesticated man, one who both tames and is tamed; the woman wanderer is a woman alone.

(And how could Robert Graves have failed to notice this point, except that, as a man, he wouldn't think of it? The author of the *Odyssey* is confident that a woman will wait for a man and that for a man, there is a woman who will wait.)

This seems an important point because what we are really talking about here is not the autobiography of the artist, male or female. We are talking about "home" as the right end of the journey, about the work of art that justifies the pain and loneliness of the long wandering. The male writer who sees himself as Odysseus in some sense already knows where he is headed and is sure of getting there; the right work of art is the one that will celebrate the return and that can sing of the journey under the promise of the return. The tragic is not a threat; all will be redeemed. All discord will be resolved into harmony.

Including domestic harmony.

Throughout *Midquest,* a certain counterpoint of one more pair of "contraries" sets up a cross-structure supporting the cross of elements, though the poem never talks about this device: it is the counterpointing of male to female. Ole Fred, the wanderer in a dark wood, Odysseus at sea, is finding his way home. Oh, "how would I ever stop, once started to come / Down? I'll rain *home* all over us" (163).

Home is there, implicit in the act of love with which the First Morning began, because Odysseus is male and because "to come" home, like many of our street metaphors, holds a more precise meaning from a male point of view than from a female one. We need metaphors for women. Meanwhile, Ole Fred finds the end of his journey where Susan-Penelope waits. Perhaps this accounts for the optimism of the recurring assertion that "no one sleeps apart." A woman poet might reach an entirely different, less sanguine conclusion.

I mention this masculine bias "in conclusion" because it is both there and delightful. We have become so divided these days, as poets and sexes, that I am afraid women readers may cheat themselves by overlooking or refusing to look carefully at this attempt by one poet-person to reintegrate the world—male and female, water, fire, air, and earth—for all of us. As a poet, a reader, and a woman, I believe strongly that there is an angle of perspective in this work that complements and enlarges any that I, for example, or another woman writer might come up with. *Midquest* is a terrifically fine and powerful poem, full of the pleasures of surfaces and the deep gratification of complex structure.

Midquest *and the Gift of Narrative*

ROBERT MORGAN

One of the rarest gifts in modern poetry is that for narrative. The legacies of imagism and modernist fragmentation seem to have stifled the special talent that can tell stories in measure. Among the poets of our time there are many with great ability for concentration of phrase and figure, for fluent improvisation with tone and allusion, and even for resonant statement. And there are many fine story writers and novelists among us. Since Frost, however, there has been virtually no one who can do both at once. Perhaps it is the unfortunate trend toward specialization that deprives us of such versatility. Or it may be the limitation of our ambitions. But part of the burden of American poetics has been the tunnel vision, not to say snow blindness, of trying to look directly upon the face of the Word and tell what it is like. In trying to be Elohists of a new world, our poets have left much of the best of the imagination to the novelists.

Of course, the art of prose is as difficult as any poetry, even though in our culture it does not carry the same aura of pretension and expectation. Poetry is something to be worshipped from afar—not read, whereas we turn to prose for entertainment, information, authority. We should value all the more, therefore, a writer such as Fred Chappell, who can combine the two arts. He is both poet and novelist, and also a short-story writer. At the same time, he is at his best in what can only be called narrative poetry. By this designation I do not mean prose broken into lines. What Chappell does best is what may be termed *lyric narrative,* implying that the local texture of the lines is as interesting and concise as lyric poetry, while the overall movement of each piece is essentially narrative. The difference between prose narrative and verse narrative is considerable: the former usually incorporates much more detail and proceeds at the pace of the reader; the latter leaves far more to implication, as in other verse, and proceeds at the slower rhythm of repeated lineation.

There is a wholeness about the work of Fred Chappell. Everything he does seems a piece of the same cloth, whether story, poem, novel, or essay, and whatever he does fits with all the rest. It is the voice that dominates and is recognizable, no matter where one starts any of his works, speaking with great richness of mind and language, deeply learned, acid at times, but always improvising, engaging whatever is at hand with all its attention, true overall to a wonderful good will and wit. Whether the subject be his parents or Linnaeus, he demonstrates the same gift for luminous phrase and detail. All his work has the tone of the gifted rememberer and tale teller delighting in his powers and flights of merry-making memory. The voice is often self-deprecating and parodic, and the references range from the learned and reverent to the grotesque and mock-heroic. There is also an enormous amount of affection here for these people and their brief triumphs and losing battles with the sad facts of their lives.

Earthsleep is the last volume of the four-volume work entitled *Midquest*. Each volume is a separate poem, and all are spoken on the same day—May 28, 1971, the Dantean thirty-fifth birthday of the poet. Each poem—*River, Bloodfire, Wind Mountain,* and *Earthsleep*—symbolizes one of the four classical elements. The centering of these poems in all of experience, midway in a lifetime, is important in more ways than the merely chronological. Though touching extremes of usage and allusion at times, the work clearly derives its élan from the middle range of experience, stressing no angle of vision over another, and rendering with utmost care and humor the lives of grandmother, parents, aging mountain Falstaffs, and storekeepers. With his fluent "prose" style, Chappell has achieved a kind of middle poetry centered in the actual, familiar as conversation, but often as wry and learnedly comic as the poetry of, say, John Crowe Ransom. He uses elaborate traditional forms for the most humble subjects, often making stilnovist terza rima a vehicle for Appalachian whoppering.

This very middleness about *Midquest* is one of its most daring features, for it enables Chappell to avoid the safe and accepted manners of so much contemporary poetry and navigate far beyond the surrealist, confessional, formalist, and agrarian limits so many contemporaries have imposed on themselves. Chappell has found a "synthetic" style that enables him to assimilate all he knows into his work. Steering a middle course, he has avoided the siren call of the safely ambiguous on the one side and the heady maelstrom of manner on the other. Starting from the harbor of a northern port, he has crossed the Equator and been baptized in new tropical waters. Like the true yarn-teller he is, he has incorporated the new figures seamlessly into his old tales.

But having said all this, I must point out that the very difference of Chappell's work puts it exactly in the tradition of American poetry. Only by turning away from the accepted poetic norms into its own eccentricities and obsessions can the American gift seem to work. It is the veering away that brings one toward the middle. Chappell follows the pattern almost exactly, turning away from the high serious and meticulously chiseled understatement of verse to an explosion of free verse, hyperbole, flamboyant experimentation with French forms, and autobiography. In the rejection of poetry for the playfulness and wrinkles of self, he finds his true Poetry. In the contrasts of form and freedom, idea and facts, sad failure and guilt against rebellious joy, we find an authentic gift.

There are formal complexities in *Midquest* that will—and should—go unnoticed until a second or third reading. The whole is interwoven and subtly counterpointed with motifs and repetitions. Characters appear and later reappear in the poems. The variety of form and tone is used as a narrative as well as a poetic pacing device. Each volume is complete in itself yet completes the whole structure, beginning with the poet surfacing from the unity of sleep at dawn, beside Susan the wife-muse, and moving through a long day of remembering and storytelling, shaggydogging and drink-singing, and outright powerful poetry, to night and the return to unity and sleep with Susan, the earth-death muse and mother.

Part of Chappell's power is his willingness to put all of himself into this work. He gives to his poetry a great reservoir of learning and lyric hymning that alternates with science fiction and fantasy, and with country music. (*"I went walking up Chunky Gal / To watch the blackbird whup the owl."*) That he is willing to invest so many facets of himself is our gain, for we come to feel the wholeness of a human being. In the gaudy landscape of our times, there is the recognition that this is truly a man, yes, seen from more angles than we normally see and with greater focus and knowledge, but nevertheless a man in touch with the absurd and the corny, and with the sublime.

Midquest is about curvature and rondure, the return of that which goes out in the morning from its bed, about the turning of the earth and the seasons, and the sweep from the marriage of all in sleep (death) out through the almost overwhelming detail and near-chaos of experience back to the unity of love and dream. The theme is also the recurrence of everything, from the smallest déjà vu to the grandest rhyme of history and the night of stars beyond human history. The central thread is perhaps the "déjàvuness" of being, as each volume recapitulates the others and repeats the whole. Thus the hill in "On Stillpoint Hill at Midnight" in *River* returns near the end of *Earthsleep* in "Stillpoint Hill That Other Shore"; the Virgil Campbell of "Dead Soldiers" in the first volume returns again and again, most notably in "Firewater" of *Bloodfire* and "Three Sheets in the Wind" in *Wind Mountain,* and finally in "At the Grave of Virgil Campbell" in *Earthsleep.* The curve from birth in water to the death-sleep in earth-muse is repeated in each poem as well as in the overall shape of the tetralogy. We are led through a Dantean/Einsteinian curved and closed universe, where every route and every sin and every happiness leads back to the place of beginning.

Another recurring image is that of the tree of fire. This flame is, of course, man himself in the pain of his inspiration. But it reminds us of the Prophet Jeremiah and his bones of fire, of the Burning Bush's I AM, and at other times, of the Tree of Life, and at least once, of the burning cross of the KKK. The fire tree is being itself, as well as power, authority, wrath, suffering, and glory. It is the exhilaration and self-destruction that is being, the spirit inside the often sad and failing flesh.

Chappell is at times a mother worshipper, as in the poems to the wife-muse and earth mother and water mother; at other times, a father worshipper, as in the many fire poems and prophet hymns to power and authority. This is another instance of the middleness of the vision that enables him to incorporate so many different points of view. Blake, for example, is almost exclusively a singer of power, and Whitman, a lover of sea and earth and elusive dusks.

It is in *Bloodfire* that the central metaphor—the middle of life—becomes clear. There we see that the thirty-fifth birthday, the being born again to the second half of one's life, means to be born to death. The implication is not just that as one passes the midpoint of one's life one becomes increasingly aware of approaching death. Rather, it is the perception that one's life has become the process of death. Every breath is an act in the long dying back into the earth. And the recognition is that life is exactly the same as death, though to be alive is the opposite of being dead.

One of the finest sections of all four volumes is "Firewood," from *Bloodfire*. It is a long-running meditation in blank verse said while the speaker splits firewood. Here we have the best of a sure prose style with the free play and compactness of a poetic gift working together:

> Flame flame where I hit now, the cat is scared, heart
> red in the oak where sun
> climbed vein by vein to seek the cool
> wedge hard where I strike now and rose
> leaves drop off as if ruin of cloud on cloud
> fell, heart of red oak strips to sunlight,
> sunlight chopped like this to pie chunks,
> like this, solid as rock cleft rock, rock
> riven by vein and vein, ah if it were all
> so easy, to hit it & see it & feel it
> buck & come clean salmon colored,
> so clean I would eat it, this neat chop
> takes down the spine of the world. (67)

The drama of the maul and wedge is paralleled by a stream of associations branching out in dozens of directions and then coming back to the job at hand. As Thoreau said, our firewood warms us twice. We feel the mental fever working up in the speaker as he labors. His struggle to cleave the knotty wood becomes the struggle of people to have their lives despite the recalcitrance of nature. The monologue builds to a climax of persuasion and abuse addressed to the wood.

> Matter, I'm gonna
> kick your ass all over this universe, matter has only
> to sit quiet thinking, My man, never you heard of
> passive resistance?, why that's the secret of the
> world, Mexican stand off is the closest you'll get
> to the heart's heat heart of the heart,
> why don't you just try the lotus position or the string

quartet or something equally restful, for never has
mere fever got you anywhere or me either come
to that, we could make such beautiful silence
together if only you'd slow down & shape up & let
things as they are have their guiltless pleasures,
and man replies saying unto matter, Wassamatta
you, you talking commie now all this strike talk,
I been sentenced doncha know to create reality
by the sweat of my brow, Bible sez so, take
that you weird pinko freak, and with this I
bring the hammer down and the wedge the old
hearthurter doesn't even *budge*. (72–73)

Chappell has integrated into hip epic story the details and names of his region as no one else has. "Chunky Gal," "Greasy Creek," and "Standing Indian" do not just give a sense of local usage, they become part of the thick texture of the style, giving at once intimacy and distance to the poetry. It is as though the speaker is of two minds at once, the mountain boy telling of the places and people of which he is derived, and the learned and wise poet who knows Latin, Italian, French, neoplatonism, and quantum mechanics. The complexity of tone is rendered most clearly in the sections about the poet's parents, in their constant harping, from the comfort of their prosperous suburban lives, on the hardness of the old days on their hardscrabble farms. There is a parodic overtone in their monologues, a teasing, as though the poet knows that even though they do miss the sweat and poverty of their childhoods, they are exaggerating all around. Even if they could travel back they would not, yet probably it was not as hard as they make it sound. This essential paradox is what Chappell communicates so affectionately, and it partly explains his enormous popularity in the South. No one has rendered so accurately the sense of displacement amid so much prosperity, and the jealous holding on to the phrases and accents of the old as both an amused conning of the self and an irreplaceable touchstone.

Typical of this half-serious teasing are the stories about fundamentalist religion. The little white churches in these poems cast cold shadows over the coves, and their preachers and doctrine are never absent long from the mind of the speaker. Whether in the mock-heroics of the terza rima "My Grandfather Gets Doused," or the mock-epic alliterative line of "My Grandfather's Church Goes Up," or the Dantean "In Parte Ove Non E

Che Luca" which, part translation, part original, tours hell with the Master and finds James Dickey in the Inferno for lechery, or finally, in the drinking hymns of "At the Grave of Virgil Campbell," we see a mind coming to terms with one of the terrors of its world through the jujitsu of humor. Since the church and its work ethic and hellfire can't be ignored, it must be defused a little with parody, while the more humble, everyday things are treated reverently. As the mighty grandmother of "Second Wind" says after the death of her husband,

> I heard the out-of-tune
> Piano in the parlor and knew that soon
> Aunt Tildy would crank up singing "Lo, How a Rose
> E'er Blooming."—Now I'll admit Aunt Tildy tries,
> But hadn't I been tried enough for one
> Heartbreaking day? And then the Reverend Dunn
> Would speak . . . *A Baptist preacher in my house!*
> That was the final straw. I washed my face
> And took off all my mourning clothes and dressed
> Up in my everyday's, then tiptoed past
> The parlor, sneaking like a scaredey mouse
> From my own home that seemed no more a place
> I'd ever feel at home in. I turned east
> And walked out toward the barns. I put my trust
> In common things to be more serious. (104–105)

There is a spirit in this work I find remarkable and rare in contemporary poetry. Much of what we read these days is often at best hardbitten and stingy, sometimes downright nasty to the reader. Though Chappell is often outrageous about himself, his family and neighbors, there is an assumption of community in all his work, a sense of belonging not just to a family and a place, and to a place in terms of geography, but also to the terrain of history. It is a community in time that is implied and evoked, a world of parents and ancestors both literal and literary, as real as the expressways and gaudy vernacular of the present.

Interestingly enough, this sureness of who he is, in a community both poetic and familial, gives Chappell a truer rapport with the contemporary culture. His imagination lives not only among the things that were but also among the things that are. That is, to paraphrase Wallace Stevens, his gift is equal to the pressure of reality. This partly explains his popularity as a poet and as a reader of his poetry. He speaks to people as they are and as he is. The authenticity is instantly perceivable, on the page and in his voice. There is no precious regionalism here, no easy agrarian indignation, no sentimental celebrations.

Since *Earthsleep* is a self-contained unit but comprises eleven sections, I will not quote extensively from it. There are too many movements and forms to do justice to in a brief essay. But with two or three passages, I hope to show something of the range and grandness of the voice and the personable wit. In the opening section, "Earth Emergent Drifts the Fire River," spoken to the Beatrice-wife Susan, we hear a song at daybreak as the poet and world waken from the earth of common sleep and all sharpens into articulation:

> speak you,
> Tell me some elder annunciation, tell me
> History is being reborn in water, in healing water
> Rise all the cities gone down, the nations who
> Died in the fire of blood take clean new bodies,
> A silver ivy of water reclaims the broken walls,
> Unguessed Atlantises poke their streaming heads
> Out of the history books, sins of the fathers
> To lordly earth overgiven rise
> Again now transformed to the great names we feed upon,
> The fertile waters of deathsleep manure the flames. (148)

The questioning continues for each of the four elements in a recapitulation of the structure of the book and of the previous three volumes.

In this poem, more than in the others, the date May 28, 1971, is both a resurrection and a foretelling of death. The concern with mortality has been threaded in the poem in general, whereas here it becomes primary. Much of the book could be considered an epitaph for the poet and others; nowhere is the subject handled with more humor and affection than in "At the Grave of Virgil Campbell." Here, in a mock-eulogy at graveside, the poet addresses his old friend in the earth:

> I've been fumbling with some epitaphs
> In case you want to try them on for size.

HERE LIES VIRGIL CAMPBELL—ONE MORE TIME.
How's that strike you? A little naked maybe.
Something a bit more classical perhaps?

>   SISTE, VIATOR.

>   VIRGIL CAMPBELL'S QUIET HERE.

>   WHO NEVER WAS BEFORE.

Or:

>   HERE'S THE FIRST TIME IT WAS SAID
>   THAT VIRGIL CAMPBELL WAS GRAVELY LAID.

Or:

>   EARTH, RECEIVE
>   YOUR PLAYFUL LOVER
>   TO HIS ONE SLEEP
>   WITH NO HANGOVER. (167–68)

After a long discourse on the possibilities of the Afterlife ("I know there's Whiskey-after-Death") and a further recounting of Virgil's likes and weaknesses and virtues, the poem ends with a salute:

What's this, it's not a hymn it's a drinking song,
Well, sometimes who can tell the difference?

To hell with the ragshank preachers
>   Who make it out sinful to think,
And down with the dustdyed teachers
>   Whose veins run Bible-black ink,
And Damn every one of those creatures
>   Who told us we oughtn't to drink!
If ever they'd taken a sip
>   (From me and Chris Sly
>   Here's mud in their eye!)
They'd had more brains and less lip.

But here's to the happy old souls
>   Who trip about clinking their chains
In time to the music that rolls
>   From the locker of Davy Jones,
And here's to the Hand that controls
>   Raw-Head-&-Bloody-Bones!

Let's have us a neat little nip
    (For we and the Host
    Forever cry, "Prosit!")
Before we take our last sleep.

Let's put on our nightcaps of moonshine
    And kneel and mumble our prayers,
In Glory we drunkards will soon shine
    Singing our spiritous airs,
And, tipsy as possums by noontime,
    We'll roll down Pisgah like bears!
So pour us a tight little drop
    (And here's to the Splendor
    Of the Holy Bartender!)
And we're ready at last for our nap. (172–73)

The section entitled "The Peaceable Kingdom of Emerald Windows" is almost an Edenic roll call of the lovers and progeny of the earth, so colorful and rich in allusion it turns out to be heaven, or at least an earthly paradise, that is described. The word that comes to my mind most often as I read here is "Celtic," because of the intensity and animism of the images:

Chortlings of the green uproar of Earth,
Tree-dream, weed-dream, the man within the tree,
Woman within the weed, babies inhabit
Tea roses, at the bottom of the trumpet
Of day lily lies the yellow tabby cat,
Blackberry vine a whirlpool of green blaze,
And kudzu the Great Wall of China, oppossum
Of apple, plum tree is a sea urchin here
By the bridge of hills, crown of whitethorn bleeds
The broken sigh of hills, the hills launch here
Windows windows, summer dream is a freshet
Of windows, raindrop how much window, raindrop
An eye of glass, it is a window of
Deep sadness, it is the lover's tear of goodbye,
Goodbye I perceive to be a human creature. (156)

Matching the wonder of landscape, beast, and flower in "The Peaceable Kingdom of Emerald Windows" is the weird threat of "My Grandmother's Dream of Plowing," in which the beloved grandmother of the earlier poems recounts a nightmare. From a new-plowed furrow she picks up a great lump of gold that turns into a goblin child "with an evil smile." She first holds it to her breast and then, frightened of the thing, wishes it would die. No sooner does she wish than it does die, and she is left with the guilt of her murderous wish. The narrator intrudes at the end:

"And then you woke," I said, "to the world you love."

"And now I know," she said, "I never woke." (180)

Near the end, the book rounds back toward the sleep of earth. In the shortline free-verse song entitled "Stillpoint Hill That Other Shore," which moves in and out of elegiac dactyls and is addressed again to Susan, the poet hymns the kinship and union of all in earth and on earth. It is a kind of marriage song, of all with the planet, and all with all.

This hill above our house,
stillpoint before
the turning begins again,
earth solid to the hand,
earth moveless in time,
comprised
of the husk and marrow of
our dead forefathers.
Unmoving in time,
only the dead are incorrupt.

Time I shall not serve thee.
You earth I have loved most blest. . . .

The peace that shall seize us
in sleepgrip,
that peace shall I tell you
be all the black frenzies of our flesh
in one green cuddle,
let us descend to our house
our bed
and invite the mornings,
the infinite anniversary mornings,
which reach out to touch us
with the hands of one another. (183–85)

The long poem and journey through all the elements, through dreams and waking memory, through comic chorus and mock sermon, end in the conjugal sleep of all earth, in lovesleep. All sink (rise) into that paradise, beyond the gaudy and hypocritical, beyond the postures and the purgatories of wakeful work and guilty dread. The very last section is the song from earth itself, among the planets and starry coordinates fading at dawn.

> Let it then be flesh that we take on
> That I may see you
> Cool in time and blonde as this fresh daybreak.
>
> No one no one sleeps apart
> Or rises separate
> In the burning river of this morning
> That earth and wind overtake.
>
> The way light rubs upon this planet
> So do I press to you,
>
> Susan Susan
>
> The love that moves the sun and other stars
> The love that moves itself in light to loving
> Flames up like dew
>
> Here in the earliest morning of the world. (187)

Chappell's Aesthetic Agenda: The Binding of Midquest *to* I Am One of You Forever *and* Brighten the Corner Where You Are

RICHARD ABOWITZ

If there is an aspect of Fred Chappell's work that has received insufficient attention, it is the radically experimental nature of his writings. Perhaps part of the reason for this lack of attention is Chappell's attempt to conceal the speculative qualities of his work. Chappell has said that his goal in his early novels was "to produce a daring and even experimental novel which would not look or feel experimental."[1] He has maintained this goal throughout his work. With the placing of *Midquest* alongside *I Am One of You Forever* and its first successor volume, *Brighten the Corner Where You Are,* it is possible to begin to analyze the qualities of Chappell's hidden experimentalism.

Chappell is attempting to combine *Midquest* and a quartet of novels (only two of which have been published) into one mammoth work. He explains: "So I began to toy with the short stories generated by *Midquest* and struck upon the notion of a quartet of novels which would balance the *Midquest* tetralogy, surrounding that poem with a solid fictional universe. . . . The four novels were to be progressively sophisticated in technique, a little model of the history of modern fiction."[2]

The placement of *Midquest,* a reactionary work, into a larger work containing four novels violates the norm which, as Joseph Brodsky has ob-

---

1. Fred Chappell, "Fred Chappell," in *Contemporary Authors Autobiography Series,* ed. Adele Sarkissian (Detroit, 1986), 118.
2. *Ibid.,* 124.

served, has existed since the invention of the novel: "The tradition of dividing literature between poetry and prose dates from the beginning of prose, since it was only in prose that such a distinction could be made. Ever since poetry and prose have customarily been regarded as separate areas—or, better yet, spheres—of literature wholly independent of each other."[3] Chappell's decision to work against the traditional separation of poetry and prose forces us to examine how this combination adds to our view of *Midquest* and how the novels deepen our understanding of the poem.

There are two major connections between the novels and the poem: an aesthetic agenda and a plot correspondence with a symbolic network of interconnectedness.

Both the poem and the novels attempt to put forth an alternative to the current hegemony in their respective spheres: *Midquest,* to the dominance of the lyric poem in contemporary poetry, and *I Am One of You Forever* and *Brighten the Corner Where You Are,* to the dominant forces in American fiction since World War II.

In his preface to *Midquest,* Chappell notes the radical intent of the book: "Ours is the time of the brilliant autobiographical lyric. . . . I wished to capture, to restore to my work other qualities sometimes lacking in the larger body of contemporary poetry: detachment, social scope, humor, portrayal of character and background, discursiveness, wide range of subject matter. So that *Midquest* is to some degree a reactionary work" (x). Because *Midquest* works against the direction of contemporary poetry, it may be fruitful to consider the novelistic character of the book as a reaction to the contemporary novel.

In *Diminishing Fictions: Four Decades of the Novel,* Bruce Bawer is extremely critical of the post–World War II American novel. Bawer divides novels published since the war into two major categories: metafictional novels and workshop novels. Of the metafictionists, Bawer says: "The chief problem with the metafictionists, unfortunately, is that they have been . . . distracted from the human condition. . . . They have been eager to define the spirit of the age, but they don't seem to think that the spirit of the age has very much to do with the human spirit." Of workshop fiction, Bawer complains that it consists of "spare, elliptical exercises in tone, metaphor, and (above all) obsessive surface detail that, although often well written,

---

3. Joseph Brodsky, *Less Than One* (New York, 1986), 176.

seem in most instances to have been deliberately shorn of passion, force, animation and originality."[4] In general, Bawer complains that postwar American fiction writers are either obsessed with obfuscating formal and linguistic pyrotechnics that alienate the reader, or they are creating bland minimalist stories with no range and ambition beyond the banal, which bores the reader. *I Am One of You Forever* and *Brighten the Corner Where You Are* can be read as reactions to these dominating modes of contemporary American fiction.

Both novels are set in the shadow of World War II, perhaps not coincidentally the same period to which Bawer dates the beginning of the decline of the American novel. It could be argued that Chappell combines the characters of the workshop novel and the techniques of the metafictional novel, using each as a corrective to the limitations of the other. But it would be more accurate to say that Chappell, as he does in *Midquest,* is returning to an earlier vision of the novel to reclaim something that has been lost.

I Am One of You Forever and *Brighten the Corner Where You Are* are both narrated by Jess and have exactly the same structure. Each book contains ten "narrative" chapters that tell the novel's "story." Also, each book has an italicized prologue and epilogue and a section between Chapters 5 and 6, all of which can best be described as epiphanies. In general, the chapters contain the elements that we have come to identify as workshop minimalism, and the epiphanies include metafictional techniques.

The characters are members of a small North Carolina town, and the novels center specifically on the family of Jess's father, Joe Robert Kirkman. These small-town characters and their problems with holding jobs, raising children, drinking excessively, visiting relatives, and living middle-class lives would be immediately recognizable to readers of the works of writers classified by Bawer as major workshop writers: Ann Beattie, Bobbie Ann Mason, and David Leavitt. Nonetheless, those readers would never mistake the characters for products of workshop minimalism, because Chappell's characters come much closer to Bawer's description of characters in pre–World War II novels than to those who thrive in the contemporary novel: "What saved these prewar novels from being mere testaments of doom was the fact that their protagonists, as a rule, were men and women of substance.

---

4. Bruce Bawer, *Diminishing Fictions: Four Decades of the Novel* (St. Paul, Minn., 1988), 14, 16.

Doomed or not, they were genuine heroes, who actively sought to construct for themselves a life built upon useful work or positive beliefs or order or happiness or love."[5] This could easily be a description of the characters in *I Am One of You Forever* and *Brighten the Corner Where You Are*. For example, Joe Robert Kirkman's attempt to bring evolution into his science classroom against the perceived resistance of the community may be misinformed, but it is still heroic. The rich variety of bizarre uncles who visit Jess's house in *I Am One of You Forever* are, for all their impassioned weirdness, certainly people whose lives and struggles contain nobility.

A reader of metafiction would also be alerted immediately that the text is working on some of the same principles that guide John Barth, William Gaddis, and John Hawkes, writers whom Bawer identifies as metafictionists. Bawer notes, however, that the metafictional technique is borrowed from the modernists. So it might be safer to say that Chappell is re-appropriating modernist devices from the metafictionists and that he is reclaiming the middle-class family from the workshop minimalists.

From the first sentence of the first chapter in *I Am One of You Forever,* Chappell subtly warns us that Jess's narration is not to be fully trusted: "The first time my father met Johnson Gibbs they fought like tomcats." Two pages later, Jess states, "They didn't fight until the next day" (9).

In Chapter 6, we are told that Uncle Zeno always begins his stories with the preamble "That puts me in the mind of . . ." (98). Yet a few pages later, "Uncle Zeno began talking without excuse or preamble as always" (114).

Another modernist technique that Chappell employs is the violation of linear narration. Characters such as Johnson and the mother appear and vanish without reason from chapter to chapter. The most important example of this lies in the middle epiphany between Chapters 5 and 6 of *I Am One of You Forever.*

In the middle epiphany, a telegram arrives informing the family of the death of their friend and farmhand, Johnson Gibbs. In Chapter 6, as one would expect, Johnson is dead. But in Chapter 7, without explanation, Johnson is alive, and again in Chapter 8, he is dead.

So what is the point of combining these small-town North Carolina residents with modernist literary devices? In the preface to *Midquest*, Chappell claims he is attempting to restore certain aspects of poetry. These novels

5. *Ibid.,* 14.

give a hint of what Chappell is trying to restore to the center of the American novel.

The clue comes in the italicized epilogue of *I Am One of You Forever,* entitled "Helen." The reader of the novel will immediately associate Helen with Helen of Troy because she is discussed earlier in the novel. Jess watches as his father, Johnson Gibbs, and Uncle Luden all mutter the name "Helen" in their sleep. The entire epiphany has a sense of uncertainty about it, beginning as it does with the modifier "It seemed . . ." (180). Jess can't explain what he is seeing: "There was a woman I had never heard of before and she was powerful in all three lives. No, that was not possible" (182). Jess stares into the darkness though he knows he "can't look into their dreams" (182). Finally, Jess tries "to sculpt from the darkness a shape I might recognize" (182). As a result, Jess is able to see a vision of Helen.

Helen may be interpreted as a representation of the creative imagination (note the word "sculpt"). Through the literary imagination, these three men are able to be joined, and their secret thoughts understood through Jess's writing and ultimately through Chappell's novel. Chappell is attempting to return to the novel the author's primary duty to understand people and, in the process, to create people worth understanding.

What *I Am One of You Forever* suggests, *Brighten the Corner Where You Are* presents even more forcibly. Chappell picks up on the clue left in the final epiphany of *I Am One of You Forever.* In that novel, Jess learns to understand others through the creative imagination. He had written, "I couldn't see into their dreams, I had no desire to" (182). In *Brighten the Corner Where You Are,* the entire narrative is based upon looking into dreams. Jess narrates events that he could not possibly have witnessed or known about in such detail.

Jess merges so completely with his father's thoughts that Jess refers to himself in the third person: "There was plenty of time, so he'd let Jess sleep in. Let him dream those incomprehensible dreams completely out of his head; let him wake up late then, having become as sane and sensible as his father" (31). This section raises questions about the narrative that are typical of modernist writers. Is this narrative a dream, and if it is a dream, whose dream is it? It cannot have been lifted from Joe Robert's memory, because sections of the text are incidents he did not witness. It seems unlikely that

Joe Robert's son would narrate Joe's dream. Again, Chappell provides us with a clue.

In Chapter 3, Chappell interrupts the narrative for a sentence in the italicized text that, until this point, has only been used in the epiphanies: "But he knows about it, Johnson knows. He stands beside us even now as I tell you our story" (61). This is in response to the unhappiness Jess's father has just experienced because of Johnson's death. Jess is the narrator of this book, but he is not a character. His role can best be seen as a voice of the creative imagination. Before being awakened to Helen in *I Am One of You Forever,* Jess is able to narrate unsteadily only those events in which he is a participant. Having become one of them forever, he is now able in *Brighten the Corner Where You Are* to tell a story that in many of its details he couldn't know. Jess is able to see into their dreams.

The final epiphany of *Brighten the Corner Where You Are* shows Jess's father attempting to pull his wife into the story he has just dreamed:

> My father giggled in his sleep and chortled, shifted in the
> bed and nudged my mother with his elbow. Did she
> understand? Did she get the joke?
> But she did not respond. My mother, too, was dreaming,
> busy with her own concerns, pursuing her own exotic life. (212)

One suspects that the next novel, following the pattern of *Midquest,* will tell of the mother's exotic life.

From these two novels it is clear that, as in *Midquest,* Chappell is putting forth a reactionary vision to the dominant school of fiction. As in *Midquest,* he is returning to the source and then moving in a direction that most of his contemporaries have not taken. This is only the beginning, however, of the connections Chappell has created between the poem and the novels.

Chappell furthers his integration of poem and novel by creating an intricate plot and symbolic correspondence between the works. At first glance, there is only a geographical similarity between the poem and the novels, the same sort of connection that exists between Faulkner's novels. *Midquest* is concerned with the story of its narrator, Fred, and his family. The poem takes place on May 28, 1971. The novels are narrated by a man named Jess. They tell the story of his boyhood and his family during the 1940s. The only connection between the two is the character of Virgil

Campbell. Campbell's purpose in the poem is to "give to the whole its specifically regional, its Appalachian context" (Preface to *Midquest*, x). It seems reasonable that his presence in the novels similarly helps to locate them in the same imaginative town that Chappell uses in the poem. This does not show the true relationship between the poem and the novels. For that, a deeper look at each novel and its corresponding poem in *Midquest* is required.

I Am One of You Forever, the first novel, is meant to enjoy a rough symmetry with *River,* the first book of *Midquest.* Like the other poems, *River* takes place in the shadow of Old Fred's past and in the present. The war in Vietnam periodically enters Old Fred's thoughts. Indeed, the title poem, "Bloodfire," is explicitly about Vietnam. Fred is too old, however, to be a likely candidate for service. *I Am One of You Forever* takes place during World War II. Jess at ten is too young to serve, but through his friend Johnson Gibbs, the war is made a vivid part of his life.

Chappell attempts to get at the same subject by moving in two different directions, by creating two different narrators and two different types of narration. The narrative perspectives are presented through an adult man watching the destruction of youth by war and a young boy watching war change beyond recognition and ultimately kill his elders and idols. The combination of the poetic destruction in Fred's imagining a war and the prose narrative of a young boy watching a war combine to more nearly connect the poem and the novel.

River attempts to tell the story of Fred's thirty-fifth birthday through different manifestations of the element of water. The epigraph concludes with this sentence from *Moby-Dick:* "Yes, as every one knows, meditation and water are wedded for ever." The one word "forever" appears in the novel's title. As in *River,* the primary metaphoric force in *I Am One of You Forever* is water. A brief look at the manifestations of water in the prologue and in the first four chapters shows the same use of the element in both the novel and in the poem:

Prologue: A river floods its bank and destroys a bridge built by Jess and his father. The family is then enveloped in a magic tear.

Chapter 1: Jess and Johnson Gibbs go on a fishing trip. The last paragraph begins, "We fell silent to hear the water. . . ."

Chapter 2: Tells the story of a practical joke in which Jess's uncle is tricked into going out onto the roof in the middle of a storm.

Chapter 3: Centers on the bizarre metaphorical transformation of a man's beard into a "creek," into a "stream," and finally into an ocean complete with a white whale and sharks.

Chapter 4: Jess, Johnson Gibbs, and the father think they hear the voice of God in a raging storm.

By choosing the same element for different genres, Chappell's use of water in both the novel and the poem creates a unifying dialogue between the two texts. To extend the metaphor, the fiction and poetry flow freely between each other, as unified as the river and sea. (The last poem in *River* is entitled "The River Seeks Again the Sea.")

In the Preface, Chappell notes that the second volume of *Midquest* concerns the father. *Brighten the Corner Where You Are* is about Jess's father being called before the school board for teaching evolution in his class. Like "Bloodfire," its corresponding poem in *Midquest,* the novel takes place during a single day in late May. Also like *Bloodfire,* the element of fire dominates the novel. The chapter titles themselves express the importance of fire and its associated symbols in the novel: "The Devil Possum," "Bacchus," "Prometheus Unbound," "Foxfire."

We learn for the first time in *Brighten the Corner Where You Are* that the last name of Jess's family is Kirkman. Kirk, the Scottish word for church, also makes an appearance in *Bloodfire.* The poem "My Grandfather's Church Goes Up" contains the curious line "the killing by fire of my grandfather's kirk" (75). In this case, the poem and the novel again provide a subtle commentary on each other.

The strangest parallel between poem and novel comes in an inexplicable—and unexplained—coincidence: Jess and Fred apparently have the same father! In the poem "My Father Burns Washington," Fred describes his father's occupations:

> One job was farming, another
> Teaching school, and on the side
> He grubbed for Carolina Power and Light. (81)

This matches exactly the job history of Joe Robert Kirkman. Though the two men have different names, as we have seen from the presence of Virgil Campbell, they are from the same imagined region. The final touch involves a story in both the poem and novel of an unusual courtship ritual between father and mother:

From the poem "My Mother Shoots the Breeze," in *Wind Mountain*:

> First time I met your Pa he took my slip
> Off. "Miss Davis, I want your pretty slip,
> If you've got one loose about, for my Science class."
> He was going to fly them Benjamin Franklin's kite. (107–108)

From *Brighten the Corner Where You Are:*

> Don't you remember what-all Joe Robert did last year when he was principal? How he flew that kite made out of his wife's old silk slip. (174)

The context of the incident has changed between poem and novel. Also, this is from *Wind Mountain* and not *Bloodfire*. This fact can, however, easily be explained if the next novel is, as I have suggested, about Jess's mother. For how these collisions in fact and circumstance will finally be resolved and justified, we must await the final two novels. Nonetheless, it is clear that both the poem and the novels must be read in consort, as one statement and one work. If Old Fred's last name is Chappell, read *chapel,* then the Kirkman family, read *churchman,* are the people filling it.

The Singer Dissolved in Song:
The Poetic as Modern Alternative
in Chappell's Castle Tzingal

PATRICK BIZZARO

Commentators have described this series of twenty-three short dramatic pieces in a variety of ways. One calls it "a throwback to the Renaissance allegory, antiquated diction and all." Another describes it as "a murder mystery in a book of poems." And still a third believes it to be an "archaic poem of arrogance and its punishment."[1] As my title suggests, I am interested in the interchangeability of form and content, in how the singer of a poem dissolves in song and yet seems to survive, in how our concern over form in contemporary verse becomes self-referential, and finally, in how Fred Chappell challenges us in *Castle Tzingal* to view poetry differently in an age when all about us weep for the loss of audience.

It seems an understatement to say, as has Michael J. Bugeja, that "the book is offbeat."[2] Chappell seems to have consciously created a book of verse that might be called "archaic" and "antiquated," since much of the effect of his message is a result of his presentation. In fact, commentators on this book write as though very little, indeed, has been thought recently

---

1. Genevieve Stuttaford, Review of Fred Chappell's *Castle Tzingal*, in *Publisher's Weekly*, November 6, 1984, p. 63; Mark Jarman, Review of Fred Chappell's *Castle Tzingal*, in *Hudson Review*, XXXVIII (Summer, 1985), 331; R. T. Smith, Review of Fred Chappell's *Castle Tzingal*, in *Southern Humanities Review*, XIX (Fall, 1985), 391, hereinafter cited parenthetically with page numbers in the text.

2. Michael J. Bugeja, Review of Fred Chappell's *Castle Tzingal*, in *Georgia Review*, XXXIX (Winter, 1985), 896.

about allegory. After all, allegory appears to be a throwback to another time, a time preromantic and extremely rational. Unlike the symbol, glorified by most postromantic theorists, allegory seems limited, offering a closed system that fails to endure once it gives up its predictable meaning. Although the symbol lives on in suggestiveness, the allegorical closes like a frozen flower until only its shape reminds us that it once held beauty, freshness, and breath. If we view *Castle Tzingal* as allegory or assess its value chiefly in its effort to revive Elizabethan revenge tragedy, we may run the risk of reducing the work to form only, separating it from its own age and from the very suggestiveness that allegorical verse offers in the postmodern era. But modern allegory, drawing from the age of rationalism, is especially appropriate to Chappell's purposes in this drama, enabling him to probe at an historical distance the most critical and, it might be argued, Romantic issues facing poets in the postmodern age. Chappell employs allegory to make a suggestion concerning the survival of art, if not of the artist, in this darkest of ages.

As postromantic dramatic poetry, *Tzingal* can be read, as Robert Browning instructed us to read drama nearly one hundred and fifty years ago, either as the workings of man in action or of action in man. As allegory, this drama can be read as two narratives strung together by events occurring simultaneously, events outside the characters as well as inside. These are crucial distinctions to make, for one of the most confusing features of Chappell's verse drama is a question of how, exactly, it is to be read. R. T. Smith, for one, points out that most of the "near-dramatic monologues" in *Tzingal* reveal "no alleged listener other than the voyeur-reader" (Review of *Castle Tzingal,* 391).

Clearly, in many of these poems, a listener is absent, an element of the communication triad dissolved, suggesting an interrelationship between Chappell as contemporary poet and his poet-hero, Marco, who sings through a disembodied voice to a range of characters who hear him in their dreams and interpret what they hear differently, idiosyncratically. In a sense, then, this work is a postmodern work, a narrative on narrative that tells two stories—one at an historical distance from the postmodern audience and the other immediate, since in Chappell's view, poetry is transcendent, even in a world like Tzingal, marked by "an ugly murk of treachery" (13). We are given characters in action, but we are also offered action in characters, often in dreams that echo later in the waking world and affect the characters' lives. Chappell offers this unactable drama almost as an answer to the enduring question of our times (at least enduring among poets and closet dramatists): Is anyone out there really listening? Does anyone hear me when I write? Can poetry survive without performance? Can we address universal troubles in specific poems? Or must we "number the streaks of the tulip," as Sam Johnson asks, hoping we can avoid such reduction of our poetic resources and, thereby, write of the individual rather than of the species? And through a process of historical distancing, Chappell requires his readers to view the events objectively and follow the logical sequence of actions in men that ultimately suggest answers to questions about meaning, achievement, and success in the postmodern age.

Poetry and Audience: "The Disembodied Voice"

Considerable unhappiness abounds among poets, many of whom have been required to reassess their view of poetry in the postmodern age. At the core of such concerns is the belief that poets must do something to develop an audience of what Robert McDowell calls "potential" (as opposed to "pocket") readers. To attract such an audience, McDowell argues that poets "would be wise to remember the past and bring some business savvy to the task of creating a larger poetry audience." What has prevented this from happening before? McDowell says that an audience of potential readers will not be developed "unless poetry apes the media's already successful and familiar products, its sitcoms and rock videos." He insists that "it is a mistake to assume a relationship between the popularity of a product and its quality."[3] What happens then to poetry? Do we diminish it to make it popular?

The suggestion that we make poetry more popular by writing *to* potential readers is not offered by mere hacks who we might easily dismiss. Dana Gioia has taken an increasingly popular and well-publicized position on contemporary American poetry. In his article "Can Poetry Matter?" Gioia seems especially attuned to Chappell's notion of the disembodied voice of the poet in contemporary America: "American poetry now belongs to a subculture. No longer part of the mainstream of artistic and intellectual life, it has become the specialized occupation of a relatively small and isolated

3. Robert McDowell, "Poetry and Audience," in *Poetry After Modernism,* ed. Robert McDowell (Brownsville, Ore., 1991), 331, 335, 334, 333.

group. Little of the frenetic activity it generates ever reaches outside that closed group. As a class poets are not without cultural status. Like priests in a town of agnostics, they still command a certain residual prestige. But as individual artists they are almost invisible."[4]

Elsewhere Gioia, a businessman in New York, has written about poetry and business, interestingly tracing the business occupations of several esteemed American poets, including Wallace Stevens, T. S. Eliot, A. R. Ammons, and James Dickey. Among the questions Gioia asks (but for the most part, rhetorically) are these: "How did their business careers affect the lives and works of these poets? Why did these men write nothing about their working lives? What personal and artistic changes did they undergo in the years they spent in jobs that were alien if not antagonistic to their vocations as poets? Were these jobs only ways of surviving until fame caught up with them? Is anything even gained by segregating them off as a distinct group of writers and comparing them to other poets whose lives seem more typical?" The intent here is honorable enough: Gioia seems as concerned as McDowell about the state of American poetry and its exclusion of certain subjects, including the world of business, by poets who have actually worked in that world. Like Chappell, he seems disturbed that the poet's voice has grown indistinct at best, silent at worst. But Gioia's underlying concern with the relationship between the world of business and the world of art merits mention here, since he seems spokesman for those concerned with material success: "For whatever reasons, the profession of poetry is a dangerous one in America, perhaps because it is so damnably difficult to succeed in any meaningful way."[5] A reader must ask if what is "meaningful" to Gioia is meaningful to other poets.

For such poets as Fred Chappell, I think, it is not. Chappell offers an alternative vision of the poet in such a society, one more accurately portrayed in *Castle Tzingal* than in any other of Chappell's works, poetry or fiction. Chappell's poet in the book, Marco, represents an orientation to poetry antithetical to the view of poetry and its importance to society espoused by Gioia, who concludes that for businessmen–poets, "working in

---

4. Dana Gioia, "Can Poetry Matter?" *Atlantic,* CCLXVII (May, 1991), 94.

5. Dana Gioia, "Poetry and Business," in *Poetry After Modernism,* ed. Robert McDowell (Brownsville, Ore.), 126, 131, hereinafter cited parenthetically with page numbers in the text.

nonliterary careers taught them a lesson too few American writers learn—that poetry is only one part of life, that there are some things more important than writing poetry" ("Poetry and Business," 132). For Marco, of course, there is nothing other than poetry, even though he is King Reynal's nephew and might have certain social privileges denied others of lower social standing. Nonetheless, for Marco, poetry is the ultimate form of truth, requiring of everyone—not just poets—the transcendent imaginings Shelley wrote about that would inevitably undermine the treachery and deceit abounding in Tzingal. Characters in *Castle Tzingal,* like people around us in our daily lives, are aligned in terms of their ability to think alternatively; what's more, they form, as it were, a hierarchy of political types, some better suited to the world as it is and others, like Marco, better suited to the world as it should or could be.

Marco, a disembodied voice in *Tzingal,* is poetry in that world. Even though he is decapitated and subsequently banished to the bowels of King Tzingal's castle, poetry hauntingly lives on through his voice, which threatens but also transcends a certain social order, because it offers an alternative vision of the world. Chappell seems to be saying that even in an age when the poet's voice has been silenced by the power of political and economic authority, a certain rebellious spirit remains. As a result, some do hear the poet's song, detached as it might be from the singer. Not surprisingly, though, the song they hear requires interpretation, and each listener interprets the song differently, personally, permitting Chappell to comment as well on perception and the reliability of narrative.

To create such a world and to comment as such on narrative in that world, Chappell relies on the power of allegory to give readers the sense that the events of the drama are at a distance from events in our world. And in so doing, Chappell offers answers to two critical questions that we must consider now more than ever: What is that world (and our own) like if in it the poet has been silenced? And what circumstances in that world (and our own) require the poet's resurrection?

Distancing the Text: "His Unanswerable Duty to Sing . . . "

Part of Chappell's success in *Midquest* comes from the methods he employs in creating setting and character. Others have spent considerable energy describing and praising the Appalachian backdrop of Chappell's poetry. Yet most of those readers are cultural outsiders, like myself, who cannot measure the accuracy of Chappell's description and who must therefore accept the setting and the characterizations a priori, surmising that much of what Chappell offers is exaggeration and hyperbole. In *Midquest* and most other works successfully employing those techniques, the reader does not know otherwise or in any case cannot judge the falseness of what's being told, except after being duped, at some point, into believing the narrator. After all, the cultural outsider is effectively distanced from the event of the poem or story or tale and is thus forced to become a reader summoned to the text by the author rather than a reader who can sit in judgment of the author's truthfulness.

Though the setting of *Tzingal* is quite different from the setting of *Midquest,* the effect on the reader is much the same. By placing the events at Castle Tzingal at an historical distance from the reader, the reader is again in the role of cultural outsider. Knowledge that the reader can bring to the text—in an activity that must occur if reading is to take place at all—is of events *similar* to the ones Chappell describes, not of the events themselves. Hence, the reader cannot judge the truthfulness of those events. This distancing requires us to see the poem in terms of likenesses and understand the poem in its relationship to similar events we have known. In effect, Chappell offers a narrative on narrative; the disembodied voice tells a tale interpreted differently by each of the central figures in the drama, underscoring the difficulty of reading Chappell's poem. As readers, we are forced to generalize from these interpretations, accepting not the truth of individual perceptions but the validity of perception that seems to lie in the multiplicity of interpretation and narration.

More specifically, poets in the world of Tzingal are treated no differently, in the final analysis, than poets in the world of McDowell and Gioia: in both, poets have been summarily dismissed. Granted, the poet experiences some feelings of prestige among certain groups but not among those who enable royalty payments, for instance. Poets, to paraphrase Gioia's catchy comparison, are like priests in a community of agnostics. Chappell portrays the kingdom of Tzingal as a past world where the poet has been banished forcibly from society. Through the ages, we have known such places. Plato banned poets altogether from the Republic, for instance. But more recently we have witnessed yet another kind of banishment, through book burnings and book bannings. Still, there is a surer and more damnable form of death than either of those, one that Marco shares with many poets today: if poets practice their art at all, they do so under certain constraints. Many have taken up the utilitarian task of writing to be understood by a wider range of people than poetry ever attracted, as if by doing so and becoming more popular, poetry will be appreciated by greater numbers of readers. But at what cost? Clearly, the status of poets in Tzingal and in our world has made it impossible for them in any socially acceptable way to influence the affairs of state or how those affairs might be perceived. No one has adequately portrayed the world as it must be without the poet's influence as forcefully as has Chappell in *Castle Tzingal*.

"This Castle Tzingal," writes the Envoy to his King, "is not well" (13). A "dark infection / Shadows" all activities, both of state and in the personal lives of the castle's inhabitants. Deceit is at the center of the world, since "all knowledge becomes of use" (2). In light of Chappell's portrayal of this world, the following reading of *Tzingal* is an effort to construe Chappell's position on the poet's role in society, as an influence on both those living in Castle Tzingal and those living in America during the last two decades of the twentieth century.

A Range of Characters:
"I have prepared to journey where degrading insult / Cannot reach"

One possible view of the modern allegory is that it offers at least two narratives. Although the events of the narratives may take place simultaneously, they are perceived as two different stories that depend for their existence on our views of the characters and whether we perceive them, ultimately, as reliable narrators. We might trace the development of Chappell's dual narrative in three characters who seem to represent the range of perceptions possible in Tzingal.

On the one extreme of characters inhabiting this world is the manmade homunculus, Tweak. As a result of what must be called genetic experimentation, which could have made him into anything the inventor wanted, Tweak represents the prototypical inhabitant of Castle Tzingal. A product of his culture, Tweak sees his entire worth as his ability to deceive: "I'm useful to the State, usefuller / Maybe than a general or diplomat. / I may find out a secret to forestall a war / Or bear a plan that threatens our defeat'' (2). Tweak, like others in Tzingal, ''could tell you stories.'' But under the guise of loyalty, he insists one thing he later betrays: ''I won't''

> —Ah no, I can't be bribed to speak. Whatever
> Could you bribe me with?
> The things I dream of are forever
> Beyond my reach, sunk deep in earth
> Or at a human height.
> . . . .
> It's a rarified temptation
> Could smudge my honesty,
> And as for what *you* offer . . .
>> Well, we'll see. (2–3)

Tweak possesses characteristics most valued by the King. Those very traits, however, will make complete loyalty impossible for Tweak, even if the homunculus was made in the likeness of his king.

In "Tweak to Petrus," the dialogue with King Reynal's envoy leading to Tweak's betrayal of King Tzingal continues:

> So. You're back again.
> Do you bear a more imaginative bribe
> Than that you offered when
> You first approached me? (25)

We find out the Envoy's new bribe—a duchy, to which Tweak responds: "There's a thought might cause my fealty to slip." Tweak puns that he's "*mercurial*," since the "Astrologer laid perhaps too much quicksilver" in the homunculus's birth. In any event, this bribe leads Tweak to reveal the truth about Marco.

> Marco is dead. That is, he's mostly dead.
> But a part of him still lives in pain and horror.
> King Tzingal conceived a jealousy of the poet;
> Gave orders for his murder.
> And then with his own hand chopped off his head.
> He ordered my father Astrologer to do it

With a burning poison, but reserved the harder
Pleasure for his own royal sword.

He fancied, you see, that Marco and the Queen . . .
Well, you need no pictures drawn. (25)

Tweak's betrayal not only thickens the plot, it also advances the narrative as the reader confronts the image of King Tzingal offered by a member of Tzingal's inner sanctum: "King Tzingal never inquires for proof. He's mad / You know. His body is a cage, his mind a beast / Harried by phantasms of guilt."

Ironically, the poet's "severed head still lives. And sees. And hears. / And feels. And knows. / And may survive for years and years, / Could live through unaccountable centuries." Like today's poets who seem invisible though determined to write as their imaginings (rather than their sense of "potential" audience) demand, "the severed head *still sings*." Tweak offers a moment of insight:

He planned to kill the poet but not the man.
And now it seems the poet may persist
Though all his sweet humanity is gone. (26)

Those who would kill the poet to nurture an audience are much like Tweak, betraying an earlier loyalty for material gain or simply elevating a desire "to succeed in [a] meaningful way," to quote Gioia, above the poet's more important business. After all, America and Tzingal have at least one thing in common: the shrewd succeed—and survive—as does Tweak. Like the poet-turned-businessman, Tweak has "no love of being loved; a minim man / Prefers to flourish by means of fear, / To cast beyond his stature giant shade" (2).

The Queen, on the other extreme, seems Tweak's foil. She actively seeks love in Tzingal, even if not the love of her husband, the King. Rather, Queen Frynna has come to love the poet Marco and longs for his return. She seems to have insight into the workings of a higher consciousness and seems capable of the kinds of imaginings that run counter to the way others in Tzingal perceive the world. She describes herself as "a captive lullabye in a land / Of battlesong" and Tzingal as a place where "no man walks; /

But sneaks or stamps or stalks. / And no one tells a tale but the telltale. / And no one thrives here but the mad / Or guilty" (5).

In "Queen Frynna Waking," the Queen awakens from "bad dreams," but dreams she has grown accustomed to. She is uncertain of the demarcation between dream and waking, between vision and real-life experience, having entered the Shelleyan realm of "divine imaginings." These dreams, she says, "bring no message I can piece to sense" (18), though the same dreams are interpreted differently by each character who has them. In this world of authoritative and controlled thought patterns, the Queen describes herself as "King Tzingal's half-mad wife." Presumably, because of her deep imaginings and sensitivity, she is deemed mad. She exists outside the realm of reality and acceptable perception as dictated by the state, as must anyone in late twentieth-century America who writes without concern for material success. Thus she is uncertain: "I do not trust myself / I cannot trust my dream." The dream fails in the poet's absence, and transcendent perceptions of a better world must likewise be abandoned. In "Queen Frynna Dreaming," she says of her lost vision:

My happy childhood is a little gray mouse
That hides away beneath the eaves
Where all these terrors hungry and mean
Cannot climb to harm his cunning little house. (32)

And as she slowly learns to interpret these visions, she concludes, to her personal demise, "I do not want this knowledge that comes to me / In song-torn sleep, in weeping dream" (33). Understanding these dreams, as she does in "Queen and Handmaid," does not offer solace or peace, because she realizes she cannot call upon this knowledge for help: "I think I understand, / And have a thing, a little thing, in mind" (37)—suicide.

Unlike the Queen and Tweak, who represent two extremes in Tzingal, the Admiral is portrayed as a transitional character in the process of reevaluating his contributions to the state and its survival. The Admiral remembers bravery at sea in brutal defense of Tzingal: "How in the rigging we'd freeze / To stone amid the biting snow / Until the bosun warmed us with the cat" (7). Now retired, the Admiral has no such experiences. Instead, he sits in drydock and counts his medals.

I pull my final duty: to bore
The queen and court and visiting ambassador
With tales of seafights long forgotten. (7)

In truth, what he does is provide a service: "I distract at table while the King / Observes, and deliberates on war." Yet the Admiral has become wise about the world of Tzingal, wise enough to offer warnings to the young and to suffer sleeplessness because of his past sins, where he sees "far-drowned sailors" and hears their "groans, / Tears, and prayers flying in the dark." But he is a man tormented by his past, by living in accord with the laws of the land.

I cannot sleep for all the tears,
For all the cries, of my drowned men.
I picture the foamsprent wave, how it receives
The tumbling snow and drives,
Drives against a lonesome reef
Its full freight of grief.
And I cannot sleep.
And the wind cannot stop. (8)

Not only does the poet represent the transcendent self, but the poet also sings so universally that everyone who hears the song in their dreams—Browning's "action in man," the only place where such imaginings can take place in Tzingal—finds its relevance to their lives. Clearly, the poet stands in contrast to those described by Queen Frynna. Married to "an iron and fruitless man," she confesses in monologue her love for Marco and his songs:

All I'd unremembered I remembered when
You struck the harp and sang the old old ballad.
Unbearable sweetness overcame my head
And heart. I gnawed my inner lip,
Recalling the voice of my gentle mother
When your voice lifted up. (5)

Marco fans the Queen's feelings, and through his greater sensibility he also causes her to contemplate images of her childhood and of her mother. The poet brings her out of her protective forgetfulness. No doubt, then, in the comparison between the poet and the mother, Chappell hoped to suggest something compelling about true poetic sensibility in an age of "drunken ambitions" and "nightmare designs" (5). In doing so, Chappell places the world of Castle Tzingal in sharp contrast with the world of the poet. Marco's effect on Frynna can be measured by her vivid recollection of a better time: "There is a child, a sunny child, / Who dances within my breast and combs / Her sunny hair and coddles a painted mammet." In the poet's absence from Tzingal, however, this child must remain silent, as she says, denying her own sensibility. She concludes, "I shall not bide here ever. / The poppy chalice shall ease my sorrow, / Or the river." Though the poet offers such balm, "No one here / Loves fair word or silken hand" (5). Imaginings of this world are limited to "dreams of knives / or the labyrinthine whispers that assail, / Asterve my wits." She laments,

All this world hates the good,
And I'm afraid that I
Will come to be of these and lose
My soul, dishonor my noble blood. (6)

Queen Frynna recognizes a higher authority measured against which her obedience to the state of Tzingal is trivial.

The Queen is not alone in this recognition. Dreams and the higher consciousness they bring about require the Admiral to reconsider his allegiance. In fact, the Admiral exchanges his obedience to the state for an obedience to a higher authority, living as the poet would require—under the aspect of eternity rather than under the aspect of temporality, bound by time and the senses. Dreams take him away, outside the limits of his body, and demand of him greater understanding of suffering humanity and his role in its plight.

As with Tweak and the Queen, Chappell allows us to trace from poem to poem the Admiral's growing recognition of the harm he has caused to others. In "The Admiral Ponders His Sleep," we see the influence of the poet's disembodied voice, how it invades even his sleep:

Last night the worst.
Never more chilling, never more clear
Have the voices of my foundered sailors

Sounded in my dreaming ear.
Am I cursed
Forever to hear them dying in my sleep?
Am I condemned to watch their falling falling
Down through the gray deep? (20)

Now that old age has descended on him, he is forced to contemplate, upon hearing the poet's song and noting it in his dream, what he has done with his life. He believes the dead sailors sing the poet's song, forcing us to acknowledge Chappell's skillful treatment of narrative, a treatment fully consistent with poststructural approaches to reading and perception. Because the Admiral can only interpret what he dreams in light of his experiences, and since Marco's song is universally relevant, the Admiral receives Marco's song as being that of deceased sailors: "'I have a sorrow that no tear can cool . . ./ I find the parts that never make a whole.'" The Admiral comments that this is "strange song for brave tars to lift / After death has enlisted them all," believing that the song is specifically directed toward him and his particular circumstances. Nonetheless, he admits that he has changed, become more poetic in sensibility, forgotten "how to be a man." He has relinquished the masculine consciousness that dominates thought in Tzingal and is nowhere better demonstrated than in the very prototype of Tzingalian behavior, in the actions of Tweak. The Admiral recognizes that "the dream-torn nights" have undone the effects of Tzingal and that he shall "receive no grace . . . , / No forgiveness" (20–21). This because "everything I did was in the line of duty." All along, what has been required is that he transcend duty to the state, as the poet does and as the Queen remembers once doing. And if no relief can be found during life, the Admiral pledges, "That too I can amend, / If the nights bring no release, / With my own hand" (21).

Narrative on Narrative: Chappell and Poststructuralism

Castle Tzingal is, in many ways, a book about knowledge, how it is gained and how it is used. There is the common knowledge of the world, the kind of knowledge a poet is not privy to and perhaps not interested in, what Tweak describes as "to know who knows, and how he knows, and why" (1).

But there is still a higher knowledge in this world, the one that comes to us in dream or vision; through these alternative ways of knowing, all truth is revealed in this sequence of poems.

Strikingly, this truth is relative. Chappell's decision to write a series of dramatic monologues signals the relativity of possible interpretations of experience. By relying on the individual mind in isolation, giving away its orientation through its very language, Chappell has knowingly or unknowingly opened an area of concern that is strikingly postmodern in its emphases.

Throughout the drama, Chappell has placed Marco's songs at equal intervals. The first, roughly a third of the way into the book and the drama's seventh poem, reflects Chappell's effort to provide adequate background so that readers might understand enough of the situation to benefit from hearing the disembodied voice of the poet. That song is followed by seven monologues commenting upon the song. To deepen the plot further, Chappell then interjects "Second Song for Disembodied Voice." The next seven poems comment on or result from the second song. And the final Epilogue is yet a third song sung by the disembodied Marco.

Chappell knows, however, that narrative is subjective in nature and that each interpretation of each song will reflect the idiosyncratic concerns of the interpreter. Clearly, some characters are so weak in consciousness that they will not hear the song at all. In "Astrologer and Page," we find that the Page had, as he says, "some troublous dream I can't remember" (22). The Astrologer denies the song altogether: "I heard the wind make music over crenellated stone; / Bad dreams wrought cries from the Admiral and Queen" (23). The inability of such characters to acknowledge the song at all might be seen as an indication of how totally absorbed they are in the limited perceptions dictated to them by rationality and by the state. They are simply obedient. And to those knowledgeable about affairs of the state, like Tweak, "This was of course a song not counted on" (26). In "Second Song for Disembodied Voice," Marco describes himself as "memory that, though silenced, / Will never cease" (30). He wonders, as Chappell would also have us wonder of contemporary poets, "Why have they killed the poet but preserved / His unanswerable duty to sing?" (30).

Marco sings universal truth and in so doing sings to the idiosyncratic concerns of all who hear him. To the Queen, Marco tells the truth of his imprisonment. In "Queen Frynna Dreaming," she is concerned with the song and who sings it, concluding "that he is brave / Beyond his death I must not disbelieve," thus granting to Marco courage that is not perhaps suited to his situation. Her solution is to join Marco in her "forever dream" (33). Similarly, the Admiral interprets Marco's song in light of his experiences at sea and his responsibility for the death of many young sailors. Through Marco's song, "the voices of my foundered sailors / Sounded in my dreaming ear" (20). He continues:

Old age is upon me, and without its honor.
How shall I bear
Each night the ripping shrouds, the blood,
The youthful shrieks and cannon-sundered air
Without stark fear? (20)

These dreams lead the Admiral to acknowledge his past mistakes committed in the line of duty to the state: "To the very last / I carried out my battle plan. / All commanding officers must do the same." Still he wonders, "*But what do the other commanders dream?*" (21). His dreams set him apart from the rest.

By permitting his characters to have individual reactions to Marco's songs, interpreting their dreams in the only way they can, and by bringing their past experiences to bear on Marco's language, Chappell accomplishes three tasks in his narrative on narrative. First, he suggests a belief, contrary to the positions of McDowell and Gioia, in the universality of poetry and in the poet's obligation to sing the transcendent and timeless song of his imaginings. Second, Chappell seems to assert that the poet must imagine deeply, so that others who hear the poet's song can also imagine intensely, an act of consciousness required for us to live freely in the world and contemplate yet a better way to live. And finally, Chappell shows that narrative is subjective. As Terry Eagleton has said about poststructuralism: "It is difficult to know what a sign 'originally' means, what its 'original' context was: we simply encounter it in many different situations, and although it must maintain a certain consistency across those situations in order to be an identifiable sign at all, because its context is always different it is never *absolutely* the same, never quite identical with itself."[6]

6. Terry Eagleton, *Literary Theory: An Introduction* (Minneapolis, 1983), 129.

The key word here is "context." We can never know the author's intention. We can at best surmise what the author intends based upon the context within which we read a work. The same must be said of narrative inside *Castle Tzingal*. Each person who hears Marco's song creates a context for understanding that is unique to the listener. That Chappell understands how readers generate contexts from their personal lives to interpret a text seems fundamental to this work and more so than to his other works, fictional or poetic.

In the end, we must acknowledge that *Castle Tzingal* has been wrongly neglected these past eight years, overshadowed perhaps by the tremendous success of *Midquest*. But in the face of demands by other poets that we turn our attention toward developing a wider audience, Chappell courageously insists on the necessity for poets to retain their vision, to seek the higher knowledge that comes through intense imaginings, and to lead those who will follow poets to those same kinds of perceptions. Unlike many others, Chappell has not given up on his vision and has not obeyed the call to duty issued by those around him. Chappell offers instead a consistent view of the poet as Shelleyan "divine legislator" and stands unobtrusively against those who would diminish the role of poetry in a dark age of universal misunderstanding and individual prejudice.

The Cultivated Mind: The Georgic Center of Fred Chappell's Poetry

DON JOHNSON

In his introduction to *The Fred Chappell Reader,* Dabney Stuart notes what is probably the most remarkable aspect of Chappell's work—the division between the rural and the intellectual impulses, the homely and the worldly visions. Stuart himself admits the "basic oversimplification" of this observation (xix). Nevertheless, any reader must acknowledge Chappell's thorough grounding in the hills of his native North Carolina in such poems as "February" from *The World Between the Eyes,* his first collection published in 1971. "February" describes in graphic detail the speaker's memories of rural hog butchering. But in the same volume, Chappell declares his allegiance to the world of letters in a eulogy to the English poet W. H. Auden.

Even a cursory examination of Chappell's succeeding volumes, from *Midquest* through the recently published *First and Last Words,* reveals that Chappell's dual role as "Old Fred," the Carolina mountain boy, and Professor Chappell, the cosmopolitan man of letters, has been maintained. I would like to make a case, however, for the perception of these roles as complementary rather than oppositional. Each one feeds into, nourishes, the other. Stuart hints at this reconciliation in his remarkably comprehensive introduction but because of the demands and limitations of his task, chooses not to develop it. He quotes an essay in which Chappell praises Virgil's *Georgics* and draws several parallels between the life of the farmer and that of the poet. Farming, says Chappell, "is the one life besides poetry and natural philosophy that still touches an essential harmony of things."[1] I

1. Fred Chappell, "The Poet and the Plowman," *Chronicles,* X (July, 1986), 14.

would go further than Stuart's observation that Chappell's tribute to the farmer "could be, and I suspect is, about himself" (xx), and argue that Chappell consistently alludes to Virgil's *Georgics* and the bucolic life it depicts in order to forge an integrative vision that makes his own roles as farmer and professor/poet/philosopher compatible. Undoubtedly, both characters exist. As Stuart points out, *Midquest,* though it is more or less autobiographical, owes its structure and many of its themes to Dante. *Castle Tzingal* combines fairy and folk tale with the Orpheus myth and the gothic novel, and *Source* depends more upon Lucretius's *De Rerum Natura* than southern or mountain literary traditions (xvi–xx). *First and Last Words* (published after Stuart's essay) is a collection of prologues and epilogues written for works ranging from the Orestia trilogy to the gospels.

Throughout these pieces, Chappell reveals not merely a passing knowledge of the art he alludes to but a thorough understanding of them as well. In fact, the most outstanding feature of these poems is that they cut both ways. They are simultaneously allusive and interpretative, first requiring that the reader have some knowledge of the originals to ensure his appreciation of Chappell's deft handling of setting and theme, and then sending the reader back to those originals with the fresh interpretations that Chappell's prologues and epilogues provide. Like the best of what Dryden would have called "imitations," these poems demonstrate the universality and applicability of other literature and art (both ancient and modern) for the contemporary world. They also are invaluable in helping us further understand that literature and art.

Chappell's poetry, its urbanity and erudition notwithstanding, nevertheless remains firmly rooted in the homeplace soil of the southern Appalachian mountains. In "My Grandmother Washes Her Feet," Fred's grandmother reminds him of his hardscrabble heritage, a family tree that the speaker imagines as a "wind-stunted horseapple," and tells him that he'll never be anything but "second generation respectable":

But it's dirt you rose from, dirt you'll bury in.
Just about the time you'll think your blood
Is clean, here will come dirt in a natural shape
You never dreamed. It'll rise up saying, Fred,
Where's that mule you're supposed to march behind?
Where's your overalls and roll-your-owns?

Where's your Blue Tick hounds and Domineckers?
Not all the money in this world can wash true-poor
True rich. (12)

The grandmother admonishes him not to grow "away from what you are";
yet when she pulls the plug and the dirty water rushes down the drain, the
speaker imagines all his "Shadow Cousins," the forebears his grandmother
had described for him in her lecture on life, as clouding the water and
running down to be absorbed into the earth. He says they would be "effigies
of soil" and that he could "seek them out"

By clasping soil, forcing warm rude fingers
Into ancestral jelly my father wouldn't plow.
I strained to follow them, and never did.
I never had the grit to stir those guts.
I never had the guts to stir that earth. (13)

In his drive for respectability, Chappell gave up farming and pursued the
life of the mind, but his grandmother's admonition that his native soil would
insinuate itself into the boy's life during moments when he would least
expect it has proved to be prophetic. He cannot abandon this turning back
to the soil, which accounts for what some might consider the tension between the rural and the intellectual elements in Chappell's poetry. But this
tension evaporates when one considers that, despite the poet's denial of his
ability to till his native soil, Chappell has indeed continued to turn the
homeplace earth over and over—*in his mind.* An increasingly internal vision
has allowed him to "cultivate" his imagination and to sow it with seed
gleaned from all of Western literature. The word *cultivate* means both to
prepare soil in order to promote the growth of plants and to improve or
develop by study, exercise, and training. The word has its origins in the
Latin *colere,* which means to cherish. Through cultivation of his mind/
imagination, Chappell has rooted in his rich native soil the exotic flora of
Greece and Rome and the vigorous ancestral cuttings of England and the
rest of Europe. In the process, he has become an Appalachian embodiment
of the three ideal figures to emerge from the *Georgics,* Virgil's didactic agricultural poem:[2] the inquiring philosopher of Book II, who is contrasted

2. Virgil, *Georgics,* trans. Smith Palmer Bovie (Chicago, 1956), hereinafter cited parenthetically with page numbers in the text.

with the reverent, more intuitive, "retired" poet (both positive figures), and the old Corycian farmer of Book IV. In his Lucretian quest for knowledge of the way the world works, the first asks that

> the sweet-toned Muses,
> Whose symbols I raise up, inspired by love,
> Find me worthy, spread before my eyes
> The planets and the stars, the sun's eclipses,
> The moon's revolving labors, the earthquake's source;
> Reveal the hidden motions of the sea,
> That force the waters up and sink them down.
> Show why the winter suns race toward the Ocean,
> What holds in check the long-delaying nights. (II, 476–83)

If these secrets are to be withheld, the poet then asks that he be allowed to "relish the country, humbly revere / Streams that glide through glades, the woods, the rivers" (II, 482–83). The Corycian farmer from Book IV would be recognized as kin by any mountain farmer who had ever tried to wrestle a living from the tilled mountain acreage no one else would plow, since he cultivated "a patch of unclaimed land alloted to him, / Not suitable for pasture, crops or wine" (II, 125–26) but through diligence and careful husbandry made it prosper. Together, these three figures from the *Georgics* epitomize the values Virgil advocated throughout his poem: unrelenting toil, self-sufficiency, and reverence for and curiosity about nature.

The *Georgics* is one of Chappell's favorite pieces of literature. In the essay alluded to above, he argues for the poem's applicability to all our lives and its very special significance for the poet. In *First and Last Words,* he draws directly upon Virgil for his "Patience" (a prologue to the *Georgics*), and he has confided to me in casual conversation that he had considered having the matured Jess Kirkman labor on a translation of the *Georgics* while narrating the projected third volume of the Kirkman trilogy, which began with *I Am One of You Forever.* But even where Virgil's influence is not directly acknowledged, the spirit of the *Georgics* pervades Chappell's work. Few poems in the language are more sympathetic to the *Georgics'* spirit than "My Mother's Hard Row to Hoe" from *Midquest.* In response to queries about conditions on the farm where she grew up, the mother repeats seven times in the space of sixty-three lines that the world she knew was "just plain

hard," or "too grinding hard," or "flintrock hard," bringing to mind
Virgil's assertion from Book I that Jove "made the path / Of agriculture
rough, established arts / Of husbandry to sharpen wits, / Forbidding sloth to
settle on his soil" (II, 122–25). Yet Chappell's mother cannot wholly relin-
quish her ties to the land. In the final five lines of the poem, she recalls
pleasant associations: the "sweet and clean and promiseful" air of morning,
the song of a mourning dove, but as if to warn her interlocutor against the
possibility of romanticizing the experience, she categorically stifles the in-
flux of pleasant memories by the final variation of her stark refrain, "You've
got to understand how it was *hard*" (152).

In "Humility" (from *Source*), Chappell creates the archetypal bucolic
refuge and fully demonstrates that the farmer touches "an essential harmony
of things." Though the picture the poem paints is ideal, it is not pastoral
but Georgic, evolving out of the context of heavy physical labor, in contrast
to the leisurely pursuits of shepherds (the singing contests, the pursuit of
maidens, the discussions of the effects of unrequited love). Rural life is
difficult and unpredictable, though it carries the potential for deep satisfac-
tion. "Humility" describes a respite from gleaning when "the village behind
the graveyard tolls softly, begins / To glow with new-laid fires" (9), a pause
whose significance deepens only when one considers the back-breaking
labor that preceded it. But the apparent reality of Chappell's first three
stanzas is undercut in the fourth when he reveals that

> This is the country we return to when
> For a moment we forget ourselves,
> When we watch the sleeping kitten quiver
> After long play, or rain comes down warm. (9)

It is a memory (or perhaps even a wholly imagined experience) that washes
over and comforts us:

> Here we might choose to live always, here where
> Ugly rumors of ourselves do not reach,
> Where in the whisper-light of the kerosene lamp
> The deep Bible lies open like a turned-down bed. (9)

Despite physical details evocative of the senses, this poem offers a landscape
of the mind that invites the imaginer into security and warmth of almost

limitless expanse deriving from the final simile, which creates a literary hall of mirrors that invites frequent and prolonged musing.

No poem could be more firmly rooted in a rural setting than "Awakening to Music." Here the poet contrasts the hard realities of retrieving stray heifers in the sleet-laced dawns of winter, the diseases and hard births the animals endured, with the soft dreams to be had when every morning he leaned into the milk cow's flank, "the grandest magic helmet / breathing." He recalls

> her red belly
> rubbing my intimate right shoulder,
> and milk-squirt slicing through the foam
> like yard on yard of brocade piling up. (11)

The afflictions that the poet associates with livestock might remind one of Virgil's account of the devastating murrain of *Georgics III.* And Chappell's description of the errant heifer's "tossing her rag-curled / forehead, tossing the silky string / of lucid snot pearly from chin to knees" (10) is worthy of the praise Addison lavished upon Virgil when he commented that in the *Georgics,* the Latin poet "breaks the clods and tosses the dung about with an air of gracefulness."[3]

Yet "Awakening to Music" extends beyond the mere recounting of farm life and deepens to become Chappell's version of Keats's "Ode to a Nightingale." Through the half-dream generated in his drowsing against the flank of the milk cow, Chappell envisions an ideal world, an Edenic garden of "warm rain on heart-shaped leaves, and dozing orchids," which is much more vivid than the world he regularly inhabits. In this visionary world, he "came to the pulsing green fountain where music is born," presumably the fountain of the muses. When the poet says,

> And all those years I went clothed in this sleep,
> odor and warmth
> of cows blanketed about my head (11)

---

3. Joseph Addison, *The Works of Joseph Addison,* ed. G. W. Greene (Philadelphia, 1868).

we must assume that he refers to the visionary sleep associated with the lush garden that colored his young life even when he was not directly stimulated by the physical presence of the cow's flank.

Keats's poem ends with the speaker's being made doubly aware of his ties to earthly reality after his experience with the song of the nightingale. Returning from his union with the bird, Keats asks, "Was it a vision or a waking dream? / Fled is that music. Do I wake or sleep?"[4] His questions are not so much attempts at understanding the experience he has just had as they are inquiries about the nature of the reality he has returned to. Is this world he will now experience less vivid than the one he has just left? Like Keats, Chappell ends his poem with questions about his vision:

> How would I get it back? Go to blood
> again, sleep the light green sleep?
> How can I wake, not waking to music? (11)

But Chappell's questions are more poignant than Keats's "Was it a vision or a waking dream?" or "Do I wake or sleep?" Chappell's "How would I get it back?" seems to imply the probability of returning to that visionary world, but his middle question posits a return to a state of near innocence as a prerequisite for recapturing the visionary moment. Consequently, when the final question is asked, the reader is inclined to answer that the speaker cannot awaken, in the sense that he "woke" to an awareness of the REAL in his youth. The best one might hope for would be a memory of having had that vision, in effect a Wordsworthian resolution to the Keatsian dilemma.

The fact that Chappell denies the easy way out is indicative both of his firm rooting in native soil and his absorption of larger literary traditions. There is no easy primitivism here, no celebration of the noble mountaineer living in ignorance and grace. One might be temporarily lulled into a primitivist stance by the beginning of "Patience: a prologue to *The Georgics*" from *First and Last Words:*

> An early summer evening.
>   The broad homophony
> Of the hive of stars immerses the dark porches where

---

4. John Keats, *The Letters of John Keats, 1814–1821,* ed. Hyder E. Rollins, 2 vols. (Cambridge, Mass., 1958).

The farmers muse. It seems that all the earth there is
Has been taken by the plow, and the hedgy boundaries
Of orchards encroach upon the sea, all the sea
There is, the planet lapped in grateful breathing fields:
Here the labor is, here the finished work. (9)

As a tribute to Chappell's ingenuity and the universality of his vision, Jim Wayne Miller notes that the reader might well place this scene in some Appalachian valley.[5] Indeed, it presents the farmer's ideal of a wholly cultivated earth, a landscape that his unrelenting toil has finally subdued:

The farmers and their animals have sculpted the world
To a shape like some smooth monumental family group,
The father mountains and the mother clouds, their progeny meadows
Stationed about them, as if posing for a photograph
To be taken from a silver orbiter spaceship by beings
Like angelic horses, who return to their home world
With pleasant report: *Leave Earth alone, it is at peace.* (9)

The poem's second section bursts this bubble, however, and exposes its opening as an unrealizable ideal envisaged by the contemplative farmer. "Always the Poet knew it wasn't that way" (9), Chappell tells us. Recalling Virgil's evocation of a world constantly on the brink of chaos owing to internal broils, foreign wars, and the individual's susceptibility to the domination of the passions, Chappell offers a disturbing testament to the precariousness of civilization: "the plow" is "disused unhonored, the farmer conscripted and his scythe / Straitly misshapen to make a cruel sword" (9). The world is imbrued in war. The shepherd, herdsman, and plowman are murdered.

But like Virgil, Chappell takes refuge in the enduring appeal of the bucolic life, which must survive if humankind is to survive. Disruption and disaster plague the world. Soldiers die because of patriotism and greed, or they return home to lord it over the farmers whose humdrum lives pale in comparison to the glorious exploits of the military. But some of these glam-

---

5. Jim Wayne Miller, Review of Fred Chappell's *First and Last Words,* in *Now and Then,* VI (March, 1989), 61.

orous soldiers ultimately become farmers. Others marry the farmers' daughters, and their sons in turn become plowmen, so that the warrior is ultimately subdued by the plodding rustic. As Keats pointed out in a letter to John Taylor, "Agriculture is the tamer of men—the steam from the earth is like drinking Mother's milk—it enervates their natures" (September 5, 1819). Though cataclysmic changes occur, farm life abides, whether in the Italian countryside or in the Appalachian mountains:

> Sundown still draws the chickens to their purring roost,
> The cow to the milking stall, the farmer to his porch to watch
> Whether the soaring constellations promise rain. (10)

Chappell ends where Virgil begins, with weather signs, with the farmer trying to fix himself and control his destiny as fully as possible in a rapidly turning world. He knows that anything approaching total control will forever elude him, but even minimal control can come only through hard labor and passionate attention to the natural world.

Fred Chappell's productivity over the past two decades provides ample evidence for his having taken to heart Virgil's injunction that "*Labor vincit omnia*"; in any case, throughout his works, passionate attention to natural detail is evident. His grandmother's wisdom nothwithstanding, it seems that Chappell has managed to wash the dirt from under his fingernails, but the intellectual row that he has taken to hoe is as difficult and challenging as the rocky soil of any mountain homeplace, and he has mixed the "ancestral jelly" his father "wouldn't plow" with the fertile soils of ancient cultures.

Images drawn from the life of the soil dominate Chappell's poetry. "An Old Woman Reading the Book of Job" and "Scarecrow Colloquy" (an epilogue to the Gospels) are, respectively, the first and last *poems* in *First and Last Words*. Both are set in rural surroundings, although they draw more from a biblical matrix than a classical one. But even though Virgil's hand is not immediately apparent, the grudgingly hopeful realism of his agricultural didactic is not incompatible with Chappell's message here.

It would be foolhardy to argue that the *Georgics* is *the* single most important influence on the poetry of Fred Chappell. Nonetheless, I do feel strongly that the poem's role in Chappell's critical background is difficult to overestimate and that it is essential in understanding the mutual dependence of the two seemingly disparate identities that manifest themselves throughout his work. In his essay on the *Georgics,* Chappell points out that although "the poem is acceptably realistic . . . Virgil is also at pains to show that he stands at some distance from his subject, that his poem is a bookish poem."[6] The assertion applies with equal validity to Chappell's own work. But just as Virgil's realism and "bookishness" reinforce each other, so too do Chappell's sophistication and earthiness. In his mind and imagination, cultivation is taken to its highest level.

6. Fred Chappell, *The Fred Chappell Reader* (New York, 1987), 12.

Chappell's Continuities:
First and Last Words

PETER MAKUCK

I had learned, maybe without really knowing, that not even the steadfast mountains themselves were safe and unmoving, that the foundations of the earth were shaken and the connections between the stars become frail as a cobweb.

—*I Am One of You Forever*

Since his tetralogy on the elements appeared under one cover as *Midquest* in 1981, Fred Chappell has published *Castle Tzingal* (1984), *Source* (1985), and *First and Last Words* (1989), all of which are linked, if not by voice, then by an abiding concern with Ultimates, with faith and art, love and war. *Midquest* is an impressive compendium of forms and voices—poems that sing and laugh, paint and ponder, rhetorically expansive poems that tell stories and have a keen interest in the character and language of vivid mountain folk. Chappell's diction in the tetralogy ranges from pure lyricism to scatology, sometimes even within the same verse sentence, whereas the range in subsequent books is narrower—the difference, say, between symphonic and chamber music. Nonetheless, from *Midquest* to *First and Last Words*, continuities exist.

Midquest, bookish but funny too, like the novels of Saul Bellow, is seriously concerned with the question of meaning. In one poem, Ole Fred says, "Everything means something/Even if it's Nothing" (171). In another, he wonders about death: "Not death, no, there is no/Death, only a deeper dreaming" (147). Elsewhere he describes passion or "bloodfire" as "the disease/necessary to know God" (91). In yet another poem, he asks, "but where/shall I sit when once this flesh is spirit?" (73). In one of the love poems to Susan, the prospect of loss threatens the speaker's faith in reunion beyond death, but at first his faith seems strong. *"We shall meet again on that other shore,"* he thinks, then plays with the phrase, "We shall meet again, we shall meet/When now touchless my hand on your breast is swimming" (51). The key word is "now"—the eternal now, which is an important dimension in Chappell's work but one that need not preclude the possibility of postmortem survival ("I'd like to believe anything is possible" [6]) or the necessity of further quest.

Though Chappell has written prayer poems and the vocabulary of Christian belief proliferates in both his early and later work ("resurrection," "grace," "chrisom," "baptism," "Christ," "Lord," "Eden," "Genesis," "temptation," "Paradise," "annunciation," "absolution," "faith," "mortal sin," "angels," "redeem," and so on), the poet's belief is not narrow or orthodox. In "Birthday 35: Diary Entry," he writes:

I'd sleep in the eiderdown of the True Believer
And never nightmare about Either/Or

If I had a different person in my head.
But this gnawing worm shows that I'm not dead.

Therefore: either I live with doubt
Or get out. (5)

Other poems in *Midquest* also make us realize that Ole Fred will not rest complacently in the fundamental comfort of a Personal Savior, for a realistic look at the human predicament (at "photos of Hitler and the cordwood dead" [65], at "snail-white corpses/bloating the Mekong and Hudson" [48]) shortcircuits belief in a personal loving God. Further, Chappell's imagination is haunted by emptiness and nothingness, the latter word recurring frequently in his work. In "Hallowind," a rich and wonderful dialogue poem about writing that features Ole Fred, Reynolds Price, and Susan, the personified and annihilating elements have the last words:

     The Rain (to The Wind)
What say we work us up some brio
And drown this silly wayward trio?
My favorite line is "Ex Nihilo."

The Wind

Leave them in peace, if peace there is
For their clamorous little species;
Let them relish their flimsy wishes.
Tomorrow and tomorrow we
Advance against them frightfully.
This night at least they have their say
Together; the force of Time
Upon their arts, upon slant rhyme
And paragraph, delays for them.
It's soon enough that we dissolve
Their names to dust, unmoving move
Against their animal powers to love
And weep and fear. (138–39)

Love is a central value in Chappell's poetry, but whether love is eternal remains to be seen. In *Midquest,* perhaps the poet often ponders the question of immortality because he so intently watches the heavens with a chilly knowledge of late twentieth-century astronomy, with a knowledge of *"vacant interlunar spaces"* (69). Chappell's skymaps do not necessarily indicate the direction of transcendence; they point to purity, wonder, mystery, as well as nothingness; they sometimes act as psychological mirrors of human projections, register positive and negative valences in the observer. At the end of Faulkner's *Sanctuary,* Horace Benbow, emotionally battered from having witnessed so much human savagery, looks on the beautiful April delta coming back to blossom and says: "You'd almost think there was some purpose to it." In the work of Fred Chappell, the night sky is a constant, a given, as is the alternately mocking and consoling delta landscape in Faulkner, the moody sea in Conrad, the eyelike sun in Flannery O'Connor, and the enigmatic heath in Hardy. In *Midquest,* we have numerous references to stars, comets, constellations, planets, pulsars: "the stars / Splash down in the filth of morning newspapers" (4); "the Pleiades / Streaked in my head like silver fleas" (16); "wrinkling stars in rings" (46); "mole-runs of starlight" (46); "our savage reverend assault upon the stars" (102); "the stark beginning where the first stars burned" (77); "the lancet / glance of the star" (69); "firepoint / constellations" (183); "the black stars whirling / collapsed to a nervous cinder" (185); "stillness like a star of ice"

(137); "love that moves the sun and other stars" (187). A typical way Chappell uses stars can be seen in the following:

> The pure spirits stand among monsters and heroes,
> Orion, Hercules, Cassiopeia,
> And Draco and the Big and Little Bear.
> And we this hour, 28 May 1971,
> Are Gemini:
> > the Twins, each each and the other
> Like the two-colored candleflame.
>
> *Torn sheet of light sizzles in the mirror:*
>
> The seeds, ignis semina, of fire
> Put forth in me their rootlets, the tree of fire
> Begins to shape itself. (56)

The method involves correspondences and analogies—ways of exploring and mapping relationships, both galactic and personal.

Chappell also pursues this method in *Source,* where again we have a profusion of starlit poems: a "powder of stars," "a granary of stars," "savage stars," "star-tangled trees," "discolored stars," "a nebula of accident," and other celestial imagery. The negative element of dread that results from contemplating the black emptiness of outer space appears in "Windows," where Chappell identifies "the gray light" that "steals across the unforgiving vacancy, / the tired source of death is that impervious space / between galaxies" (50). In the face of death and those terrible spaces between the stars, "We huddle into ourselves. Beaten by / obscure longings. . . . And the prayed-for transformation / remains stone" (50). The most positive and the loveliest stellar metaphor in *Source,* however, comes in the first lines of "Latencies":

> First point of light and then another: the stars
> come out, bright fishnet lifting from darkness those broken
> many heroes we read the mind with. (25)

In this poem, the starry configurations of myth point to latent possibilities of Time, both positive and negative. A trout troubling the river's surface "reinstates the dawn" and is "a latent prayer." A woman standing by a window reminds the speaker of a "decade of obliterate dreams," of regretted waste that causes him to say: "The window is a latent religion." But there is also a negative latency:

> Or consider the young man fishing the river. Now he
> has gone to be a soldier, he has become
> a latent garden of terrible American Beauty roses
> which only the enemy bullets can make manifest. (25)

Chappell's meditations on the heavens also suggest vacant and impervious spaces in the soul and recall both Pascal's God-bringing meditations on "les espaces infinis" and the God-less universe of Stephen Hawking (*A Brief History of Time*) or of Joseph Wood Krutch (*The Modern Temper*). What is important to Chappell, however, is that we create our own god, with either capital or lowercase. "I been sentenced doncha know to create reality / by the sweat of my brow, Bible sez so" (*Midquest*, 73). Here and elsewhere in Chappell, we have a sense of the poet as Job and are reminded of Santayana's famous statement that poetry is "religion which is no longer believed."

Castle Tzingal is in one sense an anomaly among Chappell's books in that it lacks a celestial backdrop. Indeed, *Tzingal* is an indoor, low-ceilinged narrative, the castle and most of its inhabitants locked in a godless winter of discontent, with no bucolic memory except perhaps a brief one that lives in the voice of the murdered poet:

> I'd make my song like the wind-tossed willow tree,
> Promiseful-green and all a-lilt . . .
> With sun-spangle from a pleachy sky . . .
> . . . .
> But Arcady is fled and gone
> Until I rend the guilty sleep
> Of Castle Tzingal and, like the sun,
> Wither this black scheming up.
> I am no more alive,
> And all my murderers thrive. (16)

In this volume, appearing between *Source* and *First and Last Words* (both books in which he shows himself highly successful as well at short poems, poems of less than a page), Chappell once again interests himself in character and voice to tell, in dramatic monologue and soliloquy, the grim story of Castle Tzingal, a tale of paranoia, jealousy, murder, and the persistence of poetry. Though very different, *Castle Tzingal* puts one in mind of W. D. Snodgrass's *The Führer Bunker* (as well an indoor if not underground narrative), in which Hitler's minions explain themselves, have their final say—cynical, pathetic, political, recriminating—before the last act and their final exits. It is ironic that Chappell's only book without starlight features an astronomer who is a diabolical opportunist, a denizen of a cold and starless world haunted by a murdered poet's voice, the voice of lost light and redeeming love. Of considerable importance in Chappell's work is the notion that love, religion, and art are ways to deny our nothingness. In fact, even in *Midquest's* "Hallowind," where oblivion seems triumphant, the assertion of emptiness is paradoxically a denial of it. No matter how often it is brought home to us that our lives are founded on and speeding toward nothingness, we must live them, Chappell seems to suggest, as if such were not the case. We must, with our imaginations, press back or believe as Tertullian believed—*because* belief is absurd. With great difficulty, our fictions praise creation and become a form of prayer, an act of faith. In *Midquest's* "My Grandfather's Church Goes Up," a disembodied voice says:

> *Pilgrim, the past   becomes prayer*
> *becomes remembrance rock-real   of Resurrection*
> *when the Willer so willeth   works his wild wonders.* (77)

The poet, Ole Fred often implies, is someone responsible for always being on duty, is someone haunted into song by the black yawn of Time. In "Susan Bathing" (*Midquest*), the link between poetry, religion, love, and time is deeply felt:

> that beauty too is Jesus . . .
> . . . .
>   that
> unattending beauty is danger & mortal sin . . .
> . . . .
>   I
> must cleave to speech, speech being my single knowledge, speech praise,
> though this speech clings only a soiled atomic
> instant about your bare feet before pouring fast to the black
> mouth of the pipe to smother. (19)

Through Art, Chappell implies, we are able to know solace or experience the Sacred. Art notices, art reminds. We have a responsibility to complete the world by noticing—an act of perception that recreates. "We've got to tune and turn the music ever. . . . / You wouldn't let the music of this world die. / Would you?" (115).

In Chappell's world, small natural sounds potentially aspire to the condition of music and are themselves the sources of music and poetry. In *Source*, "Music as a Woman Imperfectly Perceived" and "Awakening to Music" celebrate those soft daily sounds

in air existing and just now coming to exist,

as in a fog-quiet autumn dawn the three low
        dew-cool notes of the mourning dove
        across mist-washed grass and fence wire
suffuse themselves to hearing. (20)

Sounds awaken other senses, and we smell "wilted perfume and stiff linen" as well as the lovely woman of the title. The world, of course, comes to us through the sound of words as well and becomes more intensely itself for the sounding. At the end of "Awakening to Music," which recalls the speaker's waking in the predawn dark and stumbling to chores in the milking barn, we are presented with important questions:

How would I get it back? Go to blood
again, sleep the light green sleep?
How can I wake, not waking to music? (11)

The answer is he can't, and we can't. As Wallace Stevens tells us in *Noble Rider*, it helps us live our lives; it's connected with our survival. Stevens here is talking about the music of poetry and, quite often, so is Chappell, but from *Midquest* on, he often celebrates classical music and jazz, too. In "The Highest Wind That Ever Blew," a poem of homage to Louis Armstrong, Ole Fred says, "I couldn't count how many times / You saved my life" (99). Interesting, too, how the notion of art saving and renewing the world is underscored in the epigraph from Schopenhauer that Chappell chose for the poem: "Music is the world over again."

If music is a source of beauty and solace, if war is a source of ugliness and suffering, *Source* ponders the painful and intimate coexistence of these elements. Here and elsewhere in Chappell's poetry, the relationship between pain and beauty, peace and war is a major problem but a problem not to be solved. And therein lies the meaning. There is no bottom–line. The two elements constitute a mystery to be lived and not a problem to be solved. Further, the element of evil can be tracked to the individual self, the finger of accusation not smugly or easily pointed at others or at the external world. In "The Virtues," Chappell says, "The vices are always hungry for my hands / But the virtues stay inside their houses like shy brown thrushes" (35). Then, interestingly, he personifies the virtues and makes them feminine, indicting the warmaking side of man's nature:

> The virtues are widowed sisters;
> No man has been with them for many years.
>
> I believe they are waiting for cataclysm.
> They will open their doors
>
> When perfect ruin has taken down this city,
> Will wander forth and sift thoughtfully in the hot rubble. (35)

In *Source,* which often balances war and images of horror with those of bucolic peace, we come upon another poem about virtue, "Humility," which offers the possibility of innocence recaptured. We have a country setting bathed in "vesper light" where "the martins slide / Above the cows at the warped pasture gate" (9). Humility is a virtue one cultivates, a virtue that one can freely choose to perfect. Chappell emphasizes the element of choice in the two final stanzas of the poem:

> This is the country we return to when
> For a moment we forget ourselves,
> When we watch the sleeping kitten quiver
> After long play, or rain comes down warm.
>
> Here we might choose to live always, here where
> Ugly rumors of ourselves do not reach,
> Where in the whisper–light of the kerosene lamp
> The deep Bible lies open like a turned-down bed. (9)

All of the images tell us this is not the Bible that readily supplies appropriate quotations for various crimes needing justification. The Bible here supplies the daily bread of poetry, the possibility of grace, virtue, and peace. Like a book of poems, this is the Bible that few read or care to believe in. If the dread of nothingness (the dark side of peace and quiet) weren't enough to endure, our hunger for the power that leads to war is also a theme that makes itself felt in *Midquest* and in Chappell's subsequent volumes. The imagery of warfare is frequent and *homo homini lupus* a constant theme. There is a sense in which aggression is a form of deliverance or distraction from the painful perception of "unforgiving vacancy" between the stars— an unbearable vacancy, too, within the self. In this context one thinks of thematic parallels in Théophile Gauthier ("plutôt la barbarie que l'ennui") or Walker Percy's *The Second Coming:* "Are we afraid that ordinary afternoons will be interrupted by gunfire, or do we hope they will?" Chappell, in "Urlied" (*Source*), has a fictional Lucretius say:

> "The comfort is, there's nothing personal in it.
> The seeds of things put forth foreordained fruit,
> Nothing's wasted, nothing crazy, nothing
> Out of nowhere to attack a man for nothing." (53)

Nothing is five times repeated. It is this perception of nothingness, Chappell intimates, that either prompts song—is the primitive source of all song— or violence, for in the title poem "Source," Chappell says, "An ancient wound troubles the river" where a "perfumed barge drifts by, bearing/ The final viceroy to oblivion" (36). Faced with "oblivion," one will turn either to creation or to the destructive pursuit of power as a form of relief, of deliverance from awareness.

In the beginning was the Word, and at the end, too, there will be words, or as Faulkner put it, man's "puny inexhaustible voice, still talking," still refusing to accept the end. Chappell's *First and Last Words* is about silence and talking, about words sacred and profane, about music and silence. More perhaps than his other volumes, this is a book about language and makers, about Chappell's pantheon of favorite musicians, artists, and literary forebears to whom he responds. It celebrates the continuity of genius throughout history while simultaneously transcending linear time by enacting dialogue with the work of great artists in an eternal now. The volume is full of homages and references (mostly classical): Homer, Aeschylus, Virgil, Livy, Catullus, the Bible, Schiller, Goethe, Tolstoy, Valéry, Hardy, Einstein, Auden, Vermeer, Fragonard, Watteau, Baudelaire, and others. Though *First and Last Words* gives evidence of wide and deep reading, one would be hard put to describe it as exhibitionistic in motive. In fact, the reader's reaction to a wealth of presented ideas is like Chappell's own to the way, in "Subject Matter," Auden deals with "irrefrangible Newton at the close / of his bookish poem / that seemed somehow not bookish at all. / Seemed instead a colloquy" (47). Early in *Midquest,* Ole Fred's grandmother accuses him of being "bookish," but in that work the references (direct or indirect) to Rimbaud, Kierkegaard, Dante, and many other writers, painters, or musicians are often passed over quickly, well digested by the characters, the action, or the large canvas of the narrative. In *First and Last Words* what was backstage most often comes to the fore, stands alone, and delivers clear statements of mixed feeling. The imagistic, glittering particulars reappear now and again but less frequently than in previous volumes. For Chappell, the notion of the quest has always been important, and here that quest for the highest things is associated again with the heavens, with the charting and mapping that we find, for example, in "Voyagers," a poem based on Vermeer's painting *The Astronomer.* Though Chappell does not mention the painting (*The Finding of Moses*) within the painting, it is nonetheless clear that studying the heavens is metaphorically our proper spiritual destiny, is intimately connected with our need for guidance. Chappell's astronomer stands in a "room that silence studies like a science" with "his globe celestial, / His book that names the fixed and ambling stars, / Their ascensions, declinations, appointed seasons" (22). The illusion of order and control that naming brings to the learned astronomer is ironically treated in the poem's closure:

> The oceans after all agree
> With what the astronomer tells the stars to do
> From his room at Delft with his little silver book. (22)

We find the same sense of ourselves as vulnerable, searching creatures in "Word" where we have, in effect, a picture of the Writer as Sisyphus. Though we long for the order and seeming fixity that naming promises, we are never allowed rest or certainty, for:

With the word I set down after
the next word I set down,
all is obliterate.
                    It becomes
a blind white plain as far as anyone can see,
a clean snowfield into which we march like children,
printing our fine new names. (27)

Frustration, vulnerability, uncertainty, and a sense of loneliness notwithstanding, it is more important in Chappell's scheme of things to keep the
faith, to be a quester, a watcher of skies than not to be. That the unexamined
life is not worth living appears as more of a religious than a philosophical
idea in Tolstoy's "The Death of Ivan Ilyich," a story that prompts Chappell
to write, in "Meanwhile," these beautifully balanced lines:

At midnight in the paneled library he pours
a brandy and tries to think about his life.
He ponders instead his career which gleams
like a samovar. (13)

The "meanwhile" of one's life, Chappell and Tolstoy imply, ought to be
filled with more than "career" and society's guiding idea that "A man must
get ahead in the world." If one goes for the con and buys into such intellectual junk bonds, one then lives in a "world that breaks its first and only
promise" (13).

Chappell's *First and Last Words* is so finely structured that his poems play
against each other like wind chimes. A contrasting sense of "meanwhile"
is found in the poem "Dipperful," in which the speaker is out wandering
in the mountains on a hot day. An old country man offers him a drink,
which he gladly accepts. No career is at stake. Simply one man attuned to
another and to the surrounding hills. Ole Fred "drank the hill. Scatter of
sand-motes sparkled/When I launched the gourd's blind belly back in the
bucket,/And on my tongue the green hill sprouted ferns" (35). Unlike
Ivan Ilyich, who lived to get ahead in the world, the old country man tells
an attentive Fred:

"I never got married, you see, never had
To grub for other people. I worked enough

To keep myself sufficient peace and quiet."
. . . .

He spat again and a swoon of flies unsettled,
Then settled back. The early afternoon
Began to climb the fields. "I've talked too much,"
He said. "I wish I didn't talk so much."
When he said that, the silence had its say. (36)

Silence always takes the last word, and the quality of silence varies from poem to poem. In some cases, silence emphasizes vacancy, nothingness, loneliness, and is an aggressive, annihilating force; in others, silence isn't so much an absence of sound as a positive sensation, the barely audible music of small sounds that accompanies the night sky and, say, bats "tacking from star/to early star as if putting in at ports of call" ("The Garden," 30). Related to silence, of course, is peace and the fleeting consolation provided by music itself.

First and Last Words has fewer poems about music than previous volumes, in fact only two ("The Gift To Be Simple" and "Webern's Mountain"), which is perhaps an ominous sign of the poet's darkening vision. The book is structured in such a way that harmony brought by music is threatened by our time. First we come to "The Gift To Be Simple" in which Chappell, with aphoristic force, speaks about the curative dimension of music: "For Order is a Music of such health and delight/That in hearing it newly we come round right" (15). If music measures the health of a human soul, then we live in plaguey times, for in "Webern's Mountain," German fascism prepares "the clinical bonfire" for "Jews and poets" (37). The poem closes with this potent image:

Then it came apart, the stave-line filaments
Of gleam snapped by a mortar shell, viola
And cello strings dying under the tank treads. (37–38)

In "Observers," troubled and still pondering the unthinkable consequences of life without music, Chappell characterizes the late twentieth century as

a time of arbitrary starlight

Which is drifting toward the place where Mozart
goes unheard forever, which is punctuated by
the blackened matchstem that was Nagasaki. (44)

With fewer references to music and poems about music, music itself seems under siege, the implications for civilization grave. But the closest to topicality that Chappell comes is a powerful short poem about the national scourge of drugs, which ends, "A whole Manhattan of indifference, / A whole Miami of despair" (33). Despair indeed. What does one do when the music of civilization becomes moribund? Chappell does not provide an answer, but in key poems he has sentinel figures who remain faithful to heroic ideals in the most grinding of conditions, who embody virtues like humility, fidelity, patience, and courage.

"The Watchman" is a poem about the Trojan war and the faithful watch of a sentinel who sees, as he waits for the signal, "stars flitter stupidly overhead / Like an irritated squad of flies above a corpse" (7). Chappell nicely describes how war and endless waiting for the end enervate and make the watcher numb. He skillfully accomplishes this indirectly by reference once again to the stars:

> So many nights of silent skies
> Have darkened his capacities
> To comprehend. The arrow showers
> Of meteors no longer startle; he no longer numbers
> The familiar constellation stars.
> The Great Bear lumbers
> Over his spirit, leaving a shadow like a mortal bruise. (7)

In another war poem, "Patience," which Chappell calls a "prologue to the *Georgics,*" we find a traditional tension between country and city, peace and war. The irresistible rural setting is beautifully painted with a "hive of stars" that "immerses the dark porches where / The farmers muse" (9). The farm animals have a "patience almost mineral" and settle in sleep "to the ground like velvet boulders" (9). But men, alas, do not have this kind of patience and abhor the vacuum of peace because it has nothing to do with the power they seem to crave. Chappell tells us that poets—wrongly perceived as unrealistic woolgatherers—have known this all along, and he provides a bloody and balancing imagery of war, with "cottager mothers flung on the corpses of their children" (10). The poem concludes directly and with the implication that peace / war cycles (closely related to the book's country /

city dialectic) are a mystery to be endured with something close to animal-like patience:

> But nothing changes. The war grinds over the world and all
> Its politics, the soldiers marry the farmers' daughters
> And tell their plowman sons about the fight at the Scaean Gate,
> And the other sanguine braveries the dust has eaten.
> Sundown still draws the chickens to their purring roost,
> The cow to the milking stall, the farmer to his porch to watch
> Whether the soaring constellations promise rain. (10)

Faced with various kinds of madness, ignorance, and absurdity, one must adopt an attitude, perhaps an attitude like the one in "Stoic Poet" (a prologue to Hardy's *The Dynasts*). The attitude is presented in this way: "He gains a knowledge would cause an easy man / to embitter and grow lean. / Terrors assail him, he holds steady, / absorbing the wounds of the world's every crime" (14). But perhaps the best, most intricate poem about learning such stoic balance is Chappell's fond recollection of his teacher / mentor Allen Tate, in the extraordinary "Afternoons With Allen," which presents several sharp contrasts: the active and the meditative, the quiet and the loud. Time has made its inevitable inroads on the speaker's old friend—a veteran of literary wars, a man who has taken his stand more than once and held ground. Frail now, Tate and the speaker reminisce while watching Vince Lombardi's Washington Redskins on television. Chappell humorously creates a Paleface / Redskin contrast by emphasizing Allen's "pale pale eyes" and by associating him with Valéry's intellectual Monsieur Teste. The Redskins lose, but Tate doesn't seem to care and smiles at the "unimportant score." He says, "It's their precision I like, like a machine . . . / like well made poetry" (16). Perhaps Tate is indifferent to the final outcome because he realizes that victory is at best a fleeting illusion. In any event, historical hindsight gives added poignance and drama to this scene, for the famous coach perhaps already knew he was losing to cancer, his winning single season with the Redskins a triumph of absurd courage. And in the transitional light of a late October afternoon, we see Tate losing gracefully, sipping bourbon, smoking, and appraising writers of his generation—Hemingway, Stein, and Pound, whose "talent crumbled into rant" (16). In a wonderful closure, Chappell associates Allen, Lombardi, and heroic Priam in one bold stroke:

> For Lombardi
> He fetched out of that high magniloquent head
> A telling line of the Second Aeneid.
>
> *Forsitan et, Priami fuerint quae fata, requiras?* (16)

By having Allen conclude the poem with this untranslated, uninterpreted line from Virgil's second book of the *Aeneid,* Chappell links the fate of all three men (himself as well) and suggests something of the heroic. Chappell's stroke is bold, for the context of the line, compressing so much, means everything. It is especially important and moving to know that the line comes from the scene in which Pyrrhus, hot with freshly spilled blood, pursues Polites and kills him before Priam's and Hecuba's eyes. It is the genius of the quoted line that it is one of Virgil's great transitionals: "Perhaps now you will ask the doom of Priam?" What Priam does—an old man at this juncture—is strap on his armor to avenge the murder of his son. Hecuba, weeping and pleading with him, recognizes the gesture for what it is—futile, for Pyrrhus is much younger and virtually invincible. But Allen Tate (Chappell, too) seems to find a beautiful grace and nobility in the act, an exquisite example of dramatic refusal, an act of great courage and dignity in a situation of certain loss. And Lombardi and Tate in their different ways had also heard those heavy quick steps behind them, felt the advent of final defeat in their bones. Intransigence in the face of the inevitable. But to return to the poem's last line for a moment, it is worth noting that the music of this Latin line creates another kind of transition, the transition between sound and silence—the after-silence that announces annihilation, a theme that Chappell has been sounding through the book.

The first poem in *First and Last Words* is "An Old Mountain Woman Reading the Book of Job." In a volume that largely interests itself in reading and writing and the sister arts of painting and music, Chappell could not have begun with a better poem in terms of structure. Beyond being a signature poem with mica-like glories that recall the great bucolic strengths of *Midquest,* it first sounds the themes of light against dark, sound against silence which, among other strategies, help *First and Last Words* to achieve its impressive unity. Surrounding this lonely widow on a stormy, "starless night" is a devouring silence, an aggressive menacing darkness. Chappell sets the scene in a painterly but realistic way, reminding one of the canvases of Georges de la Tour that often feature a solitary vigil-keeper in dramatic lamplight. It is a world

> delivered to ungodly shadow.
> The darkness of her hand darkens the page.
> She straightens her bifocals in which the words,
> Reflected, jitter, then come to rest like moths.
> It is November. The woodstove shifts its log
> And grumbles. The night is longer than her fire. (5)

Young poets could learn much from Chappell's example of how to establish a setting dramatically related to character with such speed and economy. This is a poem about strength of character—an old woman's refusal to cry out or be intimidated by the hostile emptiness about her; nor will she succumb to the biblical consolation of Jesus or St. Paul. Not tonight. She tends her fire which, like her faith in God's goodness, is on the wane. We see a pitiful hunger for immortality, her own and that of her dead husband, but the poet's metaphor says it all: "The night is longer than her fire."

Alone after the death of her husband, she goes (almost perversely) to the Book of Job for sustenance. Instead of help or hope, she experiences the painful absence, remembers her husband's Job-like silence through long suffering, and herself feels "Job's bewilderment." There is no help. "St. Paul does not escape, / Not even Jesus shines clear of Job tonight" (5). The key word is "tonight," for we know she will face another day, however bleak Chappell's closure seems, however final. Pursuing again a similar kind of "balancing act" structure he described in the preface to *Midquest,* Chappell in *First and Last Words* gives us a tight book, a well-proportioned, intricate structure. Beyond the sectional symmetry of nine prologues, nine epilogues, and entr'acte, there are certain kinds of thematic and imagistic mirrorings throughout. In some way, almost all the nine poems of the epilogue echo the nine earlier soundings of the prologue. Most obviously, the echoing companion of "An Old Woman Reading the Book of Job" is "Scarecrow Colloquy." The book thus opens and closes with sentinels of the night, watchers who wait with an acute sense of absence for some loving transcendent sign, memory both consolation and torment, heaven and hell. But language, too, is consolation, and the last words of the book are those of that puny, inexhaustible voice still talking to its self-made Other, whistling in the dark, making the nothingness point to a somethingness, something to keep away the dark crows of death.

In this last word, "Scarecrow Colloquy," or "epilogue to the Gospels," Chappell again dramatizes silence and suffering without God. Though he is concerned with eschatology, nowhere does he attempt to justify the ways of God to man. The last poem, in fact, endorses a Hardyesque world, stark and beautifully frightening, presided over by a *deus absconditus*. Typically, the two voices of the poem are confronted with darkness and interstellar space. The speaker humorously greets the scarecrow in the first line as "Ragwisp" and "my Sentinel of the Stars," and tells him that he looks "as entranced as St. Jerome." Chappell's use of the possessive adjective *my* seems to establish the scarecrow as an alter ego, a kind of externalized Watcher Within. The poem can easily be seen as dialogue between Faith and Skepticism. The Scarecrow asks of the speaker some news of the "*man who nailed me up, left me to challenge / the courage of the crow*" (56). But the unitalicized, world-weary voice of the speaker tells old "Hayhead" that he is forgotten by his maker, there is no point in trying to "unfold the motive of your construction" (56). The Scarecrow feels sure that the farmer, an absent and forgetful creator, must occasionally think about that cobbled-up figure he placed in the field. Light in the farmhouse window on winter nights gives some hope to the lonely scarecrow who imagines his maker by a warm fireplace, smoking a meerschaum and dreaming of "*his friend in God, the Scarecrow*" (56). No such luck. Throughout the poem, the skeptical speaker answers "Chaffstaff" in various ways that he is forgotten and better face up to it. Godot won't arrive, and if he does, it doesn't matter, anyway. But after the speaker sarcastically tells him to keep the faith, Chappell significantly gives the poignant closure to the Scarecrow:

I have spoken in the field till my voice became an owl.
I have surveyed the horizon till I lost my buttons.
The fieldmouse heard my silence and gnawed my flesh of grass.
And still I stand here, guarding the bones of Adam. (57)

I don't mean to treat the poem too seriously, because Chappell obviously intends humor and wouldn't want us losing our buttons like the old Scarecrow. But this slapstick figure of suffering reflects and mirrors to some extent the old woman we met in the first poem. Though they refuse to submit to different fates, both are nonetheless presented as refusing to submit, as keeping an absurd faith, and we are somehow ennobled by their suffering, by their dramatic *no*. Indirectly, Chappell suggests an image of the writer as watcher and Job-like recorder who must keep the faith—something not terribly far from a statement made by D. H. Lawrence in one of his letters: "A work of art is an act of faith and one goes on writing, to the unseen witnesses."

In the best sense of the word, Fred Chappell is an old-fashioned poet, one for whom writing is a spiritual project, not merely a game with words. Chappell's poems implicitly argue against the current literary / philosophical notion that words are problematically referential, or don't have meaning, or don't mean much. Chappell knows they mean plenty and, skillfully used, are capable of providing sustenance and solace. They are the fragile vessels that bear our lives and hopes, to which Chappell bears glowing witness. What Virgil—one of Ole Fred's favorite poets—wrote in another context is equally true of Chappell's own creation: *Fervet opus*. The work is all aglow.

The Comedian as the Letter C Strikes Again

DAVID R. SLAVITT

If the epigram is mostly ignored in university classes, it may be because there is nothing much to say about efforts in this genre. An epigram is like a joke—frequently it *is* a joke—and either you get it or you don't. Exegesis is, in the former case, otiose and in the latter, hopeless. Surely, there are some classicists who read Martial and a few of the poets of the Greek Anthology, but English epigrams? Prior? Herrick? Cunningham? Kennedy? Not likely! To do so would call the whole structure of the classroom into question. Why should a tweedy older person stand at the front of the room (and get paid) while others are seated in their chair-desks, paying through the nose, and either laughing or not laughing, smiling or not smiling, but understanding almost every poem—as if poetry were written to be read for pleasure? (That is an outrageous, revolutionary, and dangerous idea.)

One would suppose that poets would all rush to write epigrams then, if only to wrest the territory of their craft back from the academicians. But epigrams are not easy to do: they are, like jokes, most demanding, take talent and training and an instinct for timing, and a sense of the absurd—a whole range of craftsmanly and human qualities that are rarely found together. There is a terrible danger in the giddy egalitarianism of epigrams, too, for these innocent little diversions also come with another quite improper suggestion—that if the reader isn't smiling, it might be the poet's fault. What is even more demanding, the brief compass of the epigram doesn't allow for much wriggle-room. A sensibility declares itself in every syllable. Because of the very tight focal length and the close scrutiny that invites, fakery is even harder here, I rather think, than in an ode or an epic.

Consider a page of Fred Chappell's witty, cagey, genial book, *C,* which is a lovely minimalist title for a hundred epigrams—minimalist but not at all small, for in my title I have played on the Wallace Stevens reference. (I should be surprised if there weren't also a wink and a wave here to an all-but-forgotten Fugitive poet, Merrill Moore, whose book of a thousand sonnets was called *M.*) Anyway, here is a little Chappell:

XXXIII   GRACE BEFORE MEAT

     As this noon our meat we carve,
     Bless us better than we deserve.

XXXIV   ANOTHER

     Bless, O Lord, our daily bread.
     Bless those in hunger and in need
     Of strength. Bless all who stand in want.
     Bless us who pray, bless us who can't.

XXXV   ANOTHER

        Bless our corn pones, Lord. But let us dream
    They might be black currant muffins with strawberry
       jam and clotted double Devon cream. (14)

Now in large measure, these pieces speak for themselves. But it is interesting to consider their slight but nonetheless powerful machinery. The first couplet with its slant rhyme has in it a very gentle joke, because if we get back far enough into the hill country of North Carolina, the rhyme is less and less slant. So we're not absolutely certain how to pronounce "deserve"— we can't quite evade the echo of "desarve," to which, because of the poem's solemn substance, we are reluctant to condescend. We are, in other words, already watching ourselves, watching our manners at that table, waiting and looking around to see what's proper and trying not to make fools of ourselves.

    Then, in the middle piece, we get a slant rhyme again, one without any side to it (bread/need), so that we wonder whether we weren't presuming too far a moment before. Only we're brought up short by the second couplet, which acknowledges human frailty, the fragility of the communion of believers, the possibility of the failures of faith. And this is generously in the first-person plural: think how different the line would be if Chappell had written, "Bless those who pray, bless those who can't." I also admire the drama of "stand," which emphasizes our feeling of gratitude for being seated here, at table.

The third piece is a bit warmer, a nice jump from cornpone and back-country food (modest and poor, if life sustaining) to the exquisite muffins with strawberry jam and clotted double Devon cream—also country food but luxurious, grandiloquent, sybaritic. In all three pieces, the game in large measure is enlivened by Chappell's toying with that not-quite-mythological notion Edmund Wilson used to entertain of an educated squirearchy. This isn't a gentleman farmer who comes out from town for the summers and on weekends to putter around a bit on his too new and too large John Deere. This is the guy in bib overalls and workboots who, in the evenings, reads Plautus and Seneca, Sophocles and Homer.

Which is one reason for the next poem in the collection to be an adaptation or rendition of—or descant on—an epigram by Martial. Much of the liveliness of Chappell's other poetry, a distinguished body of work that includes the four parts of *Midquest* as well as *Castle Tzingal* and *First and Last Words*, is this playing on the Theocritan and Virgilian changes on the old polarities of city and country, urbanity as distinguished from sophistication (or both of them distinguished from wisdom). These aren't so much Chappell's subjects as they are his tools of the trade, for he has a way of scouting out the terrain, looking to see where his reader is likely to be unprepared, and then striking from that surprising direction, taking the high tone when we might look for him to be folksy, or coming in low to avoid our intellectual and cultural radar.

The individual jokes function as building blocks, but their arrangement suggests a larger and more complicated structure. We get a range of moods and tones, some genial, some rueful, some close to nasty. He has some academic and literary figures, of course:

XXIII   LITERARY CRITIC

> Blandword died, and now his ghost
> Drifts gray through lobby, office, hall.
> Some mourn diminished presence; most
> Can see no difference at all. (10)

Or:

XXVII   ANOTHER

> Peter Puffer piped a pack of poets into
> Undeservedly prominent public view;
> Then, just to prove the power of his pen,
> Provokingly piped them pouting out again. (11)

But he can be surprisingly, abruptly generous, even lush, which is no small feat in this small compass:

LXXXIX   IN THE GARDEN

> The guitar's rubato quivered
> And died. The woman shivered
> And lifted toward the night her head.
> He set his wine glass on the tray.
> There was something fragile they had feared to say.
> Now it was said. (45)

This would be an impressive accomplishment for a thirty-page chapter in a novel and a triumph in a lyric of conventional length. Chappell's suave assurance, and his instinct for what to put in and how much more he can leave out, give us the moment, with all its larger resonances, in a perfectly achieved epigram.

At the same time, there is perhaps a darker side to this constriction. It is possible to suppose that the gesture of the choice may signify a strategic withdrawal, like that of the turtle into its shell. Epigrams are not expansive, garrulous, chatty, or unbuttoned but, on the contrary, laconic, as though the proper response to most experience was a silent patience or contempt to be broken only on rare occasions. Chappell's career seems to me a poignant lesson in the incoherence of the American poetry scene—he is the most obscure winner of the Bollingen Prize, alive or dead. That award ought to have earned him some recognition and acceptance, an audience, a right, at least, to having his books reviewed. Surprisingly few reviews of *C* appeared during the first two years after its publication.

How he feels about this is his business. But it is possible for us as readers to consider the possibility that the epigram is his response, for this is the only kind of art that can be deigned. My first experience of the form—my first living encounter with it, I should say—was as a schoolboy. I studied with Dudley Fitts, Andover's poet. And a piece of the local lore was an account about his having attended some faculty party, a birthday party, at which everyone had to bring a gift and offer a poem with it. The literary lion of the faculty (or at least the largest frog in that pond), Fitts was given the place of honor and went last. As all eyes and ears turned to him to see how he would do and, indeed, dare him to do better than the rest of them, he said his piece: "It's/from Fitts." Defensive, even aggressive, brilliant, and tiny, it was the right thing for that moment. It may be that for this moment in the culture's life and in Fred Chappell's, these are the proper, even the ideal responses. Sensibly and perhaps defensively, I shall let him have the last words. The closing poem in the book, and therefore the title poem, is modest but defiant:

C   THE EPIGRAMMATIST

Mankind perishes. The world goes dark.
He racks his brain for a tart remark. (52)

The Light of Transformation in Fred Chappell's Spring Garden

SUSAN O'DELL UNDERWOOD

The appellative "new and selected" quite often brings to mind not only a great literary retrospective but also the denouement of a poet's career. Certainly, in *Spring Garden: New and Selected Poems,* there is, along with a principal impression of vivid newness, an occasional note of retirement and nostalgia. The tone of the book is not, however, one of simple poignant reflection but one of complex and resounding revelation that comes from facing both the brief future and the past. Chappell's inclusion of poems from his previously published work, representing more than twenty years of writing, does not convey resignation, because he has also written and chosen new poems intended specifically to introduce the book's conceptual, thematic, and structural elements.

Spring Garden is divided into seven distinct sections, each marked by its own prologue, with the collection itself framed by a general prologue and an epilogue. These two poems and each section prologue, except that of "Epigrams," are written in formal rhymed and metered stanzas. Each stanza of the prologues and epilogue is composed of eight lines formed by juxtaposing two quatrain patterns—an Italian quatrain and a Sicilian or heroic quatrain. *Spring Garden* certainly contains numerous traditional poetry forms encompassing the technical range of Chappell's talents, and it reflects his principal interests as well. The book's structure also reveals the patterns of a life's work. Chappell has arranged thematically the poems that best exhibit his personal concerns, his private character, and his philosophical perspectives. The seven sections are more than thematic references, however; they serve to delineate Chappell's design. They mark his unique passions in literature: pastoral and love poems, the ideals of beauty and pleasure, the creation of character, the fantastical, the humorous, and the past, including both personal and collective history. The sections are entitled, respectively, "In the Garden," "The Good Life," "The Garden of Love," "Poems of Character," "Poems of Fantasy," "Epigrams," and "Poems of Memory." Chappell introduces and reinforces the structure in the prologues, expressing in several passages throughout the book the orchestration of his design. The opening section following the general prologue might seem at first merely to advance *Spring Garden*'s central motif—the verdant, variegated garden, but in this brief section of nine poems, including the section prologue, Chappell's changeling talents reveal a prelude to the entire collection. Within the prologue for "In the Garden" he introduces specific images correlated to the general motif. The poet/persona addresses his wife, as in all the prologues save one:

Real enough, but half-imaginary,
This garden we tend together shall provide
Ingredients . . .
Quite practical and yet quite visionary.
Lettuce we'll have, that symbol of well-being;
And one strange herb that promotes fantasies
Blithe or ominous, new ways of seeing;
And tastes that call back cherished memories.

Epigrams shall be our watercress;
Fern seed to make ourselves invisible
In order to observe the sorrowful
Or happy lives of others. . . .
. . . .
And, most important, herbs that urge to love
We'll have in plenty, for love's the serious matter
We play upon in our enchanted grove. (9–10)

Chappell reveals the idea of variety and choice in life not only through his own skill for writing in various forms and through the deliberate creation of a medley of tones and sensations; but through the motif of the garden he also incorporates the suggestion of vitality in diversity. He introduces briefly but vividly the garden motif in the general prologue, wherein the setting of the poem is May, and the poet quite aptly makes with his wife their "plans for this Memorial Day" (3). The poet/persona clarifies his station in life and describes his purpose and intent very early in the book's first poem:

> The year's at spring, but I no longer am;
> Decades have mounted, as we were told they would;
> The time has come when there's but little time
> To write daft poems and speculate on God.
>
> The day has come for us to winnow through
> The pages of my crossgrain poetry books,
> Searching for any line at all that looks
> Suitable for a volume Old and New.
> A poet loves a simple irony,
> . . . that we're harvesting these poems in spring. (3)

Chappell's inclination toward modesty or humility, his use of intimate subjects, and his capacity at the same time for broaching the broadest themes come clear from the outset.

Primarily, Chappell exhibits themes expressed throughout his works, poetic and fictional, that take on myriad dimensions and illustrate the author's complex concerns: the agrarian, the romantic, the spiritual, the dichotomy of misery and beatitude in the human experience. He reveals these themes by fixing our attention upon motifs and images that are repeated and familiar from his earliest work to his most recent— images of stars, light, bees, fire, water, flowers, birds, and music. Through these images he heightens our awareness of his common subjects: nature, love, time, death, work, the imagination, human frailty, the ephemeral, the power of faith and grace, and transformation.

The idea of transformation and the recognition of transcendence as a frequent result of transformation is central to much of Chappell's poetry and also to his short fiction and novels. Quite often, the narrative within a poem is resolved through transformational circumstances or images that allude to transcendence. Poems that concern nature, particularly those involving the agrarian life or reminiscences of boyhood farm days, often culminate in a transcendent resolution. Many poems that concern transformations or transfigurations contain images of stars or music, associated with enlightenment or supernal involvement, or bees, which are symbolic of the soul and its afterlife. There is as well a motif of ascension or climbing in several poems, and close attention is paid to the transformation of time, particularly the natural elements of sunrise and twilight. Within *Spring Garden,* Chappell has created a balance of subjects and tone; at the same time, many of the poems—perhaps Chappell's best works—include the themes of transformation and transcendence.

Although Chappell has poems that deal with dark and unresolved matters, even within poems of sober content he will incorporate a deliberately paradoxical tone of hopefulness. Scrutiny of the opening pages of *Spring Garden* reveals his customary tendency to push back the darkness only after acknowledging its existence. In the general prologue, in the epilogue, and in nearly every section prologue, Chappell ensconces "translations and adaptations" of works by poets of the Renaissance and of the eighteenth and nineteenth centuries, such as Charles Baudelaire and Paul Verlaine, who influenced him (157). It will not escape readers that he also reveals as never before his excellent talent for translating poems from Italian, French, and Latin. Through these few translated poems, selected as sources to guide and instruct readers and as foil pieces, he moves beyond the theme of reflection into the subject of death. This theme is pronounced in some of the final passages in the epilogue, and he clarifies that he writes always within the peripheral fact of death. The poet/persona deliberately sets out to "end on an elegiac note":

If a garden is the place for poetry,
Its theme will be human mortality,
Whatever subjects it may talk about,
Including love, warfare, faith in God,
The silly tragic destiny of man. (154)

Chappell continues this tone in the epilogue, appropriating an entire poem from Pierre Ronsard, a French poet of the late Renaissance. The poet/persona introduces the book's concluding poem: "Pierre Ronsard composed on his deathbed/A poem borrowed from the emperor Hadrian://And I—*with thanks*—shall borrow it again":

To His Soul

O Chappellette, flimsy marionette,
    My precious trembling wet-eyed pet,
        Guardian of my every breath,
Down you go, silent, white,
    Without a scrap of coverlet,
        Into the cold Kingdom of Death,
Without remorse, without regret,
    Without the least concern for what
        You leave the greedy world to keep;
That Prize they strain so hard to get,
    With doubletalk and bloodstained sweat,
        Would cause the sunbaked sands to weep.

    Goodbye, my friends. The sun has set.
    Now I lay me down to sleep. (155)

The inclusion of such a poem seems at first to admit a morbid fascination with death, to close the book on a pitch-black note. Upon closer scrutiny, however, the poem serves to convey a sense of peace, a vision of something greater than the world itself which, in the poet's estimation, contains petty desires, vain and futile actions. The poet/persona does not mock humanity only; the tone is quite self-effacing in its ersatz stilted beginning but moves to serene humility in the final lines.

Certainly, sentiment concerning death and queries of the afterlife, though here appropriated from another source, are common in much of Chappell's verse, particularly in occasional lines from poems in *Midquest*. The themes of mortality and eschatology are among Chappell's chief subjects, not only in his poetry but also in his short fiction and novels. Nevertheless, it is important to note that the most mournful quality in *Spring Garden* is found in the poems borrowed or in lines adapted. In the general prologue, the poet/persona translates a poem from Ronsard as his first appropriation. With this verse he introduces the subtle yet overshadowing awareness of inevitable death:

My pliant youthfulness is gone,
My stamina all broken down,
My teeth are black, and white my head,
My heart is weak, my nerves are shot. . . .
. . . .

Numerous years and numberless days
Weigh me down with illnesses,
Fears gnaw my every hope;
Though I fly onward like the wind
Every time I glance behind
I find that Death is catching up.

This Death, who means to take my hand. . .
Holds that door open through which we go
To some dark land beyond, below,
The door admitting no return. (4–5)

Although this translation advances one of Chappell's predominant themes and points to the inevitability of mortality, in the very next line the poet/persona presents an alternative ideal and theme, perhaps the light that makes shadow of the central theme of *Spring Garden*. Chappell's answer to the Ronsard poem is motivated by hope of transcendence over the mere fact of human frailty, a theme of living in the moment. Certainly, transcendence in subject or tone is central to the entire body of Chappell's work, and in this vein the poet/persona admits to Susan and to the reader about the Ronsard poem:

—But this chanson is just a little grimmer
Than I'd recalled. There may be years to come
With promise almost as pleasing as our past time
Whose blaze begins to dwindle to a glimmer.
I am precipitate to mourn so soon;
There will be other springs, and winters too,
Before the whisper-snow descends upon
The stone that marks our velvet curfew.

Carpe diem is still a proper theme
For us; it's more important to seize the day
When there are fewer left. (5)

Though this is the first instance where "carpe diem" is invoked, it is not the last. Seizing the day is a prominent idea coursing through *Spring Garden*.

In addition to this marked and deliberate stake upon the transformational act of embracing the moment, this movement to transcend the fear of the unknown, there is a singularly important element that gives the book its decided charm. A predominant vehicle for the theme of transformation and the tone of transcendence is the presence of Susan, wife of the poet/persona. It is Susan to whom he directs his comments in poems such as the one above. Her gentle and lovely manner attends nearly each prologue, so that she not only plays the role of muse for the poet but also guides the reader's perceptions.

That the poet/persona makes Susan so overtly a subject of the narratives of his prologues is surely a deliberate act of revealing her influence upon his life's work. Susan is of great consequence throughout *Spring Garden,* not just in a few verses. Although mention of her is often subtle or brief, her presence makes itself felt from the first page to the last. Indeed, Susan is the central figure in the very first selected poem—essentially the first poem of the entire book, following the general prologue and the prologue to the first section. Taken from *Earthsleep,* "Susan's Morning Dream of Her Garden" is one of several poems in *Midquest* in which she appears as a character; here, however, the poet writes from Susan's point of view in a unique stance that uses her imagined voice as the poem's very substance. She speaks, reveling in her dream:

> We whirl, my garden and I, until
> the minuet boils, the sun
> and moon and lawn and tree become a waltzing sea. . . .
> . . . .
>
> I sing as high and clear-O as a finch
> in a yellow-green willow tree,
> transparent and vivid as dragonflies. (12)

Thus from the very opening of *Spring Garden,* Susan is a conduit for Chappell's welcoming tone, and her presence sounds the theme of transcendence. She is intricately and inexorably linked to the book's principal leitmotif—the garden. In the prologue to the section "The Garden of Love," the poet/persona speaks to her of their advancing age but also praises her:

> Please believe me, Susan dear,
>   This present time is your sweetest year;
>   You flower as if newly sprung. (38)

Susan's presence, then, exudes at its most intense the hopefulness and exhilaration in Chappell's volume. She is the source of light and love, the one
fixed constant in the persona's experience.

Perhaps the most buoyant and charming poem in which she plays a role
appears in the section entitled "The Garden of Love." Although the primary theme of the poem "A Glorious Twilight" is obviously passion and
love, the central subject is Susan, involved in the luxurious act of painting
her nails. The poem is full of images of light, from which it takes its title.
The persona describes this radiant dusk:

> Susan is painting her nails
> such a brilliant shade of bright
> she seems to have sprouted 22 fingers
>
> Don't need open-toed shoes, those toes
> would gleam through blind galoshes
> like designer Northern Lights
>
> Be careful, I said, waving your phalanges about!
> You're gonna burn the house down
>
> And then the house began to bulge
> With the light of fingernails
> And lifted through the air
> Through clouds where it snows and hails
> And came to rest beside
> The pale-by-comparison moon
> And glowed on the earnest astronomer
> Like a Passion Fire doubloon. (49)

Here a translucent and passionate portrait is drawn. To the poet, Susan is
an engagingly complex woman who outshines the satellites. She is beguiling
and at once enigmatic, as are the fairly palpable women who appear in
several poems within *Spring Garden* and in many of Chappell's other poems,
as well as in his fiction.

The range of women in the section entitled "Poems of Character" is
testament to Chappell's experience and his vision of transcendence. He has
remarked on several occasions and in print that critics have not written
about his women characters. He has even commented that scholars often

remark that his work does not deal with women's experience.[1] Obviously, this is untrue, for in his portraits of many women, including his mother, his wife, and his grandmother, Chappell reveals the distance his empathy can traverse. It is therefore quite fitting that *Spring Garden* opens with the dedication, *"For my sister Rebecca."*

For "Poems of Character," Chappell has chosen a great number concerned with women. Their experiences and temperaments are varied and vivid in these poems, but they share some features with the women of Chappell's other poems, old and new. Typically, he reveals the strength, tenacity, and wholesome straightforwardness of women. In "The Widow," "The Voices," and "An Old Mountain Woman Reading the Book of Job," a trio of poems that are truly companion pieces, the poet is concerned with the fortitude of older women who have lost husbands. Although these women do not necessarily transcend the anguish of their circumstances, they have the tenacity to face their sorrow. They meditate upon their new habits, their old lives, their well-worn sorrows. "The Widow," one of the new poems and very brief, begins as if in the middle of the woman's thoughts:

And then unhappiness enfolded her
Like a sleeping rose, and she dropped through
The billows of its perfume as if rising
Through an evening mist to greet a star.
Alone inside this flower she felt no fear,
Such sharp authority her sorrow held.
Her Age of Reason opened like a Sahara. (64)

Once more, the images of nature are signs of epiphany, specifically the images of the flower and the star. The act of ascension is intermingled with the image of the desert, the opening of which is reminiscent of the blooming of the rose itself. The air of deep sorrow is overwhelmed by the very transformation of the widow's understanding of her experience.

This impression of something larger and more important than human suffering is present in several other poems about women within this section. Two pay homage to influential women in Chappell's life: his mother-in-

---

1. Fred Chappell, "Fred Chappell Interview," ed. Tersh Palmer, *Appalachian Journal,* XIX (April, 1992), 409.

law, who inspired "The Reader" from *First and Last Words,* and his grand-mother, who imparts wisdom and family secrets in "My Grandmother Washes Her Feet." The poet/persona here admits his weakness and her strength at the poem's end. He is unable to continue the family's agrarian tradition, to stare in the face the rich history of his family members. He confesses:

> I strained to follow them, and never did.
> I never had the grit to stir those guts.
> I never had the guts to stir that earth. (71)

The grandmother, on the other hand, with great grace washes from her weary legs the very ancestral soil into which she delves each day. She is accepting of her station, acknowledges her humble place. She warns her grandson, Fred, "'We sprouted from dirt,/Though, and it's with you, and dirt you'll never forget'" (70). Her fortitude derives from her ability to know herself, to face the pain of family misfortune and shame, to embrace the earthy shadows along with the light that forms them. She transcends her humble station by simply accepting humility.

Clearly, the theme of humility is to be found in many of Chappell's poems and is central to "Poems of Memory," the seventh and final section of *Spring Garden.* Here it serves not merely as theme but as vehicle to transformation and deliverance. First published in *Source,* the opening poem, aptly entitled "Humility," reveals that the most simple of Chappell's mannerisms belie the complexity within his poetry. The setting for "Humility" is, after all, the "necessary field," an appropriate image to coincide with the volume's garden motif. The poet reveals an allegorical place where the past reveals only those most tender and beloved memories:

> This is the country we return to when
> For a moment we forget ourselves. . . .
>
> Here we might choose to live always, here where
> Ugly rumors of ourselves do not reach,
> Where in the whisper-light of the kerosene lamp
> The deep Bible lies open like a turned-down bed. (134)

The idea that one might escape to such a territory is a fleeting and romantic notion, but Chappell draws the portrait of an ephemeral place with images solid and pure and durable. The most transitory dream of the imagination is offered as the surest vehicle to comfort and potential reward through understanding what is to come, through what has gone before and what has been lived before.

Within "Poems of Memory" are reminiscences from early adulthood and even borrowed memories, poems of more universal nostalgia. There are, however, a few memories of childhood, of which "Child in the Fog" is perhaps the most poignant. Once again, the idea of humility arises as an important theme as the persona is washed over by a most tenable memory of his fear of the overwhelming world away from home on his "first day of school" (138). The persona recalls his initiation, his rite of passage, the "ghosts," the "white fog leopard," the sounds of pigeons and the "silent creek" in the bleary morning hour (138). He understands now those long-ago yearnings and terrors:

> This was the rapture of humility which kept saying,
> *You are a child, you are suitable to be awed.*
> I heard the whole silence.
> My heart went white. (138)

The adult persona sees through the patina of years, working still to understand the "rapture of humility" through which he received enlightenment. He embraces the past and the poignant fact of his vanished youth. His initiation now is not into the future but into the past, an initiation full of ceremony:

> Today I will build a fire the fog will clasp.
> Childhood will burn in the grate and the white smoke
> Will go out friendly to the cotton world.
> All that I feared will attenuate in mist,
> Muffling in the hush the dripping hills,
> And the other lost children, and the one lost child. (138)

In deliberately transforming the present moment, the persona makes the past clearer, completes his understanding.

Like many other poems in *Spring Garden,* this one bears a single word changed from its original publication in *Source:* the word "cotton" is used rather than "white." Many of the previously published poems have been slightly altered, warranting interesting tasks for textual scholars. The frequent word changes are quite intricate and unique, pointing to the careful power the poet wields. Like this poem, "Forever Mountain," the final poem in "Poems of Memory," contains several one-word changes, and it also employs similar images of mist and smoke. These aspects of "Forever Mountain," especially one specific word alteration, may seem of minor significance, yet they are extremely important in the realization of the poet's ultimate message.

As in *Source,* "Forever Mountain" is also the final poem in *Spring Garden,* excepting the epilogue, which closes, as previously discussed, with a borrowed elegy. "Forever Mountain" is also elegiac in content but overtly transcendent in tone, pulling together the poet's ideals of human spirituality with many images of nature. Chappell thus reveals hope—of remembrance and of an abundant afterlife for his father, J. T. Chappell. As in many of Chappell's poems, a sense of the importance of place is central in this poem, as the persona perceives that his "father has gone to climb / Lightly the Pisgah slope, taking the time / He's got a world of" (147). Now the persona's father revels in a place beloved during his life; he has an eternity to enjoy the pleasures of nature. We are privy to his "fresh green mornings," his "noontimes in the groves of beech and maple" (147).

> By the clear trout pool he builds his fire at twilight,
> And in the night a granary of stars
> Rises in the water and spreads from edge to edge.
> He sleeps, to dream the tossing dream
> Of the horses of pine trees. . . .
> . . . .
>
> He rises glad and early and goes his way,
> Taking by plateaus the mountain that possesses him. (147)

These revelatory moments in nature contain for the persona the very essence of his father. The transcendent albeit sentimental tones of the poem resound in these images of nature—of specific trees, of water, of stars, and of the mountain itself. In the final lines of the poem, however, the reader realizes that this is not a simple poem about the father's eternity but more about the persona's experience in understanding his father's death.

In the opening line, the persona explains the culmination of his grief: "Now a lofty smoke has cleansed my vision" (147). This oxymoronic statement prepares us for the final stanza; the persona's experience frames his elegy. As his father at last ascends the mountain, the persona accepts his experience with death and grief. His use twice of the word "vision," which suggests both sight and prescience, advances the ephemeral tone:

My vision blurs blue with distance,
I see no more.
Forever Mountain has become a cloud
That light turns gold, that wind dislimns.

This is continually a prayer. (147)

The final line, with its reverberating note of supplication and hope, alters the entire poem. The persona's vision of his father is, of course, what he prays. Originally, the final line read, "This is a prayer" (*Source,* 57), but the one-word alteration strengthens the sense of the persona's perpetual observance of his own loss and enlarges his attention to his father's memory. It is a humble supplication, revealing the persona's hope of the afterlife, his reliance upon his own belief system, and his faith in the transformational power of nature.

Transcendence is most often revealed in Chappell's poetry through attention to nature—through pastoral, agrarian, or garden images. Frequently, however, the images verge upon the supernatural, delving into the spiritual or the fantastical. Although some poems concerning transformation contain mystic or magical circumstances, they do not always center on the positive. Quite often, there is no clear resolution; the tone of hopefulness is eclipsed by images of transfiguration, by the surprise of reordering the normal with the unusual or extraordinary. Many of the poems in *Spring Garden* reveal this tradition within Chappell's work. In the first section, "In the Garden," Chappell infuses a sense of the mystic into two poems concerned with his vision of the enduring quality of books, writing, and the power they have upon the human imagination. In "Literature" and "The Garden," both previously published in *First and Last Words,* Chappell's principal motif of the garden is linked intensely and intricately with the vocation of writing.

Images of writing are bound inextricably with images of flowers, verdant growth, and all the blossoming garden life. Chappell's passion for language, books, and writing are evident in the two poems. In "The Garden," Chappell uses the image of the garden as a metaphor for the act of writing; in "Literature," literature is revealed to be a result of nature's transformations. The world is transmuted in "The Garden," but now the "gardener"—the poet—plays a central role:

> The garden is a book about the gardener.
>
> His thoughts, set down in vivid greenery,
> The white light and the gold light nourish.
> Firm sentences of grapevine, boxwood paragraphs,
> End-stops of peonies and chrysanthemums,
> Cut drowsy shadows from the afternoon. . . .
> . . . .
> The gardener is a book about his garden. (14)

The work of the "gardener" is organic, changeling, and in turn transforms the writer. "Literature" turns the world into literature, and then that literature alters the world, becomes a new world. "The girls and flowers keep changing into literature," the poet tells us, as if he could not control his pen, as if books continually consume the beauty of the world. The poet describes for the reader the "hidden planet" that is literature (21).

Another poem, from the section "Epigrams," is very similar to these two poems in the idea of transformation through nature and the intertwining of literature and organic growth. "Fleurs-des-Livres," however, deals neither with the persona's own writing nor with literature in the abstract but with the work of renowned figures. The persona describes in irregularly rhymed and metered verse a fantastic marriage of books and the natural elements. Humor is wedded with myriad images reflecting the garden motif:

> It rained through my window forgotten open
> On my books of poems. They sprouted like potato eyes.
> What a clutch of impulse, groping
> For sunlight! Those tubers iridescent as ice.
>
> Whitman came up kudzu and sawbriar,
> Vines hairy and rough and muscular,
> Stretching to wrestle manfully
> Mr. Eliot's pallid celery.

Miss Moore's snowdrops glittered chirping
Beneath Laforgue's sardonic moon
Flower. The Bukowski-worts were burping.
Dickinson sprang forth bare bone.

Pope's natty tulips rank on rank.
The Roethke reseeding itself again,
Wallowing belly-deep in my dank
Library, snuffling like a hog in the rain.

And swaying above this unweedable plot
Blake's infirm Rose towered tall as the trees,
And there roared from the heart of this polyglot
A clamor like Pindar's apostrophes. (119)

The literal and the metaphoric are synthesized here, as they are in the other two poems, until one is quite indistinguishable from the other.

These three poems might well be included in *Spring Garden*'s "Poems of Fantasy," where Chappell's unique talents and his eye for magic shine brightest. This section exudes the mystical and fantastic quality of transcendence that Chappell has fostered in much of his writing, particularly in his fiction. The poet's use of the fantastic is, in fact, one of the strongest testaments to his vision of promise—that there is epiphany beyond the darkness of life and an anticipation of beauty transcending banality.

In keeping with the tightly woven patterns of this volume, the prologue to "Poems of Fantasy" contains a borrowed poem that is sheer fiction. In what is apropos for this section, Chappell incorporates a "ballade attributed to Donald Hall," a fabrication that uses some of Hall's personal observations. This subsumed poem contains contentions against fantasy and applauds the stasis of reality within literature. A fictional Hall cites evidence and opinion:

"I have no hankering to start a quarrel;
It's just that I prefer the genuine . . .
. . . .
The homely truths that poets must see plain
And take excruciating pains to tell.
The vein of Fact is the only vein to mine." (87)

He contends that it is a poet's duty to " 'draw a line / Straightedge between the real and the irreal . . . / And eschew all fantasy' "(88).

The poet / persona finely tunes his opposing logic, resolving the predominant dilemma of the section prologue with his own rationale for encompassing fantasy within so much of his poetry. Perhaps the most important general aspect of the prologues is their openness and the revelations of Chappell's motivations and inclinations. This particular prologue is perhaps most important for its explanations of the poet / persona's use of fantasy. He begins by naming predecessors who also harbored the fantastic within their poetry: "Chaucer, Shakespeare, Spenser . . . John Keats." He remarks further that if literature is devoid of fantasy

> We might as well read government reports,
> Stock market listings, actuarial
> Pie-charts, immigration figures, and all
> The thrilling records of the traffic courts.
> Someone said of American poetry
> That like the shark it must contain a shoe.
> But why must it include the factory,
> The trucks, the warehouse, and the sales tax too? (88)

Chappell's hyperbole here employed in argument convinces with cunning and invites the reader to welcome the following section of fourteen poems—one of the longest of the seven sections. Indeed, in each prologue Chappell's tone is charming, conversational; his voice takes on a reserved familiarity. For our clear understanding of "Poems of Fantasy," he calls for "herbs conducive / To midnights of phantasmagoria, / To trance and reverie, euphoria / And nightmare, specters weeping and elusive" (90). In this section lies the dark and the blithe, with that cornerstone element of fantasy guiding all, a transformational element which, for Chappell, is yet another quickening light within his poetry.

One of the new poems in this section, "The Rose and Afterward," draws its central image from the garden motif. The fantastic transformation of a single and powerful rose reveals at once the commonality and limitless mysteries of being human, the dimensions of nature and the world:

> The rose that bruised the world was not all substance.
> The spirit in it changed the spirits that it touched;

The substance of it drew each spirit to its spirit.
There was a mystery in it like a woman
With a woman's darkness and her daylight hands.

First like a cloud and then like risen mists
The rose's presence mantled sky and sea.
It was a continent of perfume. . . .
. . . .

The nations that it tinted lost all admiration
For intellectual things. The senses
Extended their domain. . . .

And then there was no knowledge of what the world
Had ever been besides the thing it was,
Whatever that might be: the history of desire
Had found its red fulfillment, the longing
That made us animal at last had made us human. (95)

The transformational quality of the rose, its overwhelming ability to alter the world, is perhaps fantasy after all; Chappell's principal themes, however, are central once more, particularly the idea of transformation and of possessing and praising the moment at hand—"Carpe diem."

This revelation of fantastical transformation is not necessarily positive, as is the case with many of the transformations described elsewhere in Chappell's poetry. The epigraph to "Observers," from the "Epilogues" section of *First and Last Words,* cites Einstein's *Relativity* as inspiration. The poem has a tone of awe, and the final lines enlarge this vision to encompass the dark side of science and human creativity. The real and the imaginary are fused in the poet's description of "a time of arbitrary starlight / Which is drifting toward the place where Mozart / goes unheard forever, which is punctuated by / the blackened matchstem that was Nagasaki" (44). Here the transformed does not transcend, but the acknowledgement of human destruction serves to enlighten.

In "Poems of Fantasy" Chappell thus exhibits his understanding of human knowledge, literature, and nature as powerful instruments against the darker aspects of human experience. The fantastical and dark opening poem, "The Sea Text," has allegorical touches and a leaning toward that which rises from ruin. It begins with an epigraph: "I'll drown my book." From this self-destructive declaration comes ultimately a transformation, a world reborn, a veritable ascension following baptism:

The gold foil leaves waver in the current,
The sea enfolds a magic it never envied:
Secret runes, strange names, whispered spells
That cause a foreknown future to be born. . . .
. . . .

Now the sea begins to change.
This musty science, gloomy and precise,
Begins to speak its language
That knows long grief and fear and every human ache.

The sea has tasted forbidden knowledge now,
But has not lost its wild and various elegance. . . .
. . . .
The waves lap the promontory embossed with glyphs;
The sea begins to evolve new sorcerers. (92)

In this imagined place and time, the abiding sea is at once the destructive force and the birthplace of new knowledge. And the text, mutable and damaged, is the seed of this knowledge.

Of course, this is fantasy, and perhaps no singular definitive meaning may be discerned. The action in the poem is revelatory and significant, however, as Chappell's thematic interests become clear: the transformational quality of nature and the hope within man's own nature to create, to study, to write, to learn, to make of this world a magic that transcends everyday experience.

Chappell also provides as his personal stay against this darkness the very act of writing. Though certainly no one reading *Spring Garden* will need a justification, the poet/persona, without hint of apologia, provides a defense for the act of poetry. The poet reflects much upon what the world considers of poetry in the first half of the epilogue, including its calls for political action and demands for a tangible product. He recognizes that today, poetry is "looked upon as a curiosity" (153). "We've nearly lost our way," he says of the world, which asks suspiciously of the artist:

"'What is he up to? What's his little game?
Philosophy and poetry? All right,
Then let him suffer with the deserving poor.'

So say the people; their leaders say the same.
But I say, Gentle Spirit, hold to the bright
Lonely path you've chosen forevermore." (153)

The "gentle spirit" that the poet/persona invokes is no muse but the very spirit of hope and transcendence that charges all of Chappell's work, the spirit that prevails despite human mortality, the spirit that is light within the darkness.

Though the tone may be typically self-effacing, the wry humor is balanced with an admission of reverence for the vocation of poetry. The poet/persona knows his task is altogether human, imperfect, but he aligns himself with those whose duty it is to think, to illumine truth:

if philosopher and poet never sat
Sorting salad greens and sipping wine
And puzzling out some weird cosmic design
In a quiet garden with a neighbor's cat,
Who knows if we'd find courage to rise from bed
And brew some coffee, skip our exercise,
Read the papers, make a livelihood,
And try new resolutions on for size.

Someone has to dream the dreams and write
Them out in the best language they can find. (154)

Nothing, then, is perfect in Chappell's garden, certainly not even his own rendering of the world and his experiences within it.

Chappell's spring garden, even in its most ideal moments, is not Edenic, not a fool's paradise, but is composed of altogether human, earthly attributes—the pleasures, anguish, failures, aspirations, limitations, and profound mysteries he embraces and in turn releases through literature. Chappell creates a poetry that looks at life square, through the brilliant, gleaming lens of language, and perpetually transforms the world anew.

Friend of Reason: Surveying the Fred Chappell Papers at Duke University

ALEX ALBRIGHT

Toby Milliver lies dying at the end of Fred Chappell's story "Thatch Retaliates." It's 1718, and he had come from Williamsburg to investigate the possibility of selling books in North Carolina. His last words, "I remain a friend of Reason in this place," are buoyant with the optimism that books and learning and ideas might one day find a home so far south, "where reading may well be counted as lacking"—as Toby had been warned, en route to his casual and senseless murder.

It's not difficult to see in that story, first published in 1979, a parable reflecting, from Chappell's point of view, a deep concern over the sometimes fragile sanctity of ideas in his home state. During the summer of 1963, a year before he first started teaching at the University of North Carolina (UNC) at Greensboro, the North Carolina General Assembly had passed the notorious Speaker Ban Law. This legislation had an early North Carolina precedent in a World War II law that was scarcely protested, but its wording and implications were much closer to the McCarthy hysteria of the early 1950s Red Scare. The law itself, entitled "An Act to Regulate Visiting Speakers at State Supported Colleges and Universities" and written by Secretary of State Thad Eure, forbade any "college or university which receives any State funds" to use its facilities to present any speaker who "is a known member of the Communist Party," who "is known to advocate the overthrow of the Constitution of the United States or the State of North Carolina," or who "has pleaded the Fifth Amendment . . . in refusing to answer any question, with respect to Communist or subversive connections, or activities."

The law slipped by as a legislative rider, overlooked by most of the legislature. Statewide protest from some key politicians, educators, and other civil libertarians was immediate. But it wasn't until the next year, Chappell's first on the job, that its implications started becoming clear. Speakers, in fact, were being banned. The ensuing struggles were then mediated by politicians in the Speaker Ban Law Study Commission, formed in 1965. Those hearings rocked the struggling intellectual atmosphere of North Carolina's universities.

Senator Ralph Scott blasted the law as "the most outrageous abuse of the legislative process I have ever seen. . . . To support this bill is to say that you don't believe in the power of human reason to seek out errors." The battle lines were quickly drawn, with Scott, William Friday, Luther Hodges, Paul Green, Frank Porter Graham, and even Barry Goldwater leading the opposition. Its strong supporters included Senate President Clarence Stone, Sen. Robert B. Morgan, and I. Beverly Lake. But it wasn't really until the Study Commission learned that accreditation by the Southern Association of Colleges and Schools was threatened that the legislature amended the law, giving authority to the individual campuses to control their respective speakers.

Even after the amendment, Governor Dan Moore, acting as head of the university system, banned Herbert Aptheker and others from speaking on the UNC campus. And then-television commentator Jesse Helms would succeed, in 1966, in having a UNC English instructor removed from his classroom for daring to assign Marvell's "To His Coy Mistress."[1]

During the Speaker Ban Study Commission hearings in the summer of 1965, Chappell was among one hundred and seventy-five university system faculty to sign a statement saying they would leave their positions if the law were not repealed. Chappell wrote a letter protesting the Speaker Ban Law to the editor of the Greensboro *Daily News* after learning the American Legion wanted to know where and who he was. Among other clues the Legion had missed as to Chappell's identity, he'd recently celebrated the publication of his second novel, *The Inkling*. Richard Dillard had just written him: "Annie, the new Mrs. D, picked it up the day it came to glance at it and refused to go to bed until she finished it. She finished it and had

---

1. A federal court ruled the amended law unconstitutional in 1968; a year later, a revised version died in legislative committee.

nightmares all night. It's really grand and marvelously weird." Reviews, including Orville Prescott's in the New York *Times,* echoed the Dillards' reaction. A publication party had prompted Donald Hall to write, "That party was truly great and I'll never forget ending up drinking the vinegar out of the cruet." Chappell's editor, Hiram Haydn, agreed that Chappell's proposed novel about Samuel Johnson "would be great," and he awaited anxiously the manuscript for *Dagon.* William Gass, Haydn also noted, had recently called Chappell "the finest living American novelist." Boston University wrote in August that it wanted to establish the Fred Chappell Archives there. (But Chappell's former professor at Duke, William Blackburn, had already begun soliciting materials for Duke's burgeoning archives from his student writers: William Styron, Reynolds Price, and Fred Chappell, among others. The first papers constituting the Fred Chappell Collection had come to Duke University the previous year.)[2]

It's easy to imagine that a young and optimistic Chappell would have been so sure of the power of art, and of reason in the world, that he could defend, reasonably, such an affront to intellectual inquiry as the Speaker Ban Law.

Chappell's letter, headlined "He Will Leave UNC-G," reads:

Watching the speaker ban hearing on television yesterday, I learned that the American Legion is trying to find out my name and address, since I was one of those professors who signed a statement saying that I would leave if the Speaker Ban Law were not repealed or amended. My address is on this letter and my telephone number is in the book. And I will leave.

The Speaker Ban Law, rather innocuous in itself, is an obvious first step toward an obviously increasing restriction of academic freedom. To continue teaching in a university which is forced to tolerate such a situation is to be

2. The Fred Davis Chappell Papers at Perkins Library, Duke University, are the primary sources for information and quotations included in this essay. In addition, background on the Speaker Ban Law comes from vertical files in the North Carolina Collection, Joyner Library, East Carolina University. Other sources are the interviews with Duke archivists Robert Byrd and Janie Morris; Chappell's letter to the Greensboro *Daily News,* which appeared on August 23, 1965, p. A6; and lyrics to the UNC-G song (no longer used), which are courtesy of Greg Brown. A much shorter version of this essay appeared in the Summer, 1992, issue of *North Carolina Review.* Grateful acknowledgment is given to the Duke Archives, and to the individuals whose letters are quoted, for permission to reprint.

personally a victim of militant legislative stupidity. I do not propose this career for myself.

To stay, to teach in the university, would be to give tacit approval to a law which is probably unconstitutional and certainly the product of bigotry. This I will not do.

A law like the Speaker Ban Law is the trademark of an institution, and I cannot support in purely economic terms the lessened respect which would attach to me professionally if I remained for very long in an inferior college. For if I cannot command the respect of my colleagues I cannot command a fair salary.

Surely these reasons ought to satisfy anyone, if reasons can. Often reasons can't. Usually those persons who don't understand ideas try to close the mouths which voice them, just as persons who can't read books burn them, and those who can't love fight.

If he was prepared at all for the mail he was to get after that letter, his preparation came from his roots, not from his Duke education. Not that he'd forsaken the former when he went off to college, as is so easy the temptation for any Carolina lad dissatisfied with the mill-and-field possibilities his hometown might have offered. For almost all of the early fiction from his first collection of thirteen stories he called *The Thousand Ways* deals at least peripherally (and most quite directly) with folks suspicious of too much education, too many ideas.

The first responding letter is the harshest, mailed the day his letter appeared, August 23, 1965: "You gave me one point to make me favor the Speaker Ban Law," the unsigned letter reads, before explaining its writer's great difficulty getting through *It Is Time, Lord*. It concludes: "I was never so appalled, disgusted, and disappointed as when I began reading the obscene, nauseating, frankly nasty details. . . . When I got through with it, I took it out to the trash can and cut it up into small bits in spite of the waste of good money. Now I feel if the law in question will indirectly purge the campus of your type mind it would be worthwhile."

A few days later, an unsigned postcard, depicting "Martin Luther King at Communist training school," arrived with the abrupt message: "Are you leaving? Good riddance!"

For one like Chappell, who has so highly valued intellectual argument and artistic expression, such bluntness was probably all the more frustrating because there was no chance for rebuttal to its anonymous belches of hate and closed-mindedness. How long would he have sat into the night articulating his replies?

Five years later, he got his chance to reply to the foes of reason, after a woman with the same last name had read *The Inkling*. "I accidently [*sic*]came upon your book," she begins reasonably enough. "All Chappells with the double P and L are of the same family. Our people have wonderful imaginations and have remarkable memories." It would seem thus far but another fan letter, made the more special because this possible relative describes how she had one day realized that her personal library contained no volumes by a Chappell. And it had so happened, as it might in a bad novel, that on that day her daughter would find a copy of *The Inkling* and bring it to her, proudly. Her letter suddenly shifts tone: "The Chappell men are known for placing women on a pedestal and no lady or gentleman would tolerate a dirty story or vulgar book in their library." She describes briefly her disgust and then proclaims: "You know where it is going—in an outside fire," as if to keep its polluted fumes from contaminating her hearth. She concludes, "My daughter says maybe Mr. Nixon will try to stop some of the dirty books being published."

Chappell writes back:

It is not my purpose in writing to distress someone without cause, or to shock without purpose. *The Inkling* is a highly disguised and of course relocated account of something which actually did take place in France in the nineteenth century; and it attempts to interpret this event in light of our present dilemmas in civilization. So when it is misread or not comprehended, I find this perfectly understandable.

But if it is taken to be a dirty or a vulgar (in your sense) book, I can only believe that the fault lies with the reader. My mother and my grandmother have read the book without undue distress, as have other ladies and gentlemen. And it is of course in many ways a religious book, the key for interpretation having been borrowed from St. Augustine. Perhaps it is merely some of the language which bothers you; but surely a modern moralist is to be allowed the same latitude of speech as, say, John Milton or Martin Luther.

In any case, I should like to be able to prevail upon you not to burn it. Why not give it to a county library or to a Veterans Hospital library? Or send it back to me—I will pay the postage. But when you speak of barbarism, you must surely realize that the burning of books is the certain emblem of that ambition.

Yours truly,
Fred Chappell

That his reply to this Chappell woman exists in the Chappell archives is but a quirk—she refused to accept its delivery, and it was returned to him. Therein lies the key to what these archives contain by way of correspondence: letters mailed to him.

Of the thirty-seven thousand or so items in the Fred Davis Chappell Collection, at least 80 percent are letters and cards he has received. The rest are poem, story, essay, and novel manuscripts (including numerous fragments), galleys, bound volumes, notebooks, files of typescripts, financial records, copies of reviews of his work, and photos. The first were collected in February, 1964: "88 items and 3 vols.," including "handscript, typescript, and proofs of the novel *It Is Time, Lord,*" and "the correspondence pertaining to its publication." Also included are manuscripts of early poems and stories, "a few letters at random from various writers," and "part of an earlier novel Mr. Chappell attempted to write." The thirteenth accession—fifteen hundred items from July, 1990—includes letters, an annotated manuscript copy of *Brighten the Corner Where You Are,* and "several handwritten notebooks containing his poetry."

The most recent (and twenty-eighth) accession—twelve hundred items from July, 1996—comprises correspondence and notebooks. To scan the pages of one of those spiral composition notebooks Chappell has kept—and there are dozens in the collection—is to see a disjointedly comprehensive catalog of Chappell's artistic and intellectual concerns for the past thirty-five years. They are filled, page after page, with his distinctive and neatly cramped handwriting, so small it could seem at first glance a cursive writing exercise, his words looking almost ashamed to be on the page, letters no bigger than old picas. Tucked among notebooks of class notes and reading lists from his Duke studies are poems and story fragments, including two titled (apparently in retrospect) by Chappell, "early bad try at *Dagon,*" and "aborted beginning of *Dagon*"; a third contains the "first handwritten draft" of it. As the years pass, you can read his class and public lectures, drafts of stories, poems, essays, and reviews, and occasional notes to himself, sometimes eerily perceptive: "People sense in me an uncertain vulnerability and go straight for my tender parts with their inquiries." He lectures on Virgil, introduces his visionary lit class and his American lit class brilliantly, and sets out occasional daily schedules. The 1980 holidays find him reading Spinoza, taking notes, and then cryptically commenting that school has begun, disrupting his reading.

One of the notebook poems, "Epitaph for a Book of Poems," reads: "I never truckled / I never pandered / I was born / to be remaindered." Another, untitled, reads in part:

> John, since they cut the Bollingen in two
> And gave one-half to me, one-half to you,
> Why don't you and I also divide
> Our audiences? One shall satisfy
> The critic, and the other one shall try
> The general reader. I'll let you decide.

A notebook story fragment, "Cock Fight," begins with a dazzling sentence but ends much too quickly:

> Well, George Lynn, you always wanted me to write a story gutbucket and slashing, a funky tale of the good ole boys and the wild and crazy things they did in the nighttime off and on their motorcycles, inside and outside the grainy low smokesteamy beer joints hooting with easy irony and neon rock and roll and I hope that you wanted me to include also the soulful girls who ringed them round, goading them on with feigned disapproval; you might prefer my leaving out the sad uncomprehending and incomprehensible parents of the loud young men.

Two folders of typescripts from a 1985 accession are crammed with essays. "Pre-Season Ramblings" satirizes creative writing programs: "Even before the typewriter covers are off, and the old similes taken out and dusted, the fans are making their predictions. What writing departments are going to show unexpected strength this time out? Who will grab the glamour reviews? and steal the hearts of millions of Americans? And most exciting of all, who is going to win and carry home those grants and prizes?" In "Teacher," he lays out his agenda for a successful writing program ("Be careful not to tamper with students' current fad writers, like Brautigan"), concluding with a list of what literature of the 1970s should survive.

The plays include "Hallowind," set in Durham, 1961, with the personae of "R. Price, Susan, Fred, the Rain, the Wind" discussing "meaning in writing."

Another folder contains speech typescripts. In "Defense of Darkness," he defends himself against two charges: "(1) that I'm a joyless writer with no sense of the fun in life, and (2) that I'm a sordid, even obscene, writer." He redefines by example obscenity in modern times: "t.v. ads, military budget, unprepared or dull teachers." In another he discusses himself as a southern writer, and in "The Family and the Individual," he claims it a mistake that he was invited to speak, apparently as "an expert on family, with slides to show." He demurs: "I am not an expert on anything, and though I have pictures to prove this, they will not be shown."

But surely one of the most interesting folders of typescripts is that of Chappell's original collection of "The One Thousand Ways," stories written almost exclusively while he was still at Duke. Only eight of the fourteen have been published: "Property of Hope," "Gothic Perplexities," "The Thousand Ways," "January," "Inheritance," "Prodigious Words," "Spies," and "Band of Brothers." Chappell remained hopeful for several years that the collection would be published, and it even appeared it would be, after his first two novels came out. In October, 1965, he received a $750 advance and contract for its publication, but by the next August, his editor, Hiram Haydn, had talked him into exchanging that contract for one to publish *Dagon*. The stories as a collection are scarcely mentioned again. Today, most of these unpublished stories retain their strength and vision, and they offer interesting hints of Chappell's future (published) concerns:

—"The Prisoner," 19 pp., is set on Joan Caldwell's fourteenth birthday. Bill Briggs, her boyfriend with a car, is watched by the neighbor boy Stonkey, a skinny kid who wants to be a forest ranger despite his dad's wish for him to be a baseball player. Stonkey, for most of the story, waits up to see Bill bring Joan home from a date.

—"The Lost," 4 pp., appears to be a fragment, about a couple going to a dull party, apparently for an English department, at the Henleys'—"All their parties start early." Folks there are excitedly asking, "Have you read Thomas Darkling?"

—"A Dog's Still Life," 5 pp., is a drinking story. The dog's a drunk. Gene wants to be a painter and paint big pictures, at least 18′ × 24′. The narrator, a writer, lives in an apartment with Gene, and they drink and discuss a variety of subjects, including the baseball legend Pepper Martin.

—"Christmas Gift," 9 pp., takes place in Troy's Grill, in the small factory / college town of Winton, North Carolina, where cigarettes are in the air. Jack Cannon is just out of prison for hitting Lora, a waitress at Troy's, with a jar. She's happy now with her husband, who's stopped drinking, and with her tips: loose cigarettes left by the factory workers. Jack affects his revenge on her by getting her husband Harry, who's absent from the story but behind the conversation they have, to start drinking again.

—"The Two Ministries," 19 pp., begins in a paper-mill town in the western North Carolina mountains. Paul Warner, a sixteen-year-old, is hitchhiking, considering the question, "What if Jesus came tonight?" He's picked up by a pair of revivalists, who in turn pick up a second hitchhiker, Ray Morris, a young heathen. The revivalists stop the car to save him, then prod him up a hill at gunpoint, leaving Warner to walk away into the night.

—"Dangers of the First Floor," 7 pp., finds the narrator and his wife, Frances, and their small child, living upstairs from yet another impractical student couple. Harold's getting his Ph.D. in Arabic pre-history, attempting to prove his theory of how diet influenced their alphabet. The narrator watches and listens to the downstairs activity of each succeeding tenant. They come and go, while he remains in school, the perpetual student.

Although the other stories have been previously published, only the title story, in *The Fred Chappell Reader,* is still readily accessible. It was one of seven out of the original collection that Chappell's editors felt strong enough to include in a collection. Haydn felt that "Inheritance," "Christmas Gift," and "Dead Soldier" should also be included, but he was overruled by Peter Jovanovich. Neither of them felt "Prodigious Words," "A Dog's Still Life," "Dangers of the First Floor," and "Band of Brothers" should be included, and apparently, the collection was never seriously considered again after *Dagon* took its contractual place, even though it was copyrighted as a complete manuscript in 1968.

A bound volume of graded papers from Chappell's Duke school days arrived in 1985: "Poetry as Reflex: Dickinson's Metric," 6 pp.; "Christopher Smart and the Doctrine of Correspondence," 12 pp.; "Johnson and the Art of Translating," 38 pp.; and "Shakespeare's *Coriolanus* & Plutarch's *Life of Cato,*" 11 pp. Other bound volumes are of his own galleys, those of other writers, and books his former students have written and sent to him.

Additional accessions include a collection of forty-one book reviews of Chappell's work in 1974; 456 items and 13 volumes, in 1985, "drafts and proofs of seven poetry collections, two novels, and *Moments of Light*"; and in 1989, "11,000 items, 18.4 linear ft.," covering 1970–89 and consisting of "chiefly letters to Chappell from literary and faculty colleagues throughout the U.S. as well as from former students. Also mail from various literary organizations; publishing companies . . . ; fledgling writers seeking his advice and the criticism of their works; and persons requesting him to speak, read from his works, or write book reviews."

Chappell, Fred Davis. 1936–
Papers, 1959–1996

There may be those who would be startled or even disheartened to know their letters to Chappell would wind up in the kind of public display an archives might be considered. When, as I surveyed his archives for this article, I chanced upon a badly typed late-night letter I'd sent Fred in 1984, all the abstractions I'd considered, when glancing at all these letters by people and names I knew, were suddenly much harder to consider reasonably. Though I've written him several times since I got my Greensboro M.F.A. in 1975, my letters were always to ask a favor: usually another job reference or, as in 1984, to commission him (for ten dollars) to be guest celebrity poet for an anthology of collard poems. And they were always rather sheepish letters, as I'd gotten farther and farther away from writing the fiction I'd tried to write for his classes. I do not know if all those letters are at Duke; there are too many others—too many boxes and boxes of letters—covering too many years. Full cataloging won't even commence until the open space after "1936– " is filled in.

That space is the stopper. When it's finally filled, it will give these archives their first closure and the opening to scholars to descend, to begin their pinning to the wall the writer they will inspect for generations. It could become increasingly easy to forget Fred Chappell the teacher, as the struggles for interpretive rights ensue. The elaborate puzzle Chappell has laid out for future scholars will be his revenge, though, for it will be impossible to even approximate the measure of him without dealing first with these archives. And these archives will never let anyone forget that Fred

Chappell has been on the job, teaching with Herculean energy for twenty-five years.

If you were one of his students, you no doubt remember the stacks of letters on his desk. You may remember, as I do, the amazement with which some of us discussed how he answered them all. But he did, with a diligence evidenced by the staggering numbers of letters among his papers. They are from students, community and school kid poets, publishers, agents, and struggling and marquee poets, friends and colleagues and family. They ask, and they give thanks for his responses, for his time.

To me, the time seems most staggering of all aspects. Here, already, are twenty thousand or so letters to Fred Chappell, from Ammons to Zimmer. The ones he wrote rest in hundreds of archives, most still personal, and many with people who will never know that, by virtue of having gotten a letter from Fred, a value came to be attached to their own papers. On the one hand, it's tempting to imagine what he might have written already had that epistolary energy been spent on poems and novels, but on the other, it may be hard to imagine Fred Chappell any other way. Clearly, from his published work and the notebooks here deposited, he's kept his teaching sacred and separate from his literary production, except in the most peripheral and oblique ways: no *romans à clef* about teaching creative writing at a formerly all-women's college in the south nor about the volumes of mail requests that grow exponentially as the budding young writer reaches his publishing and popular strides.

There are no journals, at least not in the traditional sense of what we might expect from a contemplative writer like Fred Chappell, one who has wrestled over a career with the large philosophical questions and moral dilemmas. *When,* possibly, could he have had the time? He gives strong evidence of a writer who has done the bulk of his developing themes and characters and plot, with diction and imagery, before his pen ever began its work. The stories and poems, it seems, have boiled internally until they spilled to the page. And he's been the master controller of the switch he's had to make so frequently throughout his career, from teacher to writer and back again.

By far the greatest number of these letters are from his students. It will be easiest to understand what's happened to his letters for those who've made their own writing careers—they'll eventually have their own collections. Others, like me, may question, sheepishly and uncertainly, exactly why our letters might be there, while his, the more important ones, rest stuffed in files or boxes, or stuck away in books of his he's signed, in our own "collections." But then again, those of us who've not sent our heartfully inscribed first volumes to Fred don't have to worry if our book was sent to Duke because Fred really didn't want it.

This is wending quickly away from scholarly talk, into realms of writerly insecurities. Did Fred *keep* your book? Did he give Duke *that* letter? But there is clear reason at work here—reason, as usual, that Fred has taken beyond first and obvious thought, on to a grander design. Remember the space after "1936– ." Understand the volume, the sheer weight of what's been mailed to Fred. And try to appreciate that, once again, what he's doing is for the benefit of his students. That book that seemed briefly to make the world take notice will be seen again and again, as long as scholars still use archives in this world. Some will read it for quick Fred Chappell allusions. But others will read more closely—they'll be scholars—and they'll be looking for writers to write about, "obscure" writers they can rediscover for the world.

But to fully understand what's going on, it's necessary to know exactly what this archive (or any other) is supposed to be. Janie Morris, an archivist and manuscript cataloger at Duke who's done much of the preliminary work with the succeeding accessions of the Fred papers, explains that, as is, "the archives are not in great shape for researchers." The first and easiest step, she says, has been done; a survey of each of the thirteen accessions. "It's nothing but an overview," she points out, "in which we've divided as accurately as possible the contents into archival categories."

Robert Byrd, director of Duke Archives and Manuscripts, is understandably unapologetic for the imposing shape the archives are in. He explains that what has been done thus far is to facilitate access for the present. "What we ultimately do with a collection," he reminds me, "is make it as accessible as possible for scholars." But that can't be done until three steps are completed. First, the collection as a whole has to be processed. Currently, the Chappell collection is still growing; as a result, it consists of twenty-eight separate accessions, each with repeated categories. Eventually, when it seems the collection is reasonably complete, it will be processed as a whole. That is, the categories noted by Ms. Morris will be filled with items from each accession. Instead of notebooks being stored in several different boxes, they'll be cataloged together. That's the purpose of the second step—organization, getting all the correspondence arranged, all the galleys, folders, notebooks and typescripts together. Finally, it will be descriptively inventoried and cross-referenced (so that someone searching the autograph file might find a handwritten letter from, say, Anaïs Nin to Fred).

Notebooks, Byrd admits, will be a troublesome thing, especially the kind Fred has kept: drafts of letters, poems, stories, essays, lectures, all kinds of fragments and notes, and, in some, obviously nonsynchronous elements. "It'll be quite a job when it comes down to analyzing, and settling on the level of description," he says. "Much will ultimately be left to the researcher studying his work. What we'll have done by the time the collection is fully processed is to make it so the researcher can find his information and then accurately cite it."

Letters present problems for other reasons. Although it might be tempting to discard a letter that seems inconsequential, it's important, Byrd notes, to remember "the institutional commitment to maintain the integrity of a collection, to keep all the materials within one repository." That's what also makes it archivally unwise to begin soliciting letters Fred wrote to incorporate into his papers. "We would always prefer not to break up your papers, anyone's papers," Byrd says, explaining basic archives philosophy. "That would be drawing things out of their context." Nevertheless, he adds, "It is certainly hoped that a large quantity of Fred's outgoing letters will be saved in the papers of those who've received them."

And therein lies the foundation for the enormous literary puzzle that can never be fully solved, for to solve it would require that everyone to whom Fred wrote letters also saved them all and then ultimately would wind up finding an archive to take those papers. But there will be plenty of them, to be sure, if only judging from the long list of contemporary authors represented from Fred's receiving end of things. That means future Chappell scholars will be jumping about from archive to archive, including those of Donald Hall, Allen Tate, Henry Taylor, Bernard Malamud, W. D. Snodgrass, Dorothy Parker, Maurice Coindreau, Sam Ragan, Sylvia Wilkinson, Paul Hemphill, Kelly Cherry, William Pitt Root, Wallace Kaufman, X. J. Kennedy, George Garrett, Robert Morgan, Doris Betts, Candace Flynt, Marianne Gingher, Robert Watson, Annie Dillard, Allan Dugan, Jonathan Yardley, Hiram Haydn—and dozens of others as yet in the realm of "uncollectable." A fat and impressive anthology could be gathered quite easily by simply collecting the poems and stories by some of these writers, sent with letters and notes and pleas for help or praise, many no doubt already published elsewhere—but with what changes Fred had suggested in his reply? Further, in order to even begin to solve the puzzle, everybody's got to be dead, so that all the relevant archives will be closed sufficiently enough for descriptive inventories.

This can be depressing stuff. Suddenly, it seems, we're all dead, and scholars are poring over our every word, or relatives are rifling our papers for items of consequence to sell at auction. But that's eminently unfair to the spirit of the Fred Chappell papers and to any discussion of his correspondence. For if one thing shines through the many letters there, it's a spirit filled with wit and pain and bits of triumphs and tragedy endured. You can feel Fred's struggles through rejection, and follow with delight the development (and sometimes abandonment) of peripheral writing projects. Through it all, you can still sketch a Chappell-life, from his first application for a job at UNC-G through his Bollingen Prize and beyond. In between, you can read a vivid description by Kent Cooper of a 1967 Sonny Terry and Brownie McGee concert preceded by Gibbons Rourke reading a poem (and study the enclosed candid photos of John Lee Hooker apparently taken by Cooper at either his or Hooker's home). You can piece together enough details to figure that, among Fred's forgotten accomplishments, surely one of the most unusual is his penning, to Tom Cousin's musical accompaniment, of UNC-G's "University Song," for which Fred received seventy-five dollars:

To watch the living flame blown clear,
And bravely free we gather.
May our lives endear Our University.
And may our hopes set forth from her courageously;
And may the vivid flame endure,
Our University.

Some excerpts from seven years of letters:
Acceptance of "Tiros II—August 1960," by X. J. Kennedy, for *Paris Review,* 7-14-62.

"Your postscript is absolutely enchanting. I stayed in laughter for several minutes." Hiram Haydn, 7-16-62.

"You are one of the few writers living who really understands how to correct his galleys." Herman Ziegner, 4-9-63.

"That was one signing party. . . . Did I drink a bottle of soy sauce or did I dream it?" Donald Hall, 5-27-63.

"On the dawn of your fame, I salute you. I believe that's how it's done." William Gass, 8-12-63.

"Everyone here hopes the Chappells will come to Greensboro next year. In a fit of arrogance last night Peter, Randall and I decided that very shortly our new MFA program will make us the chief literary center—provided you come too." Bob Watson, 9-15-63.

"Your piece seems to imply that anything more complex than fishing with a simple rod and a pair of flies is unnecessary and detracts from the sport." Stephan Wilkinson, editor at *Holiday,* rejecting his first version of "Trout Fishing: Ritual, Not Rapture," 1-16-64.

"Look forward to meeting you" at luncheon she's hosting, with her husband. From Mary Jarrell, 3-16-64.

"You've earned your advance!" From Hiram Haydn, on *It Is Time, Lord* sales, 3-31-64.

"It does my heart good to think you had the good judgment and will power to stay in college till you earned your degree." On a birthday card from Grandmother Davis, 5-23-64.

"Fred, you are absolutely crazy. I received your manuscript (*The Inkling*) this morning—started reading it right away. Read it all afternoon, and have just finished it (10 P.M.). It is simply wonderful. The most exciting thing I have read in years, and utterly original." Maurice Coindreau, 9-5-64.

"If you haven't yet, please sit in on one of Randall's workshop classes. If he is in a good mood and feeling frisky, it's an experience you shouldn't miss. Like going to see the last kangaroo left in the world." Heather Ross Miller, 10-3-64.

There are only small problems with *The Inkling*, "like the overuse of the word 'hunkered.'" Hiram Haydn, 12-29-64.

After reading *The Inkling* twice, "When I summed it all up, I said to myself, Fred must have been born a natural psychologist. I want you to keep up your writing, just for pastime. When you write let your mind soar up and to God who gave it. PS: Be careful to not use God's name in vain." Grandmother Davis, 8-21-65.

After thanking him for a box of Valentine's candy, "You must be a good boy, don't go down the street too far." Grandmother Davis, 2-15-66.

"Studies of castration and humiliation are not the most popular studies in the world." Hiram Haydn's early reaction to *Dagon,* 8-5-66.

In rejecting three poems for *Poetry Now:* "The oddities of diction seemed more than (the poems) could bear." David Wagoner, 9-29-66.

"I've fallen hopelessly in love with Bobby Gentry," after hearing "Ode to Billie Joe" in Seattle. William Pitt Root, 9-27-67.

"Long live Chaucer and (Willie) Mays." Hiram Haydn, 2-26-69.

"Would you please send us your shoe size?" From seventh-grade students at Goldsboro school, after Chappell has agreed to judge their student poetry contest, 4-2-69.

After accepting the visiting writer's position at UNC-G and discussing student unrest across the country: "I'm afraid that the repressions will be bloodier than ever." Allan Dugan, 6-11-69.

"I am learning to wear false eyelashes and there is no telling what kind of trauma this sort of thing may lead to." Kelly Cherry, 7-8-69.

"You shot way over my head with R. M. Bucke and Joquin Miller." Robert Morgan, 7-11-69.

"What are you wearing? I'm wearing bell bottoms. You must think the worst of me by now for not writing these past few months, but I hurt my knee and as you have probably known all these years I write with my knees." Bob Watson, 7-15-69.

"Greensboro sounds worse than usual." Kelly Cherry, 7-15-69.

"Seems funny to be sending out poems like these on the day the 1st man walks on the moon." Robert Morgan, 7-20-69.

"I'm not sure I follow everything you said about sex." Kelly Cherry, 8-5-69.

"The job (at Dutton) would be perfect if only it were for one year and not for life. . . . I have discovered Borges who just plain damn knocks me out." Kelly Cherry, 8-23-69.

"I remember well our evening at Ann Queen's almost a year ago." James Reston, Jr., 9-7-69.

"As for my own writing, it looks like I'm not going to make it." Kelly Cherry, 10-3-69.

An invitation from McCall's publishing company to write a book on the Hatfield-McCoy feud, 11-7-69.

There are none of what one might call a writer's journal in the Fred papers, no day-by-day charting of his life, because it seems that went into his letters and his living. Future biographers will have a devilish time piecing all the many parts together. Hints of grand anecdotes and fanciful stories, great acts of kindness and humor—they all abound in these papers. To judge from letters sent him after he'd responded to a correspondent's poems, he has been a consistently perceptive and precise critic for some; and for others, the home poets who wrote verse from inarticulate alienation or exuberance, he has been politer: "I hadn't realized how often green images occurred in my poems," one lady writes. But what did he say? One can only guess.

Regardless of who might ultimately win the theoretical argument over the relevance of a writer's life to the texts he writes, the archives will remain. For the Chappell scholars, they'll offer clues well worth exploring. The scholars will one day come calling on folks whose letters have wound up at Duke, wondering about that reading they've thanked Fred for or how that journal they began was helped by Fred's sending it some poems. (I hadn't noticed the number of first and second numbers of very small literary magazines he's published in until I kept coming across the letters asking for his help in getting started—a couple of poems, a story, anything.)

I met Fred six times before he remembered who I was. But by that time, I had become his student, and it was easy to see that suddenly I had become more than just another who passed his vision at still another Greensboro party. John Gray introduced me to him most of those first times. He had begun his M.F.A. a semester before me, having driven from California in an old black VW bug with bad radio, glove-box door flapping, and shattered-but-still-intact windshield to study with Fred at the urging of his friend, George Lynn, who'd come to Greensboro from Limestone College; a friend of George's had told him about Fred. At parties that spring, when Fred was still on leave, John would say, "Let me introduce you to Fred again." Then we'd stand back and watch people vying for his attention, would afterward get George to tell us Fred stories, Dickey-Chappell-Lynn drinking stories.

George teaches in Alabama now, John in New Mexico, I in eastern North Carolina. Reading some of our separate letters to Fred, I couldn't help a certain wincing nor a certain pride. (I also felt like a proofreader with no pen.) How we teach is as inextricable from what we learned from Fred as is the way our lives have grown from what he taught us after class. One of his criteria for a successful writing program is the close proximity of a public gathering place. It's hard to imagine that the Pickwick might've helped keep him from moving to the Iowa Writers' Workshop (there are letters among his papers that suggest that possibility in the late 1960s); but it's harder to imagine a purely academic M.F.A., one without beers and talk: baseball and blues as much as Milton and Faulkner.

In ways impossible to gauge, Fred has touched thousands more people through his teaching than his writing. Consider the exponential progression of the number of people he's taught that became teachers; consider that by now, we're into fourth or fifth generations of teachers who've come from him. These archives are testament to that first touch, its generation. Yet the letters will always remain secondary to the literature, and for Fred's good sense to preserve his fragments, drafts, and notebooks, future literary scholars will surely bless him, perhaps more than the biographers will curse him for having laid so wondrous and complex a puzzle as these letters, and all their myriad sources.

CONTRIBUTORS

RICHARD ABOWITZ lives in Minneapolis, Minnesota. His writings have appeared in publications ranging from the *Kenyon Review* to *Rolling Stone*. He is working on his Ph.D. in English at the University of Minnesota and is owner and co-editor of the on-line publication *CAP-L*.

ALEX ALBRIGHT is associate professor of English at East Carolina University. He has edited *The North Carolina Poems,* by A. R. Ammons, and *Dreaming the Blues: Poems from Martin County Prison.*

PATRICK BIZZARO is the author of six chapbooks of poetry, articles on contemporary poets, and *Responding to Student Poems: Applications of Critical Theory* (1993). He teaches at East Carolina University.

KATHRYN STRIPLING BYER, poet-in-residence at Western Carolina University, is the author of two poetry collections, *The Girl in the Midst of the Harvest* and *Wildwood Flower,* the latter of which was the 1992 Lamont Poetry Selection of the Academy of American Poets.

KELLY CHERRY is professor of English at the University of Wisconsin. She is the author of five novels, four books of poetry, including most recently *God's Loud Hand,* and the autobiographical work *The Exiled Heart.* She has received the James G. Hanes Poetry Prize of the Fellowship of Southern Writers and many other honors.

RESA CRANE is teaching writing and literature at East Carolina University while working on her Ph.D. dissertation on Expressivism.

R. H. W. DILLARD, professor of English and head of the creative writing program at Hollins College, is the author of two novels, a collection of short fiction, two books of criticism, and five collections of poetry, including most recently *Just Here, Just Now.*

GEORGE GARRETT—novelist, short-story writer, poet, editor, and critic—is the author of some thirty books, including the novels *Do, Lord, Remember Me* and *Death of the Fox* and the short story collection *An Evening Performance: New and Selected Stories.* He is Henry Hoyns Professor of Creative Writing at the University of Virginia.

DON JOHNSON teaches English at East Tennessee State University, where he is also Dean of the College of Arts and Sciences. He is the editor of *Hummers, Knucklers, and Slow Curves: Contemporary Baseball Poems.* His most recent poetry collection is *The Importance of Visible Scars.*

JAMES KIRKLAND is professor of English at East Carolina University, where he is also director of the Writing Center and advisory editor of *Tar River Poetry.* He has coauthored several books, including *Herbal and Magical Medicine: Traditional Healing Today.*

JOHN LANG is professor of English at Emory and Henry College in Virginia, where he also edits *Iron Mountain Review.* He has published numerous essays on aspects of southern and African American literature, especially contemporary poetry.

PETER MAKUCK is professor of English at East Carolina University, where he is also editor of *Tar River Poetry.* He has published several collections of poetry, including most recently *Against Distance,* and a collection of stories, *Breaking and Entering.*

ROBERT MORGAN, professor of English at Cornell University, is the author of many poetry collections and two collections of stories, *The Blue Valleys* and *The Mountains Won't Remember Us,* and *Good Measure: Essays, Interviews, and Notes on Poetry.*

DAVID R. SLAVITT, who lives in Philadelphia, has published more than fifty books of poetry, fiction, and nonfiction, including the novels *The Cliff* and *Turkish Delights* and the poetry collections *Crossroads, Equinox,* and *Epic and Epigram: Two Elizabethan Entertainments.* He is also a noted translator of the works of Virgil, Ovid, Seneca, and Avianus. He and Fred Chappell gave their first poetry readings together in the early 1960s at the University of Virginia as guests of George Garrett.

R. T. SMITH, a native of North Carolina, is editor of *Shenandoah* and author of a collection of short stores, *Faith,* and three collections of poetry, including most recently *Trespasser.*

DABNEY STUART, professor of English at Washington and Lee University, has published a collection of short fiction, a critical study of Vladimir Nabokov, and eleven collections of poetry, including most recently *Light Years: New and Selected Poems* and *Long Gone.*

HENRY TAYLOR received the Pulitzer Prize in 1986 for this third collection of poetry, *The Flying Change.* He is professor of literature and codirector of the MFA program in Creative Writing at American University in Washington, D.C. His most recent collection of poems is *Understanding Fiction* (1996), and he is also the author of *Compulsory Figures: Essays on Recent American Poets.*

SUSAN O'DELL UNDERWOOD, assistant professor of English at Carson-Newman College, recently received her Ph.D. from Florida State University, where she wrote her dissertation on Fred Chappell. She has published poems and essays in periodicals.

INDEX

104, 127–28, 181, 182–83, 185; "Three
Sheets in the Wind," 20, 40, 67, 68,
104, 136; "My Mother Shoots the
Breeze," 153; "The Autumn Bleat of
the Weathervane Trombone," 49, 65,
108, 110, 111, 127; "Second Wind,"
54, 66; "Dawn Wind Unlocks the
River Sky," 54, 121, 126; "The Highest Wind That Ever Blew: Homage to
Louis," 54, 182, 186
World Between the Eyes, The, 9, 170; and

Awakening to Music, 83; and Heaney, 88–
89; "Weird Tales," 36, 72–73; "February," 89–90, 91; "The World Between
the Eyes," 90, 93; "Sunday," 91; "The
Father," 91–92, 94; "The Mother," 93–
94, 96; "Heath's New Drum," 94;
"Seated Figure," 94; "Tyros II," 94;
"A Transcendental Idealist Dreams in
Springtime," 108

Young Lovers, The (Garrett), 9